D1527015

Club Cultures

Routledge Advances in Sociology

Club Cultures
Boundaries, Identities, and Otherness

Silvia Rief

Routledge
Taylor & Francis Group
New York   London

First published 2009
by Routledge
270 Madison Ave, New York, NY 10016

Simultaneously published in the UK
by Routledge
2 Park Square, Milton Park, Abingdon, Oxon OX14 4RN

Routledge is an imprint of the Taylor & Francis Group, an informa business

© 2009 Taylor & Francis

Typeset in Sabon by IBT Global.
Printed and bound in the United States of America on acid-free paper by IBT Global.

Library of Congress Cataloging-in-Publication Data
Rief, Silvia, 1971-
  Club cultures : boundaries, identities and otherness / Silvia Rief.
    p. cm. — (Routledge advances in sociology ; 48)
  Includes bibliographical references and index.
  1. Dance—Social aspects.   2. Nightclubs—Social aspects.   3. Nightlife—Social aspects.   I. Title.
  GV1588.6.R54 2009
  306.4'846—dc22
  2009004665

ISBN10: 0-415-95853-9 (hbk)
ISBN10: 0-203-87329-7 (ebk)

ISBN13: 978-0-415-95853-0 (hbk)
ISBN13: 978-0-203-87329-8(ebk)

Contents

Acknowledgements

The project on which this book is based began in 1998 at Goldsmiths College in London. Now that it finally materialized in this book, after several detours and new paths, I wish to thank my mentors, colleagues and friends who provided intellectual stimulation and support. Many thanks go to Helen Thomas, who accompanied this research over several years at its outset and who was a rich source of inspiration for sociological perspectives on the body and dance. Thanks are due to Don Slater and Mariam Fraser for drawing my attention to recent debates on culture, consumption and economy and the feminist literature on 'passing'. Scott Lash's writings on aesthetic reflexivity and Bev Skeggs' work on class and sexuality also left their mark on this book as did Nikolas Rose's reflections on governmentality and freedom discourses. He was a critical influence on theoretical and methodological issues. They and all other colleagues at the time at Goldsmiths' Sociology Department and Centre for Urban and Community Research should be thanked for all their instructive comments and constructive criticisms as well as for their encouragement and support, especially Luis Jimenez, Jakob Arnoldi, Minna Pietila, Anne-Marie Singh and George Mavromatis. I am also particularly indebted to Alan Scott, thanks to whom this project shifted into new directions focusing on the governance of urban night life. Similar thanks go to Roberta Sassatelli whose work on consumption, the body and sexuality has also been a source of great insight to me. They as well as my colleagues of the 'Cities, Regions and Cultures' group at the University of Innsbruck, especially Laurie Cohen, provided much encouragement, advice and helpful comments on earlier drafts of this work.

This book was made possible by many individuals who, over the years, have contributed as interviewees, informants and gatekeepers or in many practical ways to its successful completion. I cannot possibly name them all, but wish to express my gratitude to my friends Acala and Zoe in London, and to Glad, now in Spain. In Istanbul Sabine Küper-Busch and her partner introduced me to the city's night life and opened up many contacts to local promoters, music producers and DJs. Burcu Esenler deserves a special mention for having provided assistance with translation. Her help was indispensable and extremely kind. This book also would not have seen the light of day without the financial assistance of the UK Economic and Social Research Council (ESRC), the Austrian Ministry of Science and the Austrian Academy of Science. They all awarded grants for the initial PhD project, which enabled me to embark on this research with great concentration over several years. Earlier versions of some chapters have been presented at conferences, which I could not have attended without the financial support from the University of Innsbruck. I gratefully acknowledge the assistance of these and other funding bodies. An earlier version of Chapter 8 was originally published in the journal *Studi Culturali* which is hereby gratefully acknowledged for granting permission to reprint this article in revised form. I am also indebted to Ben Holtzman from Routledge, who has taken on this work for publication and has overseen the development of the book with much patience, courtesy and understanding.

Finally, I owe a considerable depth of thanks to Iris—for the willingness to listen, to read and to discuss and for her help with the final editing of the manuscript. I am deeply grateful for her constant support and love.

Figures

Tables

Graphs

1 Introduction

The *homo aestheticus* is a virtuoso of the 'sense of possibility' and virtualisation. (Welsch 1997: 15)

SCENERIES OF CLUBBING CULTURE

Back in 1995, Franco Bianchini spoke of the 'relative underdevelopment of urban night-life in Britain' compared to other European cities (1995: 123). According to Bianchini, the development of night-life culture was inhibited by the monofunctional British town centres dominated by shops, offices and physical structures not particularly conducive to walking the city; by poor public transport provision at night; by the temporal constraints of the licensing hours and a leisure lifestyle that was predominantly home-based (ibid.). More than a decade later the landscape of night life in many British town and city centres hardly matches this dire picture of the past.

Although the oldest club of the Mediterranean island Ibiza goes back to the early 1970s,[1] it was only in the late 1980s, when British DJs who had visited the island tried to recreate the atmosphere of all-night clubbing and dancing on the drug ecstasy (MDMA) in their home country. The so-called 'Summer of Love' in Ibiza 1988 laid the grounds for the acid-house and rave culture movement in Britain. Rave's popularity and notoriety grew with the moral panics spun around the drug ecstasy in the early 1990s. Furthermore, technological advancements allowed an ever-wider group of people to engage in music production and DJing. For a couple of years underground rave scenes staged unlicensed parties in disused warehouses and squats, open-air sites like airport hangars or in countryside locations. These scenes thrived outside the established bars and discotheques and circumvented the usual standards of regulation. After the introduction of the Criminal Justice and Public Order Act (1994) however, which clamped down on the rave scene, dance culture in Britain returned to licensed venues in the cities.[2] Since then it has evolved into a significant sector of the cultural and entertainment economy. Led by new high-capacity and well-equipped super-clubs, the bar and club scene expanded in nearly all major UK cities throughout and beyond the 1990s. Apart from London, cities such as Brighton, Manchester, Newcastle, Leeds, Liverpool, Glasgow, Bristol and Sheffield all have vibrant night-life and music cultures. What once was mainly regarded as an object of regulation and containment was promoted in cultural strategies of urban renewal. The number of studies focusing on nightclubbing in Britain probably is another indicator of the changed status of night-life culture there. The British acid-house and rave culture movement is often mentioned next to Detroit techno, Chicago house music, and the famous New York nightclubs of the 1970s and 1980s as one of the most influential centres from which dance music and club culture spread out to the globe. In general, however, the discourses on nightclubbing culture are still very UK-centred. This contrasts with the fact that over the past decade, 'clubbing' has become an international, if not global signifier of 'going out dancing'. Instead of being shaped by one or a few centres, global dance culture is more like a polycentral network. Although clubbing is somewhat less central to youth and adolescent life in North America than in the UK (Saego 2004, Thornton 1995), night-life and clubbing scenes exist, for example, in San Francisco, New York, Vancouver and Montréal. In Europe (outside the UK), Amsterdam, Paris, Berlin, Dublin, Reykjavik, St. Petersburg, Barcelona, Belgrade, Istanbul and Vienna, amongst others, have built up a reputation for their music and club cultures. Belgrade has become known for its own pop and underground club scene as well as its homemade 'hardcore techno' music (Saego 2004). The Middle East (e.g. Lebanon, Israel), Australia (e.g. Sydney), Asia (e.g. Shanghai, Hong Kong, Beijing, Tokyo, Singapore, Bombay) and Latin America (e.g. Buenos Aires, Mexico City, Sao Paolo) all have seen a remarkable growth of night-life and club culture, too. In China, the development of these scenes set in with the arrival of Western expatriates in the late 1980s and 1990s. Sanlitun, a once-staid district of embassies in Beijing, has become the city's night life 'Mecca', mainly for the wealthy urban middle classes (Eimer 2006). Apart from these well-known metropoles, many partly smaller cities have also seen a considerable expansion of music and night-life culture (e.g. Leipzig and Zurich).

Club culture has truly become a global cultural phenomenon, even if significant parts of the world still remain untouched by it. Influences and cross-fertilizations can no longer be pinned down so easily. The club scenes in various locations are interlinked through global multimedia companies, international business ventures, prominent DJ(ane)s touring internationally, personal links between agents and, last but not least, the Internet. Despite the ongoing significance of established centres of club cultural production such as the UK, international exchanges often bypass these. Whereas British companies and brands have a strong presence on the international clubbing markets, for example, in Turkey, specifically Istanbul, Istanbul music and club cultures also thrive on influences and exchanges with many other places.

While nightclubbing is very much an urban form of leisure, it has also been heavily promoted as part of the time-out experience of holiday-making predominantly in warmer regions of the world. Between 1998 and 2002 the clubbing holiday market increased in value by a third to £1.8 billion or 5 per cent of the total holiday market in Britain. Fostered by the connections to DJs and club promoters in the UK, Ibiza has been at the forefront of the clubbing holiday business hosting some of the biggest nightclubs, with capacities up to 10,000. Clubbers in their early thirties, mainly frequenting Ibiza Town and the East Coast, sometimes spend around £2,000 a week partying. In the late 1990s Ayia Napa in Cyprus became the new 'Club Capital'. At the height of its popularity it attracted more than 250,000 clubbers a season mainly from Britain, Sweden, Denmark, Russia, Israel and Italy. Major clubbing holiday destinations have emerged on other Spanish islands (Majorca, Gran Canaria, Tenerife), in Goa (India), Falaraki (Rhodes) and Malia (Crete; see Mintel 2003).

In addition to the clubbing holidays, street parades and music festivals, often staging a range of music acts besides dance music, have also grown substantially since the 1990s, both in terms of quantity and economic significance. The well-known Berlin Love Parade, which was launched in 1989 with 150 visitors, reached its peak with 1.5 million visitors in 1999. Visitor numbers fell considerably in the following years, but when re-launched in the Ruhr city Essen in 2007, it drew 1.2 million people; in Dortmund in 2008 a staggering 1.6 million people were reported in attendance. Many other festivals have emerged in cities or holiday resorts, such as the Kazantip Republic on Crim Island or the Sziget Festival in Budapest.

Even though certain elements may be common to dance and club cultures across the globe (e.g. music, fashion and drugs), nightclubbing has not become a homogeneous global culture. Despite shaping similar outlooks, lifestyles and fashions across national boundaries, club cultures remain inflected by local histories, traditions, social, political and economic circumstances; for example, local modes of night-life governance or specificities of the cultural sector, musical and dance traditions, and class and gender relations. One and the same club concept may work out differently in each context. As the London-based promoter of the queer, alternative club Wotever reflected (Ingo 2007),[3] when they hosted their event in Warsaw, where queer sexualities are a highly contentious political issue, it became a 'freedom act', whereas in Stockholm, where freedom of expression is guaranteed, it appeared as an act of 'anti-capitalism'.

The kind of practices, experiences and dance spaces that clubbing signifies in different countries, cities or social contexts varies enormously. Clubbing may refer to dance and music events in nightclubs of variable sizes and capacities (up to several thousand); to going out in smaller, hybrid venues that integrate eating, drinking, socializing and dancing in one place; to dances in venues previously designated as discotheques; or to open-air parties and festivals in the open countryside, on beaches or in the mountains. In the attempt to recreate the original 'underground' feel of the rave and warehouse parties, boats, car parks, train stations and even aircrafts have been used as clubbing sceneries (Manson 2006, Randeria 2002). Recent years have seen the invention of new types of clubbing, where people gather in underground and train stations or other public places and then dance to the tunes of their MP3-players. With the emergence of new technologies, spatial contexts of clubbing have multiplied. But also the time frame for going out dancing has been uncoupled from the core weekend nights. Clubbing events may stretch out over whole weekends and more or start on early weekday evenings as after-work clubbings. However, this is not necessarily new, thinking of Tom Wolfe's depiction (1968) of the mods who escaped their offices and jobs and danced away their lunch break in central London's basement clubs back in the early 1960s (the so-called noonday underground). Raving and clubbing have often been marked off from the dance and music cultures of the 1970s and 1980s. Yet, as this example shows, there may be more continuity to previous youth dance spaces than is commonly assumed. Night-life spaces come and go, but some also stay and regularly accommodate new trends and fashions.

In the light of the plurality of forms sketched so far, a rather wide and open definition was therefore chosen for this study: 'clubbing' denotes a cultural and social practice and a particular ambience that combines (mainly) electronic, beat-centred music of various genres, dance, fashion, drugs and sexuality in various temporal and spatial contexts of co-presence. This book does not focus on a particular musical genre or type of scenery. Nevertheless, it builds on empirical analyses of specific contexts of the production and consumption of clubbing that shall be set out below.

THE POLITICS OF CLUBBINGS' OTHERNESS

Clubbing spaces and experiences are inscribed with images of transgression, freedom and liberation. As spaces commonly associated with fun, enjoyment and leisure, they are frequently described as an other reality or an 'otherworldly environment' (Thornton 1995: 21) whose absorbing atmosphere facilitates the distantiation from routines of everyday life; paradoxically, whilst reproducing routines quite similar to everyday contexts. As Andy Lovatt expounded,

> the night-time is a liminal time in which the world of work is seen to lose its hold. A time for and of transgression, a time for spending, a time for trying to be something the daytime may not let you be, a time for meeting people you shouldn't, for doing things your parents told you not to, that your children are too young to understand. This is now being promoted as vibrancy. But this invitation to transgression, marginal in the Fordist city of work is now central to contemporary consumerism. (Lovatt 1996: 162)

Indeed, club cultures can be seen as contemporary versions of the sacred (see Chapter 4). They are not only connoted with transgression but even promoted as liminal spaces, thriving on the promise of communitas (Hobbs, Lister, Hadfield, Winslow, and Hall 2000: 712, Talbot 2007: 1–2). For the audiences, as other studies suggest, clubbing usually assumes positive notions of transgression into liminal states, in which 'other' modes of being, acting and living can be explored. By contrast, for the agents and institutions of regulation, especially the local authorities, night life cultures—despite the economic benefits they bring—often carry notions of problematic transgression that is to be contained and regulated: youthful rebellion, binge drinking or 'anti-social behaviour'. Such ambivalent views on otherness are also weaved through academic studies and theoretical perspectives on the topic. Research in the first half of the 1990s was very much shaped and propelled by the media outrage over the popularization of drug taking, particularly of ecstasy, within rave contexts. As a consequence, academic research too tended to concentrate on drugs and drug consumption. On the one hand, rave culture was dismissed as either illegal and semi-criminal, or as hedonist and de-politicized youth culture. On the other hand, such images provoked critique and, to some extent, led to the opposite extreme, the academic fetishization of rave culture. From this perspective, attention was drawn to its socially and culturally progressive elements. Raving, dancing and consuming illicit drugs came to be seen as a mystery (see also Gibson and Pagan 1998: 16). Similar to other societal reactions to youth culture, interpretations of rave culture ranged from the condemnation of delinquency to the celebration of progressiveness (Widdicombe and Wooffitt 1995: 7).

The academic discourse on rave and dance culture also pressed ahead with the critique of subcultural theory and increasingly adopted postmodern terminology. In the light of postmodern epistemological strategies, rave culture itself appeared as subversive aesthetic-political strategy. This advanced and partly reshaped the subcultural vocabulary of resistance and opposition to dominant ideology (see also Frith 2004: 176). More specifically, rave came to be imagined as an aesthetic of deconstruction, and the 'raving subject' seemingly embodied a postmodern, 'deconstructed self'. This emphasized the undoing of the logic of identity. Rave was hailed for its liberating qualities of putting the subject at or over the limits of meaning and rationality. Various theoretical metaphors were employed to illustrate such subjectivity-at-its-limits: simulation (Baudrillard 1983), body-without-organs (Deleuze and Guattari 1996), neo-tribal sociality (Maffesoli 1995), liminality and communitas (Turner 1969), other space and heterotopia (Foucault 1986). Simulation evoked a dramaturgical metaphor of role-play, posing and performing, mediated through images, models and codes. Clubbing and dance cultural practices were taken as the illustration of a postmodern, eclectic use of styles, as a 'disappearance of a culture of meaning' (Baudrillard, Krauss, and Michelson 1982: 5, as quoted in Thornton 1995: 1) and the loss of cultural and self identity in the unculture of the hyperreal (Melechi 1993: 32–33). Similarly, rave culture was interpreted (and criticized) as a politically indifferent desiring machine

(Jordan 1995) that deconstructed temporality, narrative and history into a series of perpetual presents or schizophrenic intensities (Jameson 1991: 25–28). Maffesoli's notion of neo-tribal sociality had by far the most significant impact on the development of post-subcultural theoretical perspectives in recent years (see especially A. Bennett 1999, A. Bennett and Harris 2004, Muggleton, and Weinzierl 2003b). Focus shifted to transient, multiple identifications and affiliations; shared sentiments, the release from the burden of individuality and from the pressures of forced self-construction and self-perfection in a highly individualized society (Malbon 1999). The co-presence of dance clubs was thought to foster identifications 'in the presence of differences that might normally preclude this sharing of emotional space' such as age, ethnicity, gender or class (ibid. 83). Overall, however, these strands of research tended to overemphasize the 'sacred' dimensions at the expense of the profane and routine aspects of dance and club culture, celebrating nightclubs as spaces of ecstasy, bliss and transgression. Attention tended to be directed primarily to consumption, while the production and institutional regulation of nightclubbing was neglected. In the last few years, however, this tendency was inverted, and the focus of attention shifted to the mundane aspects of night-time entertainment. The growth of the nightclubbing sector and the emergence of technically well-equipped, large-capacity clubs spotlighted the routine modes of operation and the logistic management and control of crowds within night-time entertainment. Institutional and governance dimensions of night life came to the fore. As several legal changes pertaining to the night-time economy were introduced in the UK between 2001 and 2006 (e.g. the reform of the licensing legislation, the professionalization of the private security industry), researchers began to investigate the impact of these changes. As aforementioned, for a certain period, night-time economies in Britain were heavily promoted within projects of urban renewal and regeneration; yet, the ambivalent attitude towards it continues and has led, in the context of the media outrage against binge drinking, anti-social behaviour, disorder and violence, gang wars and gun crime, to a re-problematization of night-time entertainment. In some respects, as is the case with drug taking, legal norms clash with the widespread practices and values within clubbing culture, provoking ambivalent responses from the authorities. Their modes of governing night life oscillate between law and order discourses of containment and liberal discourses of economic development and laissez-faire. Nightclubbing cultures contribute to a vibrant social and cultural life of a city. But, as was found in the UK, they also add—especially at an aggregate level—to public order problems, triggering knock-on effects on late-night street crime, particularly in saturated night-life areas. They can be culturally innovative, allowing for artistic and creative practices; but they are also subject to standardization and corporate power. Attempts to contain and regulate will always provoke unpredictable transgressions. The night-time economy raises contentious political and social issues, in big metropoles with large clusters of night-life entertainment just as well as in smaller cities. It raises questions as to where and how the boundaries shall be drawn between tolerating and containing certain kinds of practices or cultures of night life, and questions as to what scale of night-time entertainment and what forms of governance are most reasonable and most appropriate. They are ambivalent spaces. However, from this it does not follow that socio-cultural analyses should partake in these debates over the value of clubbing cultures. They can neither be simply appraised as oppositional nor can they wholly be dismissed as consumerist or escapist. Socio-cultural analysis needs to avoid both a romantic, sentimental glorification and a moralistic disapproval of these practices.

REVISITING AUTHENTICITY

Postmodern metaphors of 'subjectivity-at-its-limits' in clubbing culture (such as the concepts of simulation or neo-tribal sociality) alluded to the changing understandings of authenticity in youth and postmodern culture. Youth and popular culture studies have a long history of engaging with the theme of authenticity. Subcultural theory, for example, tended to distinguish between the authentic, resistant youth cultural styles on the one hand, and the commercialized, media-saturated youth cultures on the other hand. Later works in the 1990s addressed authenticity in relation to the legitimation and validation of cultural practices in processes of social distinction. For example, Sarah Thornton (1995) investigated the subcultural classifiers for claiming or disclaiming authenticity and value. Her historical account of popular music and dance cultures drew attention to the changing conventions of authenticity regarding live performance and recorded music. Sue Widdicombe and Robin Wooffitt (e.g. 1995, 1990, 1993) as well as David Muggleton (2000) dealt with authenticity mainly in relation to the construction of youth cultural membership, identity and style. They investigated as to how authenticity figured as a theme in discourses about the way of life of a group and as a measure of (non)correspondence between 'being' and 'doing', between 'essence' and 'appearance'. In his work on rock culture, Lawrence Grossberg (1992) took a broader perspective and described the awareness of inauthenticity as a postmodern sensibility or structure of feeling. He coined the term 'authentic inauthenticity' to point to the blurring boundary between the real and the artificial in cynicism, irony and play. More recent debates about youth post-subcultures explored how postmodern depthlessness, simulation and style eclecticism led to the weakening of subcultural group and style boundaries and undermined notions of youth cultural authenticity (Muggleton and Weinzierl 2003b, Muggleton 2000, A. Bennett 1999, A. Bennett and Harris 2004). The new forms of association and sociability (e.g. 'neo-tribes', 'sub-streams', 'scenes') formed a central subject matter of post-subcultural debates on youth dance cultures in Britain.[4]

However, the relative dominance of this theme somewhat blinded researchers to other lines of enquiry including different theoretical perspectives. Authenticity was discussed mainly with respect to style, membership and distinction, but the types of practices fostered in club cultures and their effects on the experience and understanding of selfhood and identity remained relatively unexplored. The various techniques of self that are invented and cultivated in youth cultural spaces received surprisingly little attention or, in the case of debates on clubbing, were described in rather vague concepts such as 'playful vitality', 'oceanic' and 'ecstatic' experiences or 'self-fashioning' (Malbon 1999, Buckland 2002). These terms touched upon, and tried to capture, particular modes of being and experience, but the implications for the shaping of cultural and social identities and for particular interpretive repertoires were not investigated thoroughly. More recently, such questions have been taken up either by sociologists applying concepts of reflexive modernization theory or by academics interested in knowledge, innovation and cultural learning (e.g. Sweetman 2003, 2004, Ewenstein 2004). This book aims to further develop these approaches by drawing on the notion of aesthetic reflexivity (Lash 1993) and the related debates on aestheticization and prosthetic culture (e.g. Welsch 1997, Lury 1998) in order to work towards a deeper understanding of the sensibilities and interpretive repertoires not only in youth cultures, but in contexts of popular culture more generally.[5]

Debates on aestheticization also deliberate on the question of authenticity. Welsch (1997: 5) argued that an immaterial or epistemological aestheticization shifts the modes of apprehending and conceiving of reality, blurring the distinction between real and not-real and destabilizing processes of authentication. He gave as example the virtualization or de-realization induced by electronic and media worlds. Club cultures too centre on aesthetic practices and prosthetic forms of embodiment, exposing participants to intense sensory stimulation and encouraging them to play with styles, masks and roles. Thereby, particular qualities of experience and modes of reflexivity are created. Aestheticization opens up imaginary transformation through identificatory practices of acting 'as-if.' Prosthetic self-extension involves the construction of sensuous and perceptual states with the help of particular technological or chemical means. Previous studies drew attention to the play-character of clubbing contexts. Malbon (1999), as above-mentioned, referred to play and vitality; Buckland to self-fashioning (2002). But in contrast to Malbon's rather vitalistic interpretation of experiences of clubbing, the analytical framework of this book builds on phenomenological and sociological perspectives on cognition and classification. It focuses on interpretive repertoires and how they shape particular orders of reality (Schütz 1971), informing the understanding and classification of self and other (Zerubavel 1999) as well as notions of authenticity and identity.

Virtualization affects the construction of identity. Economies of transgression such as carnival were interpreted as processes of displaced abjection (Stallybrass and White 1986: 19). This suggested that carnival did not simply invert the status order at a symbolic level, but often demonized the weaker, not the stronger social groups (ibid. 19). According to Stallybrass and White, it allowed for a temporal release into abject, yet fascinating otherness. This dynamic was linked to the subject-formation of the middle classes, who appropriated carnival whilst repudiating the social spheres where these rites originated.

> The bourgeois subject continuously defined and re-defined itself through the exclusion of what it marked out as 'low'—as dirty, repulsive, noisy, contaminating. Yet, that very act of exclusion was constitutive of its identity. The low was internalized under the sign of negation and disgust. (Stallybrass and White 1986: 191)

The repudiation of the cultures of the popular as the 'culture of the Other' was seen in relation to the constitution of 'high culture' itself. This line of thought emphasized how identity in carnival was remade through the symbolic appropriation and exclusion of an Other, accentuating the imaginary closure of identity against difference.[6] In providing spaces where insincere, playful identifications can be expressed and lived, contemporary club and dance cultures do have carnivalesque features. However, the above perspective on transgression needs to be opened up to account for dimensions of identification that do not constitute and exclude abject otherness, but that are based on the incorporation of what I shall call 'virtual otherness'. As was argued (e.g. Hannigan 1998), postmodern leisure spaces frequently erode the distinction between authentic and inauthentic, setting apart simulated, hyperreal environments from 'real reality' (Bauman 1993: 170). Virtualization propels performative notions of identity, in which identity is understood as the result of aesthetic and prosthetic stylization or manipulation. To some extent, this destabilizes binary, clear-cut boundaries between sameness and difference, and generates more fleeting, unstable boundaries to a horizon of virtual otherness. The demarcation of identity, however provisional, is thereby not only related to alterity and difference, but is also informed by a 'sense of possibility', of who or what one could be or might become (in positive or negative ways). It is not only marked off from alterity and difference, but partly blends with, and takes into account, possible becomings. This book interprets clubbing in the context of aestheticization processes. It explores, at the example of an empirical analysis of experiential accounts of clubbing, how *aestheticization* and virtualization affect modes of reflexivity, the logic of authenticity and the construction of identity. By delving into the concrete qualities of experience and the varieties of making sense in contexts of aestheticization, it puts into perspective sweeping assumptions about merely inauthentic and simulated experiences in postmodern leisure spheres.

The focus on modes of reflexivity is linked up with an analysis of symbolic and social boundary practices. Such a perspective on symbolic boundaries was opened up by Thornton's pivotal study on club cultures (1995). Drawing on Bourdieu's capital theory and notion of social distinction (1984), Thornton pointed to the symbolic oppositions in the field of dance and popular music culture that were deployed to legitimate particular practices and to draw lines of demarcation against rivals in order to stake out claims to credibility (in Thornton's terms, 'subcultural capital'; on boundary work see Gieryn 1983). She identified three main discursive oppositions that oriented boundary work in this field: the 'authentic' vs. the 'phoney', the 'underground' vs. the 'media', the 'hip' vs. the 'mainstream'. This book builds on and extends this approach by drawing from recent perspectives on boundaries in US-cultural sociology (e.g. Lamont and Molnár 2002, Tilly 2006). It uses the notion of boundary work as a sensitizing concept to study the current modes of regulation and production of night-time economies in the UK as well as to analyse the negotiation of identities and of entitlements to space. Boundary work is not just narrowly understood as a mode of distinction and status competition based on claims to authenticity or credibility, but in relation to interpretive styles of authenticating and classifying more generally, for example, when marking off play and reality; when validating and invalidating certain experiences; or in terms of the framing practices that are implied in the production, regulation, mediation and consumption of club cultural spaces. The analysis thereby brings to the fore a much broader perspective on boundaries at different levels of social practice. As outlined above, the second sensitizing concept of aesthetic reflexivity sheds light on different modalities of boundary work that do not all centre on binary oppositions. In sum, the theoretical framework, which shall be expounded in more detail in Chapter 4, draws on two debates: firstly, aestheticization and prosthetic culture and secondly, cultural sociology perspectives on boundaries. I believe that these perspectives enhance the analytical understanding of the types of practices and modes of experience fostered in club cultural spaces.

METHODOLOGY AND FIELD OF STUDY

This book started off as an investigation of practices and experiences of clubbing in London back in 1998, where one part of this research was carried out, in the period between 1999 and 2001. In 2007 follow-up research was conducted in London and Istanbul (see more details in the following). The starting and ending points of this book, therefore, stretch over a decade. Over this period not only the clubbing scenes have changed substantially, but also the academic perspectives on them. Hence, this book itself reflects the shifting focal points of academic research over the past decade. At the end of the 1990s mainly theoretical analyses of rave culture existed, which often centred on a generalized and de-contextualized 'raving subject'. Empirical research on rave and club cultures was in its infancy; the first ethnographic studies that explored experiential accounts of clubbing chiefly focused on committed participants. Even though the influence of gay culture on the acid-house and ecstasy-based dance cultures was frequently acknowledged and claims about the fusing of gay and straight scenes circulated widely, research was for the most part taking place in heterosexual scenes and implicitly talking of heterosexual clubbing experiences. Understandably, researchers tended to avoid scenes that did not correspond with their sexual identification or that they found hard to relate to.[7]

In view of this, my initial research interest was to explore different types and intensities of involvement in club cultures and—instead of simply concentrating on the experience of clubbing itself—to consider how the involvement in these scenes related to other aspects of life such as work, education, relationships and to biographical experiences in general. Further, I regarded a more pronounced focus on sexuality important in advancing the field of study. Sexuality is a key topos in the representation of nightclubs as transgressive and liminal spaces. Gay and queer clubs have become popular among straight audiences symbolizing a certain aesthetic ambience. Thus, the relation between sexualities in clubbing culture called for more intensive study; in particular, the sexual codification of scenes, the degree of mixture between straight and gay audiences and people's experiences of straight, gay and mixed spaces.

As the field was relatively unexplored at the time, preference was given to an open, qualitative research design and a data-driven analysis that was modified and narrowed down in the process. In-depth narrative interviewing was the key method of data construction combined with ethnographic fieldwork. Narrative interviews generate thick and detailed accounts close to the practices under study and organized according to the relevances of the interviewees instead of being structured by the pre-conceptions of the researcher. It was hoped that this would yield data that provided the opportunity to study clubbing experiences in conjunction with wider life experiences and everyday identities and that produced complex accounts of social settings, situations, actions and courses of events.[8] Ethnographic fieldwork was used as a form of triangulation of the interview data to gather impressions of the club crowds and settings, especially those frequented by the interviewees, and of the local organization of practices in clubs. But it was also employed in order to reflect on the conditions of 'constructing' experience in environments where giving in to sensual overstimulation and immersion in the ongoing practice are normative requirements of the setting. The aim was also to explore institutional modes of regulation and ordering (see more details below).

Interviewing took place outside the clubbing sphere, and interviewees were not approached in the clubs as this was considered too random and too obtrusive.[9] The purposive sample aimed at a mix of people in terms

of gender, sexual identification, age, profession/education, social and ethnic background and different types and intensities of involvement. In order
to avoid a bias towards 'core' participants, people who did not go clubbing regularly or had stopped going out clubbing altogether were explicitly
encouraged. Several ways were tried to access interviewees; not all of them,
however, were successful. A number of people, mainly students, responded
to a letter placed on notice boards of university colleges, but none replied to
a letter put up in a (gay) pre-club bar or to the ads placed in a popular, free
lesbian and gay weekly and in the newsletter of a black gay and lesbian community association. However, snowballing via the first group of interviewees
and partly via other acquaintances proved effective to attract a further group
of people with varied backgrounds. Given these limitations, the sample generated this way was mixed in terms of age, sexual identification and national
and cultural background, but was fairly homogeneous in other respects—it
was a predominantly white middle-class sample. As far as the demographic
profile of British club-goers can be pinned down,[10] the core consumer group
of nightclubs is aged between 18 and 24; it has a strong base in the middle
income groups and tends to be single. Students form a significant part of the
nightclub clientele. Age-wise almost half of the 23 interviewees of this study
were in the main age-group of clubbers aged between 18 and 25; a third was
in their late twenties, two interviewees were in their thirties and two were in
their early forties. In terms of sexual identification, the sample included seven
'heterosexual' females, five 'heterosexual' males, five 'lesbians', five 'gay'
males and one 'bisexual' male. However, it should be noted that this categorization is based on the (implicit) self-presentation in the interviews and
was not explicitly asked. The inverted commas mean to suggest that sexual
identification did not in all cases fall into (just) one of these categories. One
interviewee labelled himself 'pansexual', another female interviewee identified as heterosexual, but referred to bisexual tendencies and same-sex sexual
experiences. Twelve persons of this sample were students, but half of them
were also working part-time or had worked before taking up their studies;
eleven persons, amongst them several graduates, were working. More than
half of the interviewees were raised in the UK; several had moved to the UK
from continental Europe including Sweden, Germany, Poland, Greece and
Italy or from Canada, Turkey and Australia. Two had a mixed background;
one interviewee was raised in Britain by German-French parents; the other
had grown up in a Korean family in Italy before coming to the UK.[11]

   The interviews for this research were usually conducted in a college
office or in people's homes. After explaining the research interests and
the procedure of interviewing, the interviews usually started off with the
question: 'Can you tell me about your involvement in different dance and
clubbing scenes and how this related to your life?' The narrative initiated by this question lasted on average between 30 and 60 minutes, and
in some cases up to 3 hours. Occasionally, this question was perceived
to be too wide; if so, more specific exemplary themes were suggested,

for example, 'Remember when you started going out clubbing'. After the initial narration I asked the interviewees to elaborate on certain topics they had covered in a more detailed way, before moving on to issues of interest they had not mentioned. When it was appropriate, I sometimes adopted a mode of direct questioning towards the end of the interview aimed at reconstructing detailed memories of a recent night out. These questions covered aspects such as 'choosing', 'organizing' and 'preparing' for the club night; memories of queuing and admission; conversations with strangers; their first impressions and perceptions of the space; their paths through different areas of the club and their memories of dancing and interacting on the dance floor. Most interviews lasted about two hours altogether and with some persons a second interview was arranged (see Appendix). In order to re-establish a reciprocal conversation, most interviewees also wished to know things about me such as, which places I went out to, what clubs I was researching, if I had similar experiences or else. In other words, in these interactive co-constructions I tended to come across—due perhaps to my age and appearance—as a participant too.

The same applied to my ethnographic role. In most ethnographic studies of rave and dance culture, researchers considered themselves part of the field they were studying and even chose contexts of study in which they felt familiar (e.g. Malbon 1998, Pini 1997, Buckland 2002). Roles of pure participation or observation were found to be inappropriate in nightclubs, and ethnographic researchers usually took up a role as participant–observer or observant participant, who joined in instead of observing and taking notes (e.g. Malbon 1998: 46–58). Ethnographic participation in clubs meets theoretical, ethical and methodological problems. A completely overt ethnographic role is infeasible in nightclubs as the ethnographic role cannot possibly be disclosed to all participants. Given that the ethnographer is likely to be perceived as a participant, detached observation runs counter to the local ethos of involvement and is perceived as strange and out of place (so would be note-taking apart from the practical limitations posed to it). As 'one of them' the ethnographer has to take part in order to build rapport. Yet, as has been indicated above, involvement in a setting of sensual (over)stimulation—especially if it is connected to bodily movement such as dancing—makes observing and memorizing rather difficult. The inescapable distraction of the senses, therefore, interferes with the ethnographic practice in clubs.[12] This, however, is only a limitation if ethnography is simply employed to gather 'evidence', which was not the main aim of ethnographic fieldwork in the context of this study. Instead it was also used as a tool to reflect upon the conditions that shaped and confined perception, memory and the making of experience in clubs.

Contrary to the frequent ironic insinuation by clubbing participants and colleagues alike that ethnographic participation in clubbing passes off the researcher's own leisure and fun as work, ethnographic practice is a work role in a space where most other people consume leisure (see also Thornton

1995: 2). The blurring of work and leisure roles sometimes produced confusion and strain as everyday research work stretched to ethnographic night-time work in clubs. In trying to avoid studying merely those contexts that matched my personal tastes, preferences and sexual identification, I selected a cross-section of about twenty straight, gay, gay-mixed and lesbian dance clubs in central London.[13] The selection of clubs aimed to cover a variety of musical genres (especially house, hard house and techno, deep house and garage) as well as clubs that were frequented by the interviewees. Clubs that indicated trends of the nightclub industry at the time such as newly opened 'super-clubs' or hybrid restaurant-bar-clubs were also included. Due to limited resources preference was given to locations within zones one and two in central London. The clubs were visited once or twice on different nights of the week with exceptions outlined further below. All of the events and clubs were advertised in listing magazines or otherwise. Ethnographic fieldwork stretched over the period from November 1999 to March 2001, but additional visits followed between 2002 and 2004 as well as in 2007. Fieldnotes were usually taken the morning after visiting the club, starting with an open, detailed and descriptive mode of note-taking at the outset of the study. Attention was paid to the physical layout and the construction of space through the practices of the crowd; to visual structures in clubs, in particular, the conditions for, and the scope of, mutual visual perception; the characteristics of the audiences in terms of estimated age, fashion and styles or else; to modes of dancing and bodily interaction between participants; to the logistic ordering of the crowds by the club management (e.g. security checks and admission procedures); to encounters and conversations with other participants. As said before, ethnographic fieldwork and note-taking also included self-observation of emotions, bodily sensations and the structuration of perception through the organization of space and the visual, auditory and haptic stimuli.

In the course of data collection, certain modifications towards more focused study were made. Ethnographic studies of clubbing thitherto had concentrated on clubbers' experiences in a rather decontextualized way without taking into account the production, marketing, management and regulation of club spaces. I therefore decided to carry out case studies of two specific sites, a gay-mixed club and a lesbian bar-club. This involved more intensive ethnographic research in these venues, which were visited about six times each at the time followed by occasional visits in subsequent years. It also included interviews with the owner/manager respectively promoter of these places. These two clubs were selected, first, for analytical reasons (see above as well as the chapter outline) and second, because they were frequently talked about in the interviews. The case studies were informed by Dorothy Smith's (1987) concept of institutional ethnography, which brings into focus three dimensions: ideological procedures and modes of accounting, institutional processes (e.g. the organization of production and consumption) and the social relations that integrate these processes as courses of action. Following this concept in a slightly modified form, the case studies explored the promotion and image work of the clubs and how they framed their markets and target audiences; they further considered the clubs' door policies and admission procedures as a central component of institutional ordering; and they examined modes of interaction inside the clubs in the context of the former dimensions. Additional material drawn from the Internet, newspapers and magazines and interviews with the managers and promoters of several other clubs complemented this analysis. In expanding the analytical focus on sexuality, I also considered how sexuality was represented in clubbing magazines and embarked on a visual analysis based on two mainstream UK magazines. The details of this analysis as well as of the narrative analysis of the interview data are set out in the relevant chapters. Overall, the analysis was supported by additional material such as surveys of drug consumption, films, documentaries and media articles.

As mentioned above, follow-up research was conducted in 2007. This was geared towards situating the empirical analysis of this book in the wider context of the development of the night-time economy market and the transformation of night-life governance in the UK. It also intended to examine ownership and company structures as well as trends of club cultural production and market making. The main focus of this book lies on London and the UK, but in order to open up a broader, comparative perspective that allowed for reflecting upon similarities and differences between the political, economic and cultural contexts of nightclubbing cultures, another local case (Istanbul) was integrated into this analysis. It builds on a range of documents and secondary sources including licensing policies, planning policy documents, local reports on the night-time economy, statistical data, market research, company data and media articles. Additional expert interviews were carried out with licensing officers and club promoters in London and Istanbul. The rationale of this analysis and the scope and limitations of the data are expounded in detail in Chapters 2 and 3.

OUTLINE OF THE BOOK

As stated at the outset, dance and club cultures have evolved into a near global cultural phenomenon. They emerged and flourished in quite diverse urban contexts with distinct local histories, politics, economic and social structures, religious cultures, demographic trends and relations of class, gender and ethnicity. However, little is known about the interdependencies between local circumstances and the development of club cultural economies and how global and local forces come to interrelate. Chapter 2 aims to work towards filling this gap by taking into account the changing regulatory context in Britain in the past two decades. The (cultural) restructuration of post-industrial urban economies and the transformation of urban governance into an economic regional development project provided the backdrop for the growth of the night-time economy not only in Britain but also in other European cities. Based on certain night-life areas in central London, Chapter 2 also explores the consequences and effects of the implementation of the new Licensing Act of 2003 and of other legal changes, in particular, as to how local councils, which became the main licensing bodies, deal with the ambivalence of night-life entertainment, how they established new strategies of control and how they balance partly opposing interests of the various parties involved or affected by night-time entertainment. In order to open up the UK-centred discourse on club cultures, the chapter delineates the pathway of club cultural development in Istanbul, a city of a similar population size, but situated in a different cultural, political and economic context.

Following the discussion of night-life governance, Chapter 3 turns to club cultural production and market contexts, an area that is relatively under-researched and difficult to map especially at international scale. The chapter takes a closer look at the economic significance of clubbing in the leisure and recreation market in Britain and describes the ownership, company and employment structures in the night-time sector, in particular the club sector. It describes how changing regulatory contexts affected the night-time economies in terms of fuelling the trend towards diversification and fiercer competition from late-night bars. Due to the dynamics of property development and the increasing role of shareholder capital and branding, night-time venues experienced a growing pressure for profit. The strategies of market making and positioning in this context are considered in more detail and compared with similar strategies in the cultural sector. This involves, for example, the balancing of credibility (through exclusivity and social closure) and economic profit-making. It also analyses the role of sponsorship, branding and advertising as well as the internationalization of clubbing businesses. In response to stagnating markets in the UK, several companies sought to export their brands through tours, events and venues abroad as well as through more long-term international franchise agreements and partnerships. Drawing on the example of the company Ministry of Sound, the chapter illustrates these developments and sketches the forms of exchange between international organization and production companies and local (independent) companies.

Chapter 4 unfolds the analytical-conceptual framework of the book. Starting from the theorization of clubbing in the context of contemporary body cultures and leisure environments, it charts how dance clubs are constructed as 'elsewheres' that transcend the everyday and offer refuge or escape through absorbing sensual stimulation. This incites bodily involvement and idealizes transgression. This discontinuity to everyday normality is constructed at the symbolic-discursive level and is accentuated by the local organization of practices and the particular socio-spatio-technical arrangements of a club. In their 'routinization of liminal practices' (Hobbs et al. 2000: 711) clubs are set apart from, but are nevertheless implicated in the structures and routines of everyday life. In the first part, the chapter explores how this broader frame informs typical institutional features such as admission rituals, particular social conventions and modes of sociality and how it is translated into scripts of experience and situated practices of dance. The second part of the chapter focuses in more detail on the forms of embodiment in clubbing cultures. I shall elaborate the thesis that clubbing centres on aesthetic and prosthetic forms of embodiment, which help generate a liminoid atmosphere and a state of 'otherness'. Drawing on the debates on aestheticization and prosthetic culture, the phenomenological concepts of experience and reality (Schütz 1967, 1971) and cultural sociology perspectives on boundaries and classification, I shall expound how the aesthetic and prosthetic forms of embodiment in clubbing affect modes of classification and notions of authenticity and identity. This will be linked up with Ricoeur's model of narrative identity (Ricoeur 1991), which serves as an analytical tool to explore these processes in the experiential accounts of the narrative interview data.

In turning to the empirical analysis of the interview data, Chapter 5 discusses how clubbing in general, and drug consumption specifically, were narrated as a temporary transgression into a separate reality or 'world'. The order of reality ascribed to clubbing reflects back on the narrative configuration of identity and agency and on the ways in which participants evaluate performative constructions of identity. The analysis reflects upon two particular narrative devices; on the one hand, narratives of delusion and disillusion, and on the other hand, narratives of transformation. With respect to drug consumption, the ethical ambivalence epitomized in images of excess became particularly apparent. Excess seems to serve as a metaphor of transgressive pleasure as well as a moral limit or threshold to pathology. This discussion is linked to the debate about the 'normalization of adolescent recreational drug use' (Parker, Aldridge, and Measham 1998) and set against the backdrop of the discursive construction of drugs as vehicles of immersion into another 'reality'. Plot-structures and story-types in these drug-narratives point up gender aspects in the semantic field of pleasure and excess and in the ways in which agency, identity and the ethical value of these experiences were demarcated.

The analysis in Chapter 6 initially started from the question as to what club cultural involvement means for people in different biographical stages and in relation to the wider life-context. Based on four case studies of autobiographical accounts of clubbing, the chapter explores how the intersection of gender, sexuality, class and social location, ethnicity and age generates particular scripts of participation and narrative representation. The focal point of this discussion is a distinctive type of narrative: a retrospective mode of ethical justification, in which clubbing figures as a resource for the aestheticization of biography by becoming narrated as an 'identity project'; that is, as a project of self-experimentation and self-realization,[14] transformation, learning and achievement. This conjured up particular identity themes such as work roles and the participation in the production of clubbing events, stardom, romance, sexual experimentation, aestheticization of the body, the acquisition and professionalization of (creative) skills or psychological self-realization. Debates on post-subcultures emphasized that youth cultural formations increasingly centred on postmodern sensibilities, individualized identities or neo-tribal forms of association rather than being articulated around class, gender, ethnicity or age (Muggleton 1997: 199, A. Bennett 1999). Despite the broad popularity of club culture across socioeconomic groups, social divides and class distinctions (apart from sexual orientation, ethnicity or age) still play a significant role in the segmentation of clubbing scenes and in the formation of taste groups. Chapter 6 discusses in what ways the construction of clubbing as an identity project can be seen as a narrative form of social positioning articulating the social location of 'new' middle-class strata in the UK.

Dance and popular music cultures are often epitomized as realms of sexual transgression and transformations; as Lawrence Grossberg put it in relation to rock, as a 'challenge [to, S.R.] hegemonic constraints on sexuality, desire and even gender construction' (1990: 114). Rave culture likewise was read as a manifestation of the social transformation of gender roles, the opening up of sexual boundaries and 'new feminine sexualities' (Pini 2001). The other way round, in the idealization of club spaces as spheres of transgression, sexuality is a central element. The overall question addressed in Chapter 7 is, as to what role contemporary club cultures play for the reconfiguration of cultural scripts of gender and sexuality, in particular, in a broader context of the sexualization of culture (Attwood 2006), which saw the proliferation of sexual texts, the weakening of sexual identity categories and, to some extent, the mainstreaming of gay sexualities. In particular, this chapter examines how non-heteronormative sexualities and sexual diversity were represented in mainstream clubbing magazines and in what ways this challenged or reconfigured their implicit heteronormativity. The discussion is based on visual analysis of imagery in clubbing magazines (*Mixmag, Ministry*) and on narrative analysis of interviewees' accounts. It aims to compare the level of visual representation with individuals' self-understanding and their reading of practices and other actors in clubs. The media imagery emphasized non-normative modes of sexuality as performative enactments and opened up scenarios of (playful) identification.

The wide popularity of gay night-life venues and 'villages' among straight audiences, the increasing number of mixed nights and the emergence of new labels (e.g. 'polysexual') since about the late 1990s suggests an opening up of sexual boundaries on the clubbing scenes. However, this is contrasted by the scepticism of many cultural analysts who point to the risk that gay space becomes 're-heterosexualized' (Casey 2004) or permeated by the 'new homonormativity' (Duggan 2002) arising from the fetishization of particular segments of gay culture at the expense of the further marginalization of others. At the backdrop of this debate, Chapter 8 presents the ethnographic case studies of the two bar-clubs in London—a gay-mixed and a lesbian venue. It explores to what extent sexual identity boundaries are de-emphasized in these spaces. Of particular interest is how the spatio-institutional features impact on the (de-)institutionalization of sexual boundaries, e.g. how these affect the practical negotiation of identities, of notions of belonging and entitlement to these spaces. Both these clubs veered between, and aimed to balance, different institutional frames ('territory of identity' vs. service and consumption space), producing complex and disjunctive borderscapes through the entanglement of sexual and aesthetic codifications. This provokes contestations over spatial inclusion whereby identity boundaries were mobilized and reconfigured. Different types of boundaries and boundary work were accentuated in these clubs producing an ambivalent mixture of heterogeneity on the one hand, and normalization and differentiation on the other hand.

In sum, this book explores contemporary club and dance cultures as a manifestation of aesthetic and prosthetic forms of life. These help cultivate particular forms of reflexivity and modes of experience that shape new devices for symbolic boundary practices and for the understanding of identity and authenticity. It offers exemplary empirical analyses of how such forms of experience are mediated by particular technologies intervening into the sense system of the body (e.g. music, visuals and drugs); the structures and contexts of nightclubbing economies; the institutional modes of ordering and regulation; and the wider social discourses and media imageries. Contemporary clubbing culture is not only a topic of study in its own right, but allows for exploring a range of issues relevant to different fields of research. This includes, for example, the study of the body in contemporary culture, leisure and entertainment; the significance of prosthetic embodiment and virtualization for the constitution of subjectivity; the role of night-life entertainment and experiential consumption in culture-driven urban restructuration; the governance of the night-time economy; the features and development of (global) cultural economies and the role of popular cultures in the remaking or transformation of gender and sexual identities, class, ethnic and 'race' relations. While this still leaves many more voids to be filled, the book aims to provide a fresh theoretical outlook on, and to open up new lines of empirical inquiry into, the study of contemporary club and dance cultures.

2 Urban Renewal and Night-Life Governance
London and Istanbul

As earlier studies argued (Chatterton and Hollands 2003; Hobbs, Hadfield, Lister, Winlow, and Waddington 2003), the rise of nightclubbing culture can be seen as one manifestation of the growing importance of cultural and experience economies for urban development in post-industrial settings (Scott 2000). Since the late 1970s urban regeneration strategies sought to redevelop de-industrialized and often impoverished urban centres and to reinvigorate urbanity through residential living, consumption and leisure facilities (Lovatt and O'Connor 1995) or through centres of cultural production and consumption (a more recent example is the Tilburg Pop Cluster in the Netherlands). To some extent, these strategies also implicitly or explicitly incorporated night-life entertainment; especially in Italy (Rome), Denmark (Copenhagen), Sweden, the Netherlands, Germany and France such policies had been probed in the late 1970s and 1980s in response to the demand of the increasing student population and new urban social movements (e.g. gay and black activism or 'Reclaim the Night' in the Women's Movement; Bianchini 1995: 122).

This is closely related to the transformation of urban governance in the context of neoliberal deregulation in Western Europe since the 1980s (Brenner and Theodore 2002). In this process, urban governance was remodelled into an economic regional development project, in which place-marketing became a central strategy in the competitive struggle for investment and in which a business and management perspective and a market logic gained increasing ground in all areas of regulation. Various mechanisms became widely accepted, amongst others, private-public partnerships, the delegation, transfer and shifting of responsibilities and the integration of stakeholders into some stages of the policy making process. A key characteristic of urban policy in this context has been the increasing attention given to the role of culture in the development of cities (Bassett, Smith, Banks, and O'Connor 2005). Culture came to be seen 'as the magic substitute for all the lost factories and warehouses' (Hall 2000: 640) and as a crucial asset within inter-urban competition, illustrated by the 'cultural arms race' (Richards 2000) towards the European Capital of Culture prize.

De-industrialization, 'neoliberal localization' (Brenner and Theodore 2002: 364–365) and the transformation of urban development strategies also affected the role and governance of urban culture and night-life entertainment. Central elements of the governance of night-life entertainment are licensing, planning and policing. Due to legal changes in the UK, licensing has been given much attention in recent years in the research of night- · life entertainment (Talbot 2004, 2006, Tierney 2006, M. Roberts 2006). It can be considered a liberal form of 'governing at a distance' (Valverde 2003, Rose 1999b) without the State directly interfering with citizens. Especially for areas of consumption considered problematic, it is seen as a more effective form of regulation than direct control, as it is supposed to create self-governing bodies who substitute for the role of the police through a 'de-centralized micro-management' of 'spaces, temporalities and activities' (Valverde 2003: 239, 248). Licensing is a mode of state regulation that channels the supply structure of the market and regulates the opportunities for consumption. Licensing also regulates by turning the objectives of policing (preserving order) into conditions of the license, defining and imposing in varying degrees roles and duties, conditions of operation and demanding the constant self-surveillance of license-holders, who in turn demand particular modes of conduct from their clientele. However, apart from licensing, planning and land use classes are of equal if not greater importance for shaping urban geographies of night life as measures can be included in development plans that prevent the start-up of new venues in certain areas. Licensing often has less-effective tools for regulating the number of night-life venues, the size of night-life clusters or the geographic spread of the scenes. In addition, policing and security, and not to forget public transport, are also important ways in which evening and late-night urban entertainment is governed (GLA 2002: iv).

Against the backdrop of economic restructuration and the transformation of local governance, many urban centres experienced a substantial growth of consumption, leisure and entertainment facilities over the past two decades. Especially since the early 1990s certain urban areas went through a downright night-life boom with restaurants, bars, music and dance clubs and other venues springing up. As for the development of night-life scenes centring on electronic, beat-centred music, one central common factor can be identified at least in urban contexts in Europe. Electronic dance-music scenes flourished especially where a great amount of cheap or free space for such activities was available—whether the remnants of deindustrialization such as disused warehouses and industrial buildings; or run-down, dilapidated inner-city areas and living quarters with low rents. The availability of such infrastructures facilitated dance-music scenes and the cultural sector more generally, but as a single factor it certainly does not explain the emergence of these cultures.

Despite common elements, neoliberal restructuration is strongly path-dependent and embedded in local economies, institutional frameworks and regulatory regimes as well as in local cultural and political traditions (Brenner and Theodore 2002: 349, Le Galés 1998: 501). Accordingly, licensing, although it is an essentially liberal form of governance, can be connected to different (political) rationalities, 'regimes of justification' (Valverde 2003: 244) and cultural traditions; hence, it regulates and shapes night-life cultures in different ways. The economic transition and the trend towards the closing down of non-profitable industries was probably more marked or abrupt in some countries than others, especially in Thatcherist Britain, 1990s Eastern Germany (e.g. Berlin, Leipzig) and Eastern Europe after the fall of the Berlin Wall and the disintegration of Soviet rule. By contrast, other cities, due to other planning structures, features of the building stock and dynamics of gentrification had less inner-city spaces that could be accrued for night-life culture. Or, due to demographic characteristics cities have a greater or smaller share of youth population to which such music and dance cultures would appeal. For example, one reason for the growth of clubbing culture in several Asian metropoles is that these have a large, increasingly affluent youth population interested in Western fashion, music and lifestyle, which prompted clubbing companies, many of them from the UK, to tap into these markets as home markets stagnated.

As these introductory remarks indicate, this chapter considers night-life and clubbing culture in relation to post-industrial economic restructuration and the transformation of urban governance. It aims to provide some background to the broader economic and political context that enabled the growth of bar, club and night-life scenes in London and the UK. In particular, it delineates how the adoption of cultural strategies of (urban) development prepared the ground for a revaluation of night-life culture and affected the status of the night-time economy in urban governance. The chapter then describes the key changes in the governance of night-life entertainment in Britain in the past decade and reviews the practical implementation of the changed licensing and planning objectives in London, discussing the policies that some local authorities have devised in order to gain more control over the development of the night-time economy. While the main focus of this chapter is on London, the final section depicts another case in a similar metropolitan setting in Istanbul. This opens up a comparative perspective on similar issues as well as local specificities in terms of politics and the role of culture, night-life governance and urban planning.[1]

London and Istanbul lend themselves to comparison for several reasons. Both are mega-cities of roughly 8 to 10 million inhabitants, with over 20 million residents in the wider city-regions. Population forecasts expect further growth as both cities are important migrant destinations: London especially for young, ethnically diverse adults who seek education and work opportunities, self-expression and exploration of identities; Istanbul mainly for poor populations from rural areas in Turkey, but also to an increasing extent for professionals from abroad. While London's 'global city' status is undisputable, Istanbul too attempted to mould itself along this image, but, as commentators suggest, is a less full-blown 'global city' despite transformation towards such a model (Keyder 1999). The economic liberalization initiated in the early 1980s led to the formation of the advanced service sector and new business districts and a wealthy urban middle class as well as to the intensification of a 24-hour-city life. However, in the 1990s the textile sector was still the most rapidly growing area of employment in Istanbul (ibid. 22). Although London is the most affluent city-region in the European Union, income inequality and poverty is extreme in both London and Istanbul.

In both cities processes of devolution in the last two decades ushered in a more pronounced emphasis on local and regional governance. With the abolition of the Greater London Council by the Thatcher government in 1986, functions were devolved to the local boroughs (e.g. the responsibility for entertainment licensing; Talbot 2007: 49). After the election of the Labour Government in 1997 the metropolitan authority of London was reinstalled in 2000 (Greater London Authority), and policy areas such as policing, elements of transport, fire and emergency services, economic development and strategic planning were brought under metropolitan control (A. Harding 2006). By contrast, in the 1980s Istanbul not only gained new influx of foreign investment, but also received a major injection of state funding and was granted more autonomy as a city (Keyder 1999: 16). Decentralization and devolution-type political reform started in the 1980s, enforced by the programs prescribed by the International Monetary Fund and later continued with the EU-accession process. A two-tier system of greater metropolitan and district municipalities was introduced. Yet, due to a strong central state apparatus the transformation towards participatory urban governance was more limited in Istanbul (Erkip 2000: 375, Kocabas 2005: 27) than in London. Nevertheless, night-life entertainment in both cities was directly affected by the new rationales of urban governance, planning and licensing.

Both Istanbul and London have big night-life clusters in their centres with a long tradition and history, but which also pose challenges for the local authorities such as overcrowding and public order problems. In addition to these centres, important night-life clusters are located in other areas in close proximity to residential areas. Although both cities aspired to become a 'world city', the image of the modern 'European' city and its urban social and night-life culture also served as an ideal in the development of urban centres and in the governance of night-life entertainment. In Britain, these images of continental night life centred on the notion of diverse audiences pursuing a variety of activities in the city centre (Tierney 2006: 454, O'Connor and Wynne 1996: 9). In this respect the licensing law with the 11pm pub closing time, the rationale of which dated back to the liquor licensing law from the fifteenth and the entertainment licensing law from the eighteenth century (Talbot 2007: 4), gradually came to be perceived as an antiquated barrier to diversity and choice in night-life culture. In Istanbul too, an image of 'European-ness' was increasingly embraced with the accession process to the European Union, in the context of which local governance and licensing were reformed and various projects were launched to raise the cleanness and safety-standards in urban centres and tourist areas.

Cultural strategies of urban renewal have gained importance in both cities; however, these were interpreted in different ways. In the UK, these were tied in with the cultural and creative industries agenda. Evening and late-night economies came to be regarded as important for tourism and, especially in the 1990s, for urban renewal and economic development. It led some UK cities—more so than London—to actively encourage the development of the night-time economy in their centres. Growing sections of the tourist guidebooks are devoted to the bar and clubbing scene. Clubbing in this discourse is seen as a key factor in creating an atmosphere of excitement and hedonism and a cutting-edge street culture that attracts the young and creative. These in turn are seen as a key factor in positioning London as a 'world city' (GLA 2002: 9–10). In Istanbul cultural strategies of urban renewal were more strongly focused on promoting the city's architectural and historical heritage, its cultural traditions and art for tourism. Despite the long tradition of cultural and night-time entertainment activities and the significant presence of bar and music scenes in the centre of Istanbul, night-life culture, whilst being promoted by tourist guides and officials, has not been incorporated by the political elites and local governments into their projects of urban renewal.

CULTURE-DRIVEN URBAN RENEWAL AND THE GOVERNANCE OF NIGHT LIFE IN THE UK

Following the example of redeveloping run-down urban areas through prestige cultural facilities probed in the US in the early 1980s, Britain was one of the first European countries to consider the potential of culture for urban regeneration, inter-urban competition and economic growth, city marketing and urban social cohesion (Lovatt and O'Connor 1995: 129, Bassett et al. 2005: 132). Such cultural strategies of urban renewal began to take hold with the Thatcher government, who in the aftermath of the Brixton riot of 1981 targeted inner cities, blamed as sites of the 'British disease' of strikes and industrial unrest, as resources of economic development and urban regeneration. The city councils, many of them under Labour Party rule, had to deal with free enterprise, deregulation and a more flexible planning system. A series of legislative changes was introduced restricting local government, freeing private capital's access to public land and development contracts and creating semi-autonomous bodies outside the control of local government. O'Connor noted the paradox that a culture-based urban renewal was initiated by a 'quasi-political body dominated by a free enterprise ethos with an anti-cultural bias' (O'Connor 1999: 85). Traditional forms of arts and culture were used as vehicles for economic development. Together with the neglect of local politics and democracy, such programmes frequently met opposition or cynicism from local cultural intermediaries (ibid. 83–85; Stoker 2004). However, from the 1980s onwards, cultural policy discourses shifted from the former accentuation of access to high culture to a market discourse that fleshed out new, albeit contested and elusive, concepts of the 'cultural' beyond the traditional arts concern. Spurred by city marketing imperatives, this governmentalization of culture (T. Bennett 1998: 30) spanned the subsidized cultural sector as well as the cultural and creative industries. Britain was one of the first countries to map the cultural sector and make its activities visible and governable. Acknowledging the economic value of cultural production and consumption, the Greater London Council adopted the term 'cultural industries' in 1985 before its abolition (O'Connor 1998: 3). New Labour carried over earlier policies in its vision of 'creative Britain' in order to boost the knowledge economy (Bassett et al. 2005: 136). A more vigorous policy and research orientation sparked off in the 1990s (Pratt 2004). The contribution of the cultural industries to job creation and economic growth was to be recorded. In 1998 creative industries in Britain were officially categorized with industry codes (SIC codes, Montgomery 2003: 297). As mentioned before, New Labour's policy approach was one of devolved governance, whereby the system of elected local government was to be transformed into a system of local governance that involved a wider range of institutions and actors, elected leaders, key stakeholders and managers in local politics. Thereby, local and regional bodies such as the local authority became one of many actors in local service delivery. Together with privatization and marketization this also reduced the importance of the former 'command and control' strategies (A. Harding 2006). Both the Conservative and following Labour governments prepared the ground for new horizontal linkages to, and partnerships with, the private sector or non-statutory organizations as well as managerialism. The Conservatives, in their deep mistrust of the public sector, bureaucracy and the local authorities under Labour rule, tended to give more weight to the responsiveness to consumers, while the Labour governments put more emphasis on localism, on the responsiveness to the local community and on a pragmatic orientation towards a range of service delivery models to choose from (Stoker 2004: 11). Local authorities were entrusted with the task to promote and enable the economic and social wellbeing of their areas—economic development and competitiveness, regeneration, environmental sustainability and social cohesion (A. Harding 2005: 70–73). Through the process of devolution and regionalization the cultural industries were linked to a regional economic development agenda. New institutional structures such as regional cultural consortia were implemented in order to develop local strategies of cultural development (Pratt 2004: 31–33).

The 'Creative Britain' (Smith 1998) discourse also brought forth the adoption of ideas of 'cultural quarters' (Montgomery 2003) or the 'creative city' (Landry and Bianchini 1995, Landry 2000) within urban regeneration strategies, the earliest examples of which date back to the late 1980s (Sheffield) and early 1990s (Manchester). These concepts had a major influence on the reshaping of many British city centres through cultural and architectural prestige projects such as museums, concert halls and waterside developments. Cultural quarters were part of a larger strategy of encouraging mixed-use urban developments in inner urban areas (Montgomery 2003: 293). Up to the 1990s night-life entertainment was not assigned a very prominent role within cultural strategies of urban development. As Lovatt and O'Connor rightly stated,

> as an object of cultural policy it has been strangely marginalized. It seemed that this night life was not a legitimate object of attention other than as something to be regulated and contained. Despite its inextricable link with the image of the vibrant city it was primarily an object of attention for agencies concerned with licensing, health and safety, planning and policing. It was a heavily regulated zone of space and time; a location for transgression conceived in terms of social disfunction. In short, a problem. (1995: 130)

However, gradually cultural quarters were also linked to leisure consumption such as eating, drinking and socializing in restaurants, cafés, bars, pubs or nightclubs. It was recognized that cultural quarters, if they were to be conducive to creative work, also had to offer facilities for forging particular lifestyles and forms of social association (Montgomery 2003). As Montgomery pointed out, 'successful cultural quarters will almost certainly have a strong evening economy' (ibid. 297). Other case studies also pointed to the significance of the night-time economy for the reproduction of social and business networks of the cultural economy (Crewe and Beaverstock 1998: 304). Eventually, evening and night-life entertainment came to be seen as relevant factors in the process of urban renewal (Hobbs et al. 2003: 18). A symbolic indication of the growing importance attributed to the late-night economy was the transfer of alcohol and entertainment policy from the Home Office to the Tourism Division of the Department for Culture, Media and Sport (DCMS) in 2001.

It was also argued that the increasing acceptance of night-life culture was a consequence of the pressure coming from the rave movement or was even a manifestation of the incorporation of rave culture. Talbot (2007: 13–14) claimed that the normalization and regulation of dance culture was a tactic of the police and government to deal with the illegal party culture. There is some plausibility in the argument that by granting extensions of opening hours the authorities tried to bring the rave scene within the remit of the licensing structure. Some club owners had begun to negotiate longer licensing hours through offering cooperation with the authorities and the police and by expanding the scope of (self-)regulation (ibid. 15). This normalization of dance culture can be seen as an example of the 'propertising' of culture (Skeggs 2005). Certain qualities and values were appropriated and resourced for the 'night-time economy', whilst others remained marginalized, excluded or criminalized. A telling example of this is the Ministry of Sound club in London, which obtained a 24-hour license in 1991 after it got clubbers to testify that the other premises they frequented were 'unsafe, unregulated and illegal' (Garratt 1998: 286; see also Talbot 2007: 15).

Similar points have been made about the emergence of gay night-life clusters in British city centres in the 1990s, another development that was partly linked to urban renewal through strategies of cultural appropriation. In the US such clusters have been discernible since the 1970s (Collins 2004, Castells 1983), and in London too, some small clusters existed since the 1970s and 1980s, as gay venues in Britain could only legally be opened since the 1967 Sexual Offences Act came into effect. Nevertheless, a gay subculture of entertainment existed in London since the late seventeenth century. In a comparative analysis of gay villages, Collins (2004) identified typical patterns of the development of such clusters. Most of these spaces emerged in urban areas of decline that had become associated with sexual and legal liminality (e.g. prostitution) and where rents were relatively low. With the widening of the services and venues gay areas often become popular and fashionable destinations for audiences outside the gay clientele raising controversial issues about entitlements to space, a point that will be more fully discussed in Chapters 7 and 8. This scenario certainly applies to Soho in London, where gay venues emerged after the crackdown on the sex and porn industry in the early to mid 1980s, which had freed up commercial premises for new uses. However, while the formation of gay culture and entertainment in Soho never received any explicit municipal support by Westminster Council, the gay villages emerging in Manchester, Birmingham, Newcastle and other cities in the 1990s were directly supported by members of the city councils and planning departments. Gay villages suddenly received such support and attention as they came to be seen as vehicles of gentrification and as signifiers of style, of up-market consumption and cosmopolitanism and of a social and public life that reminded of the continental European city (Skeggs and Binnie 2004a).

The 24-hour city was another concept which brought forward the revaluation of night-life culture. It recast the night-time economy as a strategy for reducing night-time crime and creating safer city centres through attracting a greater diversity of people and facilitating a wider range of entertainment activities. This would improve the city image and draw investment, thereby stimulating the local economy and improving employment opportunities (Heath 1997). The concept was first propagated by a consultancy report in 1991, later by Manchester's Olympic bid in 1993 and the 'Twenty-Four Hour City' conference held in the city in the same year. It took hold increasingly in the mid-1990s when Sunday opening and extended trading hours were permitted in retail. The spectrum of schemes varied between the promotion of just an evening economy or a full-blown 24-hour city with different emphasis given to the overall goals of development. Manchester, Leeds and Cardiff set the pace, whereas the concept was less widely and more slowly adopted in London.

Manchester and Leeds were also at the forefront of lobbying the central government for reviewing the licensing laws (Heath 1997). However, the night-time economy saw an immense boost long before the legal reforms were introduced in 2003. The Conservative government initiated a moderate promotion of the 'evening' economy in 1993 and licensing regulations were relaxed continuously throughout the 1990s. The restrictions posed by the law were circumvented either through special permissions for late-entertainment licenses excluding the sale of alcohol or through special hours certificates allowing the sale of alcohol after 2 a.m.. More special hours certificates were in force in 2001 than in 2004. According to data from the Department for Culture, Media and Sport, the licenses for public houses, bars and nightclubs increased roughly by 21 per cent between 1980 and 2004 (see Mintel 2006: 18).[2] Entertainment licenses in Scotland even rose by 400 per cent between 1980 and 2004 as Scotland had not yet had a high supply of restaurants and pubs (Mintel 2006: 19). Similar trends applied to London's borough of Westminster: Between 1992 and 2000 the number of venues with a public entertainment license (required for late-night music and dancing, but also including other activities such as film or theatre) increased more than two times, and the licensed capacity of these venues rose from 33,400 to 127,900 (GLA 2002: 23). According to data from Westminster Council, who estimated the capacity of premises with entertainment licenses in 2002 at 179,295, the growth was even more marked (Westminster 2008: 130). The West End, in particular, could accommodate 80,690 people in 2002 (Westminster 2005: 93).

A key factor for the rise of the bar and nightclubbing market was the significant rise in student numbers through the expansion of higher education. Between 1991/92 and 2001/02 overall student numbers in the UK increased by 75 per cent from 1.2 million to 2.01 million; with Leeds even showing a 120 per cent increase (M. Roberts 2006: 332, 336). A survey by John Moores University Liverpool in 1996 indicated that 70 per cent of all new students chose to study in Liverpool because of the famous Cream club (Garratt 1998: 302). Large student villages, as Tim Butler pointed out, 'helped sustain a burgeoning central city, night time economy' (T. Butler 2005: 178).

The introduction of the new Licensing Act in 2003, therefore, merely institutionalized a process of relaxation of certain regulations that had already been at work since the 1980s. These laws had seen little substantial modifications for almost a century. With the Licensing Act 2003 (fully implemented in November 2005) statutory closing times were abolished and flexible closing hours were introduced, which make possible 24-hour entertainment and liquor licenses for seven days a week. Instead of separate licenses for music and entertainment obtained from the local authority and for the sale of alcohol obtained from the magistrates court, under the new regime every venue is granted a single premises license with varying conditions depending on the operating schedule. Under the old licensing regulations late-night drinking was only possible in a hotel, in a restaurant together with a meal until midnight or when it was ancillary to entertainment (i.e. music and dancing). This effectively meant that nightclubs were the only place to go in order to have a drink after 11 or 12 p.m. Because of the single license, restaurants, pubs and bars can now stay open and sell alcohol longer.

As has been argued, the Licensing Act of 2003 belongs to a new institutional landscape of crime control, in which the state is no longer the only or primary provider of crime control, but citizens too are made responsible for reducing criminal opportunities through increasing informal controls and self-policing (Newburn 2001: 837). This reflects precisely the type of networked community governance through local partnerships promoted by New Labour (Stoker 2004; Moran, Skeggs, Tyrer, and Corteen 2003: 13). In terms of night life, new surveillance and policing networks were created through local initiatives, best practice charters and quality labelling schemes relating to safety, the prevention of crime, disorder or drug consumption and dealing. A complex array of agents is involved in the provision of security in the night-time (Newburn 2001: 841) as the new licensing model tends to turn over the governmental work of preventing disorder to the private sector through 'responsibilization' (Valverde 2003, Rose 1999b). The framework of 'security' is based on the rationale that 'those who live off risky consumption should also be responsible for managing the risks associated with the business' (Valverde 2003: 238). In other words, public disorder problems became increasingly framed as negative externalities to be covered by the alcohol and night-time industry. In practice this meant that the provision of order and security and the management of risk were made into conditions of the license. License applicants have to submit a schedule of operation that spells out how the license holder aims to comply with the legal regulations. With the new Licensing Act the sanctions for breaching licensing conditions became harsher (Talbot 2006: 161). Via the 'personal license holder' in the name of a person present on the premises to supervise the sale of alcohol, a member of staff was made responsible for preventing drunkenness and disorder. Security in night-life entertainment was put on a new footing by the Private Security Industry Act 2001, which set up a national scheme for training, vetting and registering door supervisors. Licensed premises such as bars and nightclubs may only employ trained and licensed door supervisors, mostly hired from security firms. Private security is the main policing agency within night-life entertainment. For example, in 2002 and 2003 about 4,000 door supervisors stood against forty police officers at work on a typical weekend night in the Manchester city centre, and only thirteen police officers policed about 125,000 people in the West End (Hobbs et al. 2003: 104, GLA 2002: 31).

The technique of responsibilization perhaps covers up the ambiguity that has always characterized the State's attitude towards night-life entertainment and alcohol consumption arising from the conflict of interest between capitalist reproduction and fears of the 'other', 'lower orders' (Talbot 2007). Waving with the pint in one hand and with the 'don't binge drink' and 'don't cause public nuisance' board in the other, state policies are trying to strike a difficult balance between enabling the development of the night-time economy, of which the state profits through taxes—according to the Late-Night London report (GLA 2002: 24), back in 2002 over £12 billion per annum were raised for the government on duty and value added tax on alcohol—and curbing or criminalizing the negative consequences caused by these very same economies. Visions of economic growth stand against the moral panics of urban disorder hyped by the media (Talbot 2007; M. Roberts 2006; Jayne, Holloway, and Valentine 2006: 458).

These contradictory tendencies perhaps became more pronounced with the concentration of new functions in the local authorities. With the Licensing Act of 2003 licensing was transferred from the magistrates, which had been the licensing authority (for the sale of alcohol and public drinking) more than four centuries, to the local authorities. This was in recognition of the fact that licensing is not only an instrument of regulation, but also closely connected to planning and local development. Licensing and planning of the night-time economy are two of several policy areas now installed at local authorities, where the goals of economic development and social cohesion may run into potential conflict. Through the devolution of responsibility these inherent contradictions are passed on and delegated to the license holders and self-governing bodies at the premises, who can be held liable for the misconduct of their patrons. Yet, they are often powerless to prevent disorder (Talbot 2006: 161) and operate in an environment where socio-cultural codes clash with the legal norms as in the case of widespread, widely accepted and even expected drug consumption. Clubs have to implement a drug policy and demonstrate the willingness to share intelligence on drug use and drug dealing with the police. This is a somewhat hypocritical measure with little effect except perhaps for deterring punters from bringing big amounts of drugs to the premises. Even license authorities themselves admit to the impossibility of preventing drug consumption by audiences who may be taking drugs before entering the venue. The main aim, in which the interests of both club operators and authorities frequently coincide, is preventing the premise from becoming a destination for drug dealing and from gang violence resulting from conflict over drug markets (Hobbs et al. 2003).

The new licensing law provided the local authorities with little discretion in granting or refusing licenses. They have to accept license applications unless formal objections are made by the police, by residents in the close vicinity or on the grounds of health and safety. In this respect, other legal changes such as the 2005 amendments to the Town and Country Planning (Use Classes) Order 1987 fitted the local authorities with stronger instruments at the level of planning. On the one hand, planning policy in Britain shifted from zoning to mixed-use especially in town centres, which meant a strong move to encourage more residential living in central areas. On the other hand, the former A3 Food and Drink use class was disaggregated into three more specific classes in order to give local authorities more influence in securing a preferred balance of uses in certain areas and in tackling the impact of the evening and night-time economy.[3] Nightclubs, which previously were not specified in any use class and which did not need any planning permission, were defined as *sui generis*, subject to obligatory planning permission for any material changes (Mintel 2004: 39). In effect the amended order entailed that conversions of class A commercial premises into shops, restaurants and cafés were generally permitted and encouraged whilst conversions into class A4 (drinking establishments) or nightclubs fell under closer consideration by local planning authorities. In addition, 'cumulative impact' policies can be applied to areas of great concentration of night-life venues. For example, quantitative restrictions put on the number of certain uses set in the Unitary Development Plans can help curb the growth of the night-time economy in these areas. In these zones, the possibilities of obtaining planning permissions for new night-life venues are severely limited even though license applications would be successful. Another strategy pursued by a local authority in London is to retain small plot-sizes to discourage the emergence of super-pubs that promote 'high-volume vertical drinking'. Planning policy, therefore, is a much more contentious field than licensing. Although the Unitary Development Plans,[4] which contain guiding policies for the future ten years, have to be certified by the mayor of London for conforming to the overall Spatial Development Strategy, these development plans are principally made locally in each London borough under the responsibility of locally elected councillors. Even if the scope for the residents' voice is limited at the level of licensing (confined to formal representations for residents only immediately affected), strong resident lobbies, especially in wealthy areas, sometimes succeed in making their interests heard at the level of planning, even more so as residential living in town centres is supported by government policy (for examples, see Chatterton 2002: 42–43).

In contrast to the initial expectations that a revitalization of urban centres through the expansion of the night-time economy would help reduce public order problems and alcohol-related street crimes, the dominant view emerging in the late 2000s suggests precisely the opposite. Research testifies rising crime figures in night-life clusters. For example, Hobbs et al. (2003: 39) reported a 225 per cent increase of assaults in the centre of Manchester from 1997 to 2001. According to the Manchester crime audit in 2001, the incidents taking place in and around the Gay Village more than doubled the number recorded in any other part of the city centre (ibid.). Similarly, the Late-Night London report (GLA 2002) found that the locations with the highest concentrations of late-night street crime are the West End (Soho), Camden, Croydon and Ealing—all areas with a high density of late-night venues. However, not all night-life hubs have high numbers of late-night street crime, just as late-night street crime occurs very widely across London (GLA 2002), an issue that shall be discussed more fully further below (p. 36-38).

A shift of opinion can also be noticed in academic, media and political discourse. In the 1990s academics who were closely linked to a popular-culture research agenda criticized the marginalization of night-life culture within cultural policy and emphasized its potential for urban renewal. Throughout this decade such voices have become more silent as the enthusiasm for cultural quarters and urban renewal strategies has cooled off and has been superseded by the critique of increasing corporate power and standardization, gentrification and social exclusion, as well as alcohol, violence and public order problems. National and local governments have come under attack for aligning themselves too easily with the interests of the alcohol industry. Regular media outrage about binge drinking, alcohol-related violence and disorder in city centres[5] also contributed to this re-problematization of night-time entertainment.

Recent legal changes illustrate these tendencies towards the re-problematization and criminalization of night life; for example, the Criminal Justice and Police Act 2001, which introduced on-the-spot fines for alcohol consumption in designated public places; the Anti-social Behaviour Act 2003; the Clean Neighbourhood and Environment Act 2005, which specified, amongst others, noise offences; and the Violent Crime Reduction Act 2006, which regulated the introduction of 'alcohol disorder zones'. These measures reinstated a culture of control and containment. The chief rationale for licensing in the past and present has been and still is the prevention of public disorder and crime relying on the almost default assumption that consuming night life ends in drunkenness and disorder. Ambiguous discourses of economic development and creativity on the one hand and of law and order on the other hand frame the governance of night life and hence produce 'ambivalent spaces' where pluralistic forms of expression are accommodated yet subject to surveillance and control (Chatterton 2002: 25).

As this overview showed, the relaxation of licensing restrictions underpinned by neoliberal economic restructuring and cultural strategies of urban renewal was counterbalanced by public order policies. Nowadays, the provision of night-life entertainment is not so much considered as a cultural policy responding to the demands of urban collective actors or as a strategy of urban regeneration rather than from business, planning, security and public order perspectives. To some extent, this tension, manifest in both the Conservatives as well as the Labour governments of the recent two decades, arose from internal fragmentations between central government institutions (M. Roberts 2006: 335). While the Department for Culture, Media and Sport (DCMS) emphasized the economic benefits of an expanding night-time economy, the Office of the Deputy Prime Minister (ODPM) overseeing local government took a more regulatory stance. As Talbot quite rightly argued, this also indicates that contradictory attitudes of government towards drinking and popular entertainment going back to the nineteenth-century tension between economic laissez-faire and the moral discourses of containment (Temperance) still have not been resolved (Talbot 2007). Obviously, it is not necessarily a contradiction or new that economic liberalism is combined with authoritarian policy approaches (Brenner 2001: 799). Especially as the economic value and significance attributed to the industry increases, efforts are stepped up to minimize (or downplay) what could be perceived as negative side-effects.

The Implementation of the New Licensing Act in London

The first year after the implementation of the new Licensing Act (2005–2006) saw a 10 per cent increase in premises licenses in England and Wales. According to the latest statistics published by the Department for Culture, Media and Sport (DCMS 2007), roughly 83,000 of all 123,000 premises licenses authorized to sell alcohol included the sale of alcohol for consumption on the premises. This roughly matches the number of licenses that also included entertainment facilities such as live music, recorded music or dancing (premises licenses and club premises certificates). The report also showed that 98 per cent of new premises license applications were granted and less than 1 per cent of all licenses had been subject to review, the majority of which were either modified in terms of opening hours or had new conditions added.

These data seem to confirm a view often aired in the literature or in the media. This suggests that the new licensing system intensified a process of deregulation leading to an uncontrolled growth of the night-time economy and contributing to an increasing (youth) binge-drinking culture and to disorder and violence in the city centres. The emphasis on alcohol and the focus on young people are considered as the main problems of the development of late-night entertainment (GLA 2002: vii). Contradictory stances have emerged on the role of local authorities in these processes. The question has arisen if the new licensing authorities are either too permissive in granting licenses (M. Roberts 2006: 333) or too weak, since the licensing and planning laws do not seem to give them much scope for control. As outlined above, moral panics about the British 'binge-drinking culture' provoked law and order responses demonstrating serious acting by the authorities. These, however, became sandwiched between polar allegations of liberal permissiveness on the one hand and of a socially biased, moralistic authoritarianism on the other hand. Several authors argued that the planning and licensing systems favour large businesses and companies that can afford highly professional legal representation to contest and overturn negative licensing decisions in court appeals, while the resources that local authorities have to withstand such appeals are limited (M. Roberts 2006, Chatterton 2002: 42, Talbot 2007: 18). Indeed, Westminster City Council lost several lawsuits in trying to refuse applications for extended opening hours (Chatterton 2002: 42). However, as examples in the following discussion will show, local authorities have adopted several strategies to regain more control over the development and operation of the night-time economy and are far from entirely powerless. The questions beg address as to whether the local strategies, backed up by the crime and disorder legislation of the past few years, have not come at the expense of intensified disciplinary power and overregulation; whether the measures of control and containment are justified by, and are a fair and appropriate response to, the problems at hand; and what impact these instruments are likely to have on night-life culture.

UK nightclubs are frequented by roughly 15 million visitors each year. London alone regularly draws an estimated number of 500,000 people to its nightclubs on a Saturday night. This is more than all the people who visit all of London's top-ten visitor attractions combined in a week (GLA 2002: ii). London's West End and Soho area (part of the city of Westminster) is the largest entertainment and night-life centre of the city and the whole country. In some hotspots, such as Leicester Square, night-time use even outweighs daytime use on weekend nights given the pedestrian flow. The number of visitors leaving the underground station on a Saturday after 8 p.m. is twice as high as on an average weekday and reaches its peak between 10 p.m. and 1 a.m. (GLA 2002, Westminster 2005: 94). In Old Compton Street in Soho too, levels of pedestrian flow are about the same at midnight as at around midday (M. Roberts and Turner 2005). Other considerable concentrations of night life exist in the town centres of many other parts of London including the City of London (especially the city's 'fringe' area in Shoreditch), Victoria, Kings Cross, Camden, Knightsbridge, Islington, Croydon and many more (GLA 2002). The capital's night-time economy is also recognized in the London Plan (GLA 2004),[6] the main planning strategy of the mayor, as 'a major contributor to London's world city status' (ibid. 138). The promotion of the night-time economy was explicitly adopted as part of the economic growth strategy of the capital:

> Strengthen the offer of London's economy. Sustain and promote the rapid expansion of retail, leisure and cultural industries, including the night-time economy, that are key to London's economic base and are the most rapidly expanding sectors of expenditure. (GLA 2006: xx)

The London Plan also defined the strategic importance of the various clusters of night-time activity in the city, which identified the West End as an 'internationally important cluster' (GLA 2006: A3) and the Covent Garden/Soho area 'as the country's most important concentration of night time activities' (ibid. 349). Other night-life clusters near or adjacent to the 'central activity zone' are considered to have strategic, 'sub-regional importance'. Regarding such areas of 'strategic importance', the mayor's best practice guidance published in 2007[7] endorsed mixed-use development and diversification in town and city centres, but warned that residential development should not compromise the areas' viability for the night-time economy (GLA 2007: 14). The local strategy of managing night-time entertainment is to be coordinated with other local strategies and is explicitly linked to tackling issues such as anti-social behaviour and crime. The main policy set out for night-time economies states that boroughs should

> where appropriate, support evening and night-time entertainment activities in central London, City fringe areas and town centres and where appropriate manage their impact through policies such as Entertainment Management Zones. (GLA 2006: 166; policy 3D.4)

This proposition followed earlier recommendations made by consultants in 2002 (GLA 2002). Such zones were envisaged for areas of existing entertainment and night-life hubs or for locations where growth of entertainment uses was planned. The key idea of these zones is a co-ordinated planning and management approach through local partnerships and networks in order to tackle the impacts of the night-time economy. The concept of entertainment management zones also overlaps with Business Improvement Districts especially proposed for areas of night-time economies. Similar to the US model, this scheme seeks to raise funding for local measures of improvement based on an additional levy on rates paid by the local businesses. Despite being pushed by local authorities such as Westminster Council to acknowledge and deal with the negative side-effects of the concentration of night-time economies in particular areas, the former mayor, Ken Livingston of the Labour Party, took a more moderate stance on curbing their growth by emphasizing, as has been said, the wider strategic importance of night-life clusters. This position, approving of diversification and entertainment management zones, but sceptical of policies of dispersal, constraints on growth and opening hours or the designation of areas of saturation or 'alcohol disorder zones', certainly posed a counterweight to the strategy advocated, for example, by Westminster Council, governed by the Conservatives.

Clustering of night-life activities is usually welcomed by venue operators, as a high choice of venues attracts more visitors, strollers and potential customers to the area (Crewe and Beaverstock 1998: 303). Although the concentration of night-life venues to some extent makes possible a more cost-efficient deployment of resources to manage the impacts, such economies of scale, however, tend to give rise to concern by local authorities.

This typically involves issues such as overcrowding, congestion, shortage of public transport and parking facilities, taxis and licensed minicabs;[8] street fouling, vandalism and shortage of resources for policing, servicing and cleaning the area; a substantial rise of noise, nuisance and safety complaints by residents; and the impacts of 'high-volume drinking' usually referred to as problems of anti-social behaviour, disorder or criminal offending. Inner London boroughs face increasing population densities and polarization between groups with high and low stocks of cultural and economic capital. Gentrification in inner areas is especially shaped by middle-class professionals, but also young adults often seek to live in inner city areas that offer opportunities for entertainment, exotic difference and excitement such as those with a vibrant culture and night-life scene (T. Butler 2005: 176–177).[9] Fast-paced residential redevelopment has often turned areas previously used only for commercial purposes into mixed-use hubs in which commercial and residential premises exist in close proximity. Often it is the same developer whose gentrification strategy is to co-develop residential, shopping and entertainment facilities (Shaw, Bagwell, and Karmowska 2004: 1991). More often than not the young professional gentrifiers are not only frequent users of night life, but also the most articulate and vocal in representing their interests against its negative side-effects (Chatterton 2002: 43). Residents' aggregate power of voicing their concerns about the night-time economy often depends on their income and social status. However, not all areas show the same relation between the local residential population and the consumers of night life. Bigger night-life clusters attract many visitors from outside the area, which runs the risk of creating a (tourism-oriented) enclave disconnected from the life of the local population (Shaw et al. 2004: 1997).

With the close proximity of night-time entertainment venues and residential areas, balancing the various interests of the parties involved has become a challenge for local authorities. Due to the contentious issues posed by governing the night-time economy, authorities are evermore assembling a (local) knowledge and evidence base as a footing for policy making. Especially crime data are used to justify the implementation of 'special policy' areas and the refusal to grant new licenses for bars, pubs and nightclubs in these areas. Analyses of crime data (e.g. drawn from the Crime Reporting Information System) seem to suggest a clear link between clusters of night life, the closure times of licensed premises and peaks in violence and criminal offences on weekend nights (Hobbs et al. 2003; GLA 2002, 2007). Impact studies imply that areas with a high density of night-time entertainment also have higher levels of disorder and night-time criminal activities such as common assault, wounding, pick-pocketing and theft. On the one hand, this is explained by the fact that the presence of a large number of (intoxicated) people in a certain area increases the potential targets and opportunity structure of crime (Urban 2007); on the other hand, it is assumed that alcohol consumption as such increases the propensity towards anti-social behaviour and violence. In its revised licensing policy, Westminster Council presented data suggesting that nightclubs are more prone to violent crime than any other type of licensed premises given the number of reports per premises (Westminster 2008: 64). However, given that the number of registered nightclubs is much lower than that of other premises, this ratio is not surprising. In absolute numbers, reports of violent crime were highest in restaurants (especially those closing after 1 a.m.), followed by nightclubs (Westminster 2008: 139).[10] While under-reporting is taken into account, crime figures often are not tested for the impact of increased reporting due to the deployment of enlarged policing resources; they lack comparison to the level of daytime crime and to areas with high levels of crime but not dominated by the night-time economy. It has also been argued that many of the offences are of relatively minor nature including street crimes such as vehicle thefts, pick-pocketing or common assaults, including the operation of unregistered minicabs, which is frequently cited as a source of crime (Urban 2007: 55–56). Westminster Council reported that 43 per cent of violent incidents occur under the influence of alcohol misuse (Westminster 2008: 135). This is significant, but still leaves 57 per cent of incidents where the influence of alcohol is not so clear. With inebriation people are more vulnerable to losing things, but often report lost items as stolen (Urban 2007: 55). They are also more likely to lose tempers when large crowds are congregating and competing for limited food and transport facilities or access to a nightclub (Westminster 2005: 97). Although evidence from emergency departments shows that there is a strong relation between alcohol consumption in the night-time economy and violent assaults in bars and on streets (Hobbs et al. 2003: 37), to some extent, incidents of disorder and violence are also knock-on effects of limited resources, tighter security policies and slower access to venues rather than being inherently caused by alcohol consumption as such. While assault and public order offences generally seem to rise in areas that have a high density of licensed premises, in some cases such as hotspots of gay night life, it is difficult to disentangle the causes of alcohol, overcrowding and homophobic hate (Hobbs et al. 2003: 102–103). For the majority of offences no arrests are made, therefore, it is impossible to determine the proportion of crime that is directly alcohol related (Urban 2007: 58). In addition, those people arrested may be tested for drugs, but are not tested for alcohol (ibid.). Although drug consumption is particularly prevalent amongst visitors of nightclubs, it was found that drug dealing in the streets peaks in the late afternoon and is not particularly linked to the night-time (GLA 2007: 9, 22). Methodological limitations also apply to the data on disorder as complaints made by telephone are likely to be categorized in different ways by operators depending on their subjective understanding of what constitutes incidences of noise, traffic or anti-social behaviour and disorder (Urban 2007). Roberts and Turner found in a study on London's Soho that 'detailed police statistics do not support a picture of exceptional crime' (M. Roberts and Turner 2005:

171). While crime data generally support the claim that a temporal-spatial connection exists between the concentration of night-time entertainment and the prevalence of disorder and crime, more detailed analysis is necessary to establish what precisely explains such incidents and how they come into existence as statistical facts.

It quickly becomes clear to any visitor that London's West End is an area where the scale and intensity of entertainment and night-life activity is unique. As has been pointed out earlier, the encouragement of mixed-use developments in inner urban areas since the late 1980s and early 1990s has led to a parallel growth in residential population and in consumption and leisure functions such as the night-time economy, whose users are mainly drawn from outside the borough. Westminster City Council encouraged residential development especially in the Soho/Covent Garden area, where the population grew by 15 per cent in the 1990s (GLA 2002: 27). Since 1991 almost 9,000 homes were built in Westminster with more than 2,500 in the city centre (M. Roberts and Turner 2005: 174). As a borough with a large share of wealthy and outspoken residents, residents' groups began to organize and voice concerns since the early 1990s. In 1999 a petition was signed by 600 residents about the decline in the amenity of the centre because of increasing entertainment uses (Westminster 2005: 107) and in 2000 two residents' groups commissioned reports on the area. The growth in resident population enabled Westminster City Council to justify the strong line it has taken for a number of years in trying to curb (the growth) of the night-life entertainment economy in the borough. Fearing the rise of an 'Ibiza culture' (GLA 2002: iv–v, 27), the council stipulated that there should be no further promotion and expansion of the night-time economy in the West End and the City of Westminster.

Already in 1993 and 1994 parts of Soho and Paddington were designated as 'stress areas' in order to enforce action against breaches of planning and licensing controls (Westminster 2005: 107). Since June 2000 Westminster City Council operated a policy for 'stress areas' and limited licensing and planning permissions for night-time drinking and dancing premises. It allowed changes in uses only where this was believed to help reduce the 'cumulative impact' of the night-time economy, for example, the splitting-up of very large nightclub venues or the substitution of such venues for other types of night-life entertainment with fewer customers or lower levels of alcohol consumption. Another measure was to encourage such developments that added greater diversity to the provision of entertainment, e.g. restaurants and premises servicing a seated audience or offering food along with drinks. Certain ratios of tables and chairs were sometimes added as conditions to the license as a method of designing out alcohol and disorder problems. An area management and improvement approach was launched in Leicester Square, Covent Garden and Chinatown which brought the introduction of 'al fresco' dining until 1 a.m. in the former two areas. City Guardians and a Civic Watch Project were set up, CCTV was extended in the West End and legal changes increased police power to stop street drinking and seize alcohol and receptacles. Despite the abolishment of statutory closing hours through the new licensing act, the core hours usually granted for premises supplying on-sale alcohol have not changed significantly and extend to 11:30 p.m. Mondays through Thursdays and midnight on Fridays and Saturdays. Only few central London venues open later during the week. On weekends less than half of the bars and nightclubs stay open after 11 p.m., many of them closing at 1 p.m. (GLA 2007: 7). Contrary to expectations, the promotion of restaurants was not without negative side-effects either. Public nuisance, especially noise issues, emerged because activities such as kitchen cleaning or waste removal continue long after licensable activities have ended. As a study of Old Compton Street in Soho found, noise and disturbance was not foremost due to boisterous behaviour or people shouting in large groups, but rather the effect of large numbers of people making use of a confined physical space. Much of the noise impact was seen to come from traffic in the early hours of the morning when the area is serviced by deliveries and refuse collections, taxis and minicabs (M. Roberts and Turner 2005).

This measure of defining areas where special policies can be applied was introduced in the Guidance issued to the Licensing Act 2003. It enables local authorities to declare 'special policy areas' where there is evidence of increase in crime, disorder or public nuisance. Such policies typically include special conditions and controls that are placed on licenses (see for example Urban 2007) or the refusal of new licenses unless it can be demonstrated that the new premises will not add to the cumulative impact. Special policies deviating from the general rules of the licensing law can be defined for such areas; for example new license applications for certain types of venues or applications for longer hours or 24-hour opening will not be granted (Westminster 2008). In England and Wales there are currently 71 cumulative impact areas, 17 per cent of which are in the Greater London area and 18 per cent in other metropolitan districts (DCMS, Licensing Statistics 2007). Special policy areas have become key instruments of local councils to increase power and control over the development of the night-time economy in these quarters. While the licensing act only enables authorities to refuse license applications if relevant representations are made by the residents in the vicinity or by other authorities (such as the police, the fire brigade or the health departments), in special policy areas the burden of proof can be reversed from the local authorities to the licensees. It is the licensees who have to prove that their activities do not negatively contribute to the 'cumulative impact' in the neighbourhood. License applicants have to provide a risk assessment of crime and disorder and have to show how the operation of premises will promote the prevention of crime and disorder (Westminster 2008). Such special policy areas were mainly created in zones with a high density of night-life venues.[11] However, there is ongoing debate about the determination of such areas. Due to challenges to local authorities' licensing functions via court, legal interpretation influences this specification, which can generate quite arbitrary boundaries and unintended effects. On the one hand, boundary drawing can be problematic as some venues have to be included within the line even if the issues are not as significant as those arising from other venues located nearby. On the other hand, venues located just outside the special policy zone might contribute to the 'cumulative impact' of the area just as much as those inside the boundary. Premises inside the special policy areas could be used for other uses not subject to licensing, but with their own negative impacts (GLA 2007: 42). Special policy areas might also lead to a displacement of growth of night-time venues to nearby areas as operators might take advantage of the closeness to a night-life cluster, but without the licensing restrictions imposed in the special policy area. Some operators inside such policy areas indeed fear that they cannot compete against venues with longer opening hours and against areas where the continuous development of new venues helps sustain visitors' attraction. In order to foreclose saturation just outside the special policy zones, it is likely that cases will be made for redrawing and expanding rather than for removing the special policy areas once they have been established. In addition, authorities might not want to yield the power they gained with this mechanism.

The criteria of saturation and 'cumulative impact' are necessarily of an arbitrary and hence political nature. Despite efforts to base licensing and planning on clear evidence about the impact arising from certain venues, for many incidences and disturbances no particular venue can be made accountable. Accordingly, Westminster Council assumes that cumulative impact arises mainly from the numbers of pubs, bars, and music and dance premises: 'Pubs and bars present opportunities for crime and they can also give rise to disorder' (Westminster 2005: 41). General survey evidence is presented about the links between alcohol consumption, crime and anti-social behaviour; yet, locally based evidence to substantiate such claims is often limited. Nevertheless, as a consequence of the necessity to base policy measures on clearer evidence, an increasing amount of information is produced and stored in integrated data collection systems. This information, comprising of police statistics of reported crime by premises, noise monitoring, ambulance call-outs and complaints, is used to determine a risk rating of premises, on the basis of which the frequency and intensity of further inspection and surveillance are determined (Westminster 2008: 85). Such information may not always be assessed as to whether it is correct or biased, stereotyped and manipulated based on evidence, on convictions or only on hear-say and subjective judgements (for a case analysis of how stereotypes and institutional racism may influence the perception of disorder and impact, see Talbot 2007).

Two other ways in which local licensing authorities can bring their influence to bear on the regulation of night life are by imposing mandatory conditions on licenses and by revoking licenses on the basis of police objections. Through the conditions added to licenses, license holders can be required to implement measures of self-regulation and self-assessment such as a CCTV system, to make extra contributions to funding schemes for security patrols, cleansing operations, enhanced public transport and public toilets and to participate in local partnerships such as the Pubwatch scheme (Hackney 2005: 55). Through the new legislation that enhanced the police powers of surveillance, licensing authorities have more information and evidence at hand that enables them to revoke licenses. For example, Westminster City Council revoked the license of Home club after a police operation against alleged drug suppliers. As a consequence, the corporate group owning the club went into liquidation (Chatterton 2002: 24). Westminster police has drawn up a list of nightclubs with crime incidents, and several nightclubs have been confronted with the threat that a revocation of their license will be demanded by the police (Edwards 2005).

The scarcity of the resources of both the police as well as the licensing authorities entails that resources of surveillance and control tend to be concentrated on such venues that have been identified as 'problematic' (Talbot 2007). This way of deploying resources involves a boundary drawing between good and bad, responsible and irresponsible licensees and consumers. While those deemed as responsible or well-managed face less hurdles in the licensing process and get away with things more easily, those identified as 'problem' cases are subject to increased surveillance.[12] This politics of normality and differentiation of agents reflects a moment that is not untypical of devolution under New Labour as Gerry Stoker pointed out; namely a lack of trust in the institutions of devolved governance (Stoker 2004: 82). Those on whom responsibilities have been devolved, in this case the licensees, have to earn the trust of the superior authority. Only if such trust can be gained does the relation become more egalitarian and partnership-like. Again, the questions arise as to on what grounds relations of trust are established, and which licensees and types of companies are seen to fit into the categories of 'business competence', 'good management' and 'cooperative' in the prevention of crime and disorder.

Differentiations of race and class continue to inform notions of order and disorder, responsibility and irresponsibility (Talbot 2006, 2007). As Talbot found in her case study (2007: 114), call-outs to the police by black licensees may be construed as weakness rather than cooperation leading to the avoidance of contact with the authorities, but risking role encapsulation. There remained serious problems of transparency regarding 'third party' influence in the licensing process, especially of police accountability (Talbot 2006: 167).

As this discussion has shown, the recent licensing reform and night-life governance in the UK has strongly been framed by the prevention of crime and disorder to such an extent that the latter is even cast as the prime goal of night-life governance. Policies often imply a default key assumption that alcohol consumption per se is the cause of violence, anti-social behaviour, public nuisance and crime. Alcohol appears as a readily identifiable, simple cause for the problems of the night-time economy, which leaves other, more structural issues out of view. It also suggests that people's behaviour is more or less determined in certain ways by their alcohol consumption. There is little acknowledgement that social drinking, socializing and dancing in the public sphere may help establish relations of trust and solidarity, reciprocity and connectedness between strangers and diverse social groups (Jayne et al. 2006). As Tiesdell and Slater argue, 'regulatory structures create (or reduce) opportunities for disorder but do not determine subsequent behaviour and conduct' (2006: 140). Despite the growing recognition that the night-time economy can have benefits for the economic, social and cultural development of an area, there is a strong notion in public and legal discourses of the current decade that the night-time economy is a source of 'pollution' and social dysfunction in need of control and 'cultural engineering' (Talbot 2006: 162). Against the intention of encouraging a more rational and less moral approach to licensing, the new licensing regime has not been purged of its moral subtext. It has been characterized as a form of policing that is 'reinforced by a discourse of moral hazard' (Talbot 2007: 107). Especially with the reversal of the burden of proof in special policy areas, licensees (in varying degrees) have been put on the margin of becoming offenders and of being criminalized. Besides its inherent moralism, the new regime of night-life governance has also been criticized for its authoritarian measures that 'become normative to the self-regulation and informal policing activity of the sector' (Mimique 2007) and enforce premises managements into 'deference' and subordination to the moral order (ibid.). For example, one London borough employs so-called 'licensing enforcement officers', who are operating undercover. Instruments such as the 'special policy area' illustrate the disciplinary power at work in the strategies of surveillance, normalizing judgement and spatial containment (Foucault 1977). Indeed, the fingerprint scanning system introduced as a pilot in a town in South Somerset in spring 2006[13] illustrates how disciplinary power extends its reach to the consumers, who are equally separated into 'good' and 'bad' customers. Prising open the premises to such measures of control and other conditions may be the price to be paid for being granted longer hours by the licensing authority. As this example shows, enforcing (self-)regulation through 'governing at a distance' does not only target the licensees and managers themselves, but uses them as mediators for enforcing (self-)regulation on the audiences of these spaces. Critics question the necessity of such intensive or over-regulation that would render 'every aspect of the functional operation of a bar . . . a condition of regulation' (Mimique 2007). The necessary and appropriate degree of regulation of night-life cultures will always be a contentious point between the interested parties. However, it is rarely acknowledged that night-life governance is not external to night-life culture, but is always already implicated in, and part and parcel of, the cultures that become objects of regulation. Particular forms of governance also shape the character of a night-life area and culture. Over-regulation, or whatever is perceived as such, is likely to either distort the good consumed, taking the fun out of going out to bars or nightclubs, or to provoke and amplify precisely the transgressions that are sought to be contained and controlled through various measures of regulation in the first place. As is well known, there are inevitable limits of manipulating an environment and solving problems of security through regulatory means (Tiesdell and Slater 2006: 152). Tim Newburn reminded of Jane Jacobs' famous point that 'no amount of police'—and, as might be added, no amount of regulation—'can enforce civilization where the normal, casual enforcement of it has broken down' (Newburn 2001: 845, Jacobs 1961: 31–32).

ISTANBUL: ECONOMIC LIBERALIZATION, URBAN RENEWAL AND THE NIGHT-TIME ECONOMIES

In the 1950s Istanbul counted only one million inhabitants. In a quite rapid process of growth and immigration it has become a mega-city of more than ten million people within a few decades (Ergun and Dundar 2004). Economic liberalization introduced in the early 1980s and the attempt to mould a global-city image have profoundly altered the urban social and cultural fabric and reshaped the urban centre as a district of culture, consumption and (night-life) entertainment. This prepared the ground for the emergence and growth of an electronic music and clubbing scene. Economic liberalization and political reform of the past two decades were characterized by contradictory moments. A liberal market economy was moulded with a traditionally strong central state apparatus. Despite the growth of the service and financial sector, the manufacturing sector (textile) continued to be the most rapidly growing sector of employment in the 1990s (Keyder 1999: 19–23). This went along with an increasing social polarization between a wealthy class of well-educated professionals and an immigrant population from rural Anatolian areas. The political arena reflects this social and cultural heterogeneity with the ongoing struggle for hegemony between secular, laizist parties and the reinvigorated Islamic parties, who gained votes and government since the early 1990s. The attempt to position Istanbul as a global city has been mingled with an orientation towards European governance structures during the EU-accession process. Although cultural strategies of urban renewal and development have also gained importance in Istanbul, the night-time economy has not come to be seen as a key element in such programmes. On the one hand, this specific, uneven path of development has given rise to quite specific features of club and night-life culture and governance in Istanbul. On the other hand, despite the local circumstances, many similarities can be noted to the club and night-life scenes of other contexts, not least because of the integration into international networks of club cultural production. As London, Istanbul has a central district with a longstanding tradition of night life, culture and entertainment. This area (Beyoglu) had seen relative decline between the 1950s and the 1980s due to cultural homogenization, migration to the sub-urbs and an abandoned, dilapidating old housing stock (see more details in the following parts). By the early 1990s, only a few bars existed in the area. But since then it has undergone a massive transformation through urban renewal programmes, gentrification and the development of a bar, café, restaurant and night-life culture. Today, the density of night-time venues in certain parts of Beyoglu is quite similar to the West End/Soho area in London, with an estimated number of two million people passing through during weekends, mainly drawn from outside the area.

In what follows, I shall first situate the emergence and the transformation of night-time entertainment and of the club and dance cultural scene in the wider economic and social changes and the cultural visions and politics in the city. After outlining the structure of the cultural sector more generally, I shall elaborate on the development of music and club culture. In the final part, a more detailed focus is put on the growth of the night-time economy in Beyoglu in the context of local cultural politics and the governance of night life in the city. Notably, the transformation of Beyoglu occurred against the backdrop of conservative Islamic council governments since 1994, which opens up the question as to whether or not certain forces and processes were at work that even the conservative Islamic AK party did not want, or could not afford, to resist.

With the military coup in 1980 that ushered in a regime monitored by the International Monetary Fund, Turkey shifted from a centralized, pro-tectionist import-substitution model to a market-oriented, liberal economic growth strategy (Erkip 2000: 372). In 1984 the free-market economy was introduced in Turkey. This entailed privatization programmes and the open-ing up to foreign capital, of which Istanbul absorbed a major share (Erkip 2000: 372; Keyder 1999: 14) and which was mostly invested in producer services and tourism. This led to an increasing presence of multinational company branches, partnerships and foreign firms and also to a dramatic increase in population, partly through immigration from the Middle East, the Balkans, the Caucasus, Russia and Western Europe. The extension of the service sector breeded a new employee group of highly paid and edu-cated professionals at income scales similar to their world counterparts and located between 'global and local values and lifestyles' (Erkip 2000: 372; Keyder 1999: 24). This was accompanied by a restructuration of the retail industry with new consumption spaces and patterns emerging. As Keyder remarked, 'Istanbul in the 1980s lived through its own version of casino capitalism and yuppie exuberance' (1999: 15). The urban geography was reshaped through gentrified business districts, office buildings, five-star hotels, new luxury housing projects in suburban areas, private universities, shopping centres and boutiques, an emerging fast-food sector, ethnic and world cuisines and an expanding night-life and entertainment sector (ibid.).

At the same time however, wages in manufacturing decreased between 1980 and 1990 (Erkip 2000: 372) and contributed to the social polarization and cultural fragmentation of the citizens into segments with vastly different incomes, expectations and lifestyles remade in, and mediated by, consumption (ibid.; Stokes 1999: 125; Keyder 1999: 24). The International Monetary Fund and the EU-accession process also prescribed political reform programs of decentralization and devolution starting in the 1980s, when some state powers were passed to a two-tier system of greater metropolitan and district municipalities. Since 1994 Istanbul Metropolitan Municipality has been under the rule of conservative Islamic parties, first the Welfare Party and currently its predecessor, the centre-right, conservative Justice and Development Party (AK Parti) led by Recep Tayyip Erdogan.[14] Aside from foreign investment, Istanbul gained a major injection of state funding and more autonomy as a city (Keyder 1999: 16). However, the transformation towards a participatory urban governance phase was limited and hampered by the conservative central state apparatus, as well as conflicts over values and objectives within the city administration (Kocabas 2005: 27, Erkip 2000: 374–375).

With the Constitution of 1982, legal restrictions on the media and the formation of associations were lifted. This resulted in the expansion of civil society organizations and of NGOs devoted to human rights, environmental and women's rights (Ünsal 2006: 2). It massively changed the media landscape of a country that had been fairly isolated from the influence of foreign media, especially Western media. State television had been introduced in Turkey in the 1970s; by the end of the 1990s there were more than twenty local TV channels and cable service in middle-class residential areas, numerous radio stations and foreign language as well as Turkish print media (Keyder 1999: 12). Market liberalization also had important impacts on the local music cultures. The harmonization of Turkish copyright law made it possible for foreign companies such as Warner Bros and PolyGram to move into the Turkish market. The influence and market share of these foreign companies brought more homogeneity at the top end of the market, yet they far from dominated the local music scene. Instead, as Stokes explained, 'media deregulation and new production technology brought an explosion of new sounds to people's ears in 1990' (Stokes 1999: 129) and partly prompted a new form of local patriotism, for example, through the emergence of FM radio stations.

Economic liberalization and immigration from the Anatolian countryside at an estimated rate of 200,000 per year in the 1990s also intensified cultural divides in a city that always has been ethnically heterogeneous but disunited, with most communities living side by side but separately (Keyder 1999: 4–5). An especially great divide opened up between the secular middle-class urbanites and the migrant population, which intensified othering processes (Robins and Aksoy 1996: 7, 20). Such socio-cultural cleavages also exist in the youth population. A small privileged segment enjoying (university) education at (private) educational institutions in Istanbul, Western Europe and the US at one end of the spectrum stands out against a large segment of young people at the other end of the spectrum living in disadvantaged communities on the peripheries of the city. They lack adequate access to educational and job opportunities and are confined to a limited universe of the home, the coffee house and neighbourhood streets and do not feel they are able to 'live their youth' (Boratav 2005: 204–205, 212). Inequalities in educational chances are perceived by young people themselves as a major source of difference among youth (ibid. 208). The Turkish state university system is based on difficult entry exams and allows students relatively little choice as to where and what they can study.

The Reconfiguration of Cultural Visions and the Cultural Sector in the City

Istanbul counts as the cultural capital of Turkey. Fostered by the city's strong Muslim and non-Muslim bourgeoisie, it has a long-lasting tradition of urban popular culture revolving around music, theatre, dance and drink. From the beginning onwards, the Turkish popular press, cinema and music industries have been based in the city (Stokes 1999: 125), which until today accommodates the media and broadcasting companies; numerous museums, galleries and exhibition spaces; entertainment industry venues and small, medium and large cultural initiatives (Ünsal 2006: 3). Usually clichéd as the bridge between two continents and civilizations, the period of market liberalization in the 1980s went along with a reinvention of Istanbul as a global and cosmopolitan city and a melting pot between Eastern and Western culture. The version of cosmopolitanism propagated in the context of the 'global city', however, was modelled on an European-style elite urbanity and hardly dealt with the cultural diversity and fragmentation that arose from the immigration processes (Robins and Aksoy 1996: 12–13). The cultural visions of the ruling AK Parti have also been complex and contradictory. In its local election campaign in 1994, Recep Tayyip Erdogan's Welfare Party tried to address the fears of its electorate in the poor peripheries of the city by distantiating itself from the vision of the Western global city, and by giving more emphasis to an 'alternative global city'. This was a strategy to 'impart a new cultural identity to those excluded and marginalized by the imagery of the global city, on the basis of a new symbolism building on the imagery of a folk Istanbul or deep Istanbul' (Bora 1999: 53) invoking the Islamic, Ottoman tradition (Stokes 1999: 124–127). Yet, when Erdogan's party won the local elections, it also had to accommodate itself to cultural forms more akin to urban cultures of Western metropoles and to more pluralistic cultural policies (Robins et al. 1996: 25). Visions of Islamization had to be negotiated with the existing urban cultural geography.

The social, cultural and political divides also materialize in struggles over the control of space and public morality (Keyder 1999: 23–25). Ultimately, the debate about the relationship between Islamism, secularism and Western culture is about the meaning of 'Turkishness'. It not only pervades the political arena, but is commonplace in public culture as people negotiate appropriate everyday comportments, ways of walking, dressing or talking. Amongst others, this contest over cultural values in everyday practices occurs at the level of gender. Although the anonymity of the metropolis opens up opportunities for varied expressions of femininity, the public comportment of women and female youth carries a particular symbolic burden being subject to negotiation and social control especially at neighbourhood level. Gendered use of public space at night with females socializing in private space is therefore common especially in disadvantaged communities (Navaro-Yasin 1999: 60–61, Boratav 2005: 214).

Cultural activities in Istanbul and Turkey generally, range from traditional folk culture to contemporary urban culture, from the artistic expressions of local communities to well-respected international arts events. As Klaic pointed out, the Turkish state views culture primarily as a factor for tourist promotion (Klaic 2005–2006: 12), the state cultural infrastructure has not kept up with the increase in population and hardly caters for all population and diverse lifestyle groups (ibid. 13). Public engagement in culture is limited. Despite a rising number of public-private co-operations, this model has not been embraced very enthusiastically by private actors. Other important cultural operators are political parties (cultural initiatives), companies in the cultural industries, non-profit non-governmental organizations or non-profit companies, foreign cultural institutions, and universities, some of which also run cultural centres (Klaic 2005–2006: 15, Ünsal 2006:1). A rising number of university courses in arts management and university education taken abroad have created a growing segment of highly qualified cultural professionals who seek adequate career prospects. Private sponsorship by family and banking foundations or companies plays a vital role for the cultural sector in Turkey. Many cultural institutions or cultural centres are privately funded (Klaic 2005–2006: 10, Ünsal 2006: 4). A large player in Istanbul is the Istanbul Foundation for Culture and the Arts (run predominantly on private resources), which has been operating for thirty-four years and which introduced contemporary foreign arts to the Turkish public (Klaic 2005–2006: 6). One of its projects is Istanbul Modern, a large facility in the post-industrial complex of Karaköy harbour. Apart from private sponsorship, cultural spaces partly also develop in semi-private contexts. Small-scale theatres or workshops are sometimes even set up in private cellars or attics (Klaic 2005–2006: 11). As this brief overview indicates, the cultural sector in Istanbul comprises both well-established institutions as well as local and informal networks and spaces (Ünsal 2006: 6). While the latter are often located in peripheries and neighbourhood contexts, most of the institutionalized cultural production addresses the middle classes and international audiences and takes place in the centre, especially in Beyoglu, between Galata Bridge and Taksim Square (Ünsal 2006: 3–4). The urban centre is therefore a highly symbolic space as it is mobilized for promoting a certain vision of the city as an international cultural capital. Istanbul's self-presentation as European Capital of Culture in 2010 can be seen along these lines. However, as mentioned before and as will be elaborated in more detail later, this vision of the city as a global cultural capital is neither the only one, nor is it without controversy as various cultural and political actors and institutions aim to shape Beyoglu according to their particular interpretation of this or of other visions of 'culture'.

MUSIC AND CLUB CULTURE IN ISTANBUL

It has been suggested that the neoliberal economic policies introduced since the 1980s also played a significant role in the emergence of club culture in Istanbul (Schroeder 2006: 7). Despite the traditional agenda tied to the internationalization of the city and the increased power of Islamic parties at local government level, economic liberalization opened the Turkish market to global consumer trends. A growing number of international and local media popularized and idealized Western urban middle-class lifestyles. With a historically high rate of population growth, Turkey also has a very young population, with more than 40 per cent in the 0 to 25 age group (Boratav 2005: 204). As a concomitant of these developments, the cultural and leisure sectors for the middle- and upper-middle-class youth has expanded. The foundation of private, partly US-funded universities in Istanbul as well as the exposure to university education in Western European or Anglo-Saxon countries contributed to a growing segment of young professionals and students embracing the fashions and lifestyles of these contexts. Similar to the UK, Istanbul saw the emergence of an 'underground' party movement in the 1980s: parties were organized in film studios, factories, old buildings, train- and underground stations, ships, ancient churches, airports and more. Yet, as a local party organizer of the time explained in an interview (Kayar 2007), although many of these events claimed to be 'underground', they were in fact manufactured by organization companies for a largely middle-class clientele. Electronic dance music was introduced in Istanbul in the early 1990s when Club 19 and Club 20 replaced Top-40 hits with techno and other electronic music styles (Schroeder 2006: 10, 24). Until this time, Taksim/Beyoglu, today's centre of night life in Istanbul, harboured hardly any bars or clubs. At the beginning of the 1990s a number of big clubs opened up in the centre, the most prominent being Taksim Nightpark located in an old paint factory, which was redesigned by Nigel Cox. Especially from the mid-1990s onwards Beyoglu experienced a night-life boom with growing numbers of bars and small clubs, catering to diverse music scenes and audiences, but remaining a hub for jazz and rock genres until today. Important influences also came from the clubs in popular tourist resorts such as Bodrum (e.g. Halikarnas), Kusadasi and Alanya. A different scene emerged along the European side of the Bosporus north of the city centre in Besiktas municipality. In the late 1980s, the first open-air clubs opened up in an area that had previously served as a small port. Today, this area hosts a number of highly upmarket open-air restaurant-bar-nightclub venues focusing on wealthy and celebrity crowds, house music and long drinks, with admission charges of €40 per night and more. In terms of average local purchasing power, going out to bars and clubs in Istanbul is a lot more expensive compared to other European contexts.

Similar to other cities, de-industrialized sites and factories have been adapted for party and night-life entertainment. Former ports and beaches likewise have been accrued for open-air clubs and festivals. Especially the latter have become more significant over the years. Istanbul hosts more than ten annual international music festivals, nearly half of which are oriented towards electronic dance music. These are large-scale festivals comparable to those in the UK or in other European cities and take place at open-air sites with several arenas. The most well-known dance-music festival is the Dance and Techno Festival, which has existed since 1998 and attracts around 20,000 people (Schroeder 2006: 10–11).

The growth of the clubbing and night-life scene was accompanied by information and mediation networks. Local radio stations such as Dynamo and Future Generation took on pivotal roles as promoters and sponsors of big events. In addition to foreign music and listing magazines such as the local spin-off of the London-based *Time Out*, local music magazines distributed through bookshops and cafés in Beyoglu and Internet platforms have emerged.

As in other contexts, the club scene in Istanbul is largely dominated by small, independent operators. But the late 1990s also saw the start-up of professional music organization and production companies (Schroeder 2006: 12), which either specialize in event organization or engage in diverse aspects of club cultural production such as hosting music events, parties and festivals; managing clubs; running club music radio channels and DJ booking agencies; producing CDs and distributing the music of independent labels (ibid.). In 2006 twelve music organization and production companies were based in Istanbul, with the bigger ones owning a record label, a club and an organization company. Unlike in London, where bigger companies grew out of a successful club or clubbing event and brand, several of them initially started as organization companies and only later opened a club to have a performance space (e.g. Pozitif). Some of these organization companies shifted from organizing clubbing events into event organization and promotion, which was facilitated by the similarities of these formats. Where once the main focus was to organize parties and clubbing events with the help of sponsoring and advertising, it then turned towards organizing promotional events by using party formats. With the need to produce more professional events in order to compete in a saturating market, the production costs for clubbing events have grown. As organization firms competed for big-name international DJs, the local prizes for such high-credibility artists went higher than at international level. It became increasingly difficult to balance the image of 'underground' parties with the growing need for sponsorship and the sponsors' demands to attract the target audiences for their products. Due to the rising production costs (DJs, artists, rents, technology) and the status of sponsorship in the cultural sector of Istanbul more generally, corporate sponsorship plays an important role in the financing of clubs and events, even those marketed as 'underground' (see also Chapter 3).

Several of the organization and production companies in Istanbul have or had partnership agreements with multimedia companies based in the UK, such as Renaissance in Nottingham and Ministry of Sound in London. The Istanbul-based companies engage in a range of organization services and seek co-operation with companies abroad for the exchange of artists. Yet, co-operation with the aforementioned UK brands in particular seems to suggest a more one-directional cultural flow in which the British companies use the organization services of local companies to accrue new markets for *their* music products, radio programmes and club cultural brands. Local companies organize tours and venues; they obtain permissions and arrange accommodation and transportation, but the core elements of music and event production such as sound and lighting systems, music styles and DJs are done by the foreign firms themselves (Schroeder 2006: 13).

Nevertheless, as documented by Fatih Akin's documentary *Crossing the Bridge* (2005), Istanbul has a lively and diverse local music scene, in which many musical traditions and influences are fused; popular and electronic dance music genres from the West too are merged with Turkish musical traditions. Advanced technologies of music production and distribution have given rise to multiple cultural networks and flows that partly bypass the traditional, corporate channels. Musicians and DJ(ane)s from Turkey or of Turkish descent are part of the international music networks and participate in the club scenes across Britain, the Netherlands, Germany, the US and Canada (Schroeder 2006: 13–15). As everyday practices in certain public spaces, music too is a highly politicized cultural form, through which symbolic differences between 'the West', 'the East' and 'the Turkish' and corresponding political agendas and social relations are negotiated (Stokes 1999: 123–124).

Overall, electronic dance music has not necessarily become a mainstream taste. According to Schroeder, clubbing first became the preserve of the (upper-) middle-class youth identifying with Western culture, but eventually trickled down to lower-middle and working-class ranks and since diversified into special-niche markets of wealthy groups, urban middle-class professionals, sexual minorities or else (ibid. 9–10). Saego (2004: 98–99) noted a 'distinct contrast between the mainstream Anglo-American pop, "corporate" rap and R&B sounds' dominating chic, expensive establishments frequented by foreigners and members of the local business elite, and those clubs specializing in house, techno and trance music, much of which is produced by Turkish-Germans in Germany. These latter clubs attract a much younger clientele who also visit the open-air summer 'rave' events and festivals. In addition, the local pop music (*yeni türku*, i.e. new Turkish pop) retains a distinct character and is popular with local audiences. Live music events of various genres continue to be important especially in the night-life scenes in Beyoglu. Even though less-privileged groups of youth have been drawn to electronic dance music and clubbing, social divisions are evident in the segmentation of club cultural scenes as well as in the semantics of 'clubbing' and 'underground', which the vernacular associates with upmarket events for wealthy middle-class and celebrity audiences.

Beyoglu: Night-Time Entertainment, Urban Renewal and Governance

As said before, Istanbul's night-life scene is mainly located in the central district of Beyoglu, which counts as the most 'European' or international quarter of the city and nowadays is the major entertainment and shopping district in Istanbul. Beyoglu was a settlement founded by Genoese merchants, and the majority of the population in the nineteenth century was of foreign, mostly European origin and upwardly mobile (Keyder 1999: 6). This is still reflected in its population structure today. Less than a quarter of the population in Beyoglu is Muslim (Ergun 2004: 396). In the nineteenth century Beyoglu was the international, commercial and artistic centre of the city, where most embassies and consulates, grand hotels and theatres were located. Beyoglu is bordered by Taksim Square in the northeast; by Tarlabasi high street acting as the main traffic route in the north and west, on the other side of which lies the poverty-stricken immigrant quarter Tarlabasi; and the Bosporus along the south and east. The core of the centre stretches along the pedestrianized boulevard of Istiklal Caddesi, sometimes referred to as the 'Street of Sound' (Sherwood 2006), which runs in a north east/south west direction. As other districts in Istanbul, Beyoglu has been a neighbourhood in transition during the previous decades. Until the 1960s it continued to serve as a multifunctional centre of business, residential living, entertainment and shopping. Beginning with the pogroms against the Greek population in the 1950s and intensified by the decentralization of economic activities, suburbanization and highway construction in the 1960s and 1970s, Muslims, Jews, Greeks and Armenians from high-income groups left the old city centre for more modern suburban housing in the outskirts. The decline in residential living led to the dilapidation of the historical housing stock, which also was not particularly suitable for modern office and business development. The percentage of firms located in Beyoglu had dropped from 30.4 to 15.5 between 1960 and 1990 (Dokmeci, Altunbas, and Yazgi 2007: 156). According to local commentators, by the 1980s, Beyoglu was run down. Its night-time entertainment was dominated by *pavyons* and *gazinos*[15], the former mostly frequented by men. In the 1980s Istiklal Caddesi was still an almost exclusively male space at night. However, the boom in night-time entertainment venues, especially of restaurants, cafés, bars and clubs since the 1990s has transformed night-life audiences and public space alike. Many of the empty houses have been adapted as multi-storey bars and clubs with rooftop terraces. Nowadays, Beyoglu attracts a dominantly young, but socially mixed audience strolling the streets and visiting a wide variety of night-life venues ranging from restaurants and cafés to upmarket-style bars, Turku-pubs and rock or jazz clubs. Istiklal Caddesi is crowded 24 hours, day and night. It no longer matches the image of adolescent male dominance at night, as women of all kinds, with or without male company, make a self-confident, matter-of-course appearance in day- and night-time public space.

Change began in the 1980s, when Beyoglu and the Historical Peninsula were declared as first-degree business districts and a tourist centre in the Metropolitan Area Master Plan 1980 (Ergun and Dundar 2004: 727). Urban renewal projects were developed and in 1985 a famous Beyoglu company established an organization for 'beautification' and 'preservation'. The project for pedestrianization started in the second half of the 1980s. In 1988 Tarlabasi Caddesi was constructed, and in 2000 a subway line opened in Taksim Square connecting the centre to the north of the city (Dokmeci et al. 2007: 159). In addition to the state-led urban renewal projects—since 1993 Beyoglu is a land-marked area and has increasingly been promoted as a cultural centre—gentrification took hold in the 1990s, mostly led by artists, architects and intellectuals, who renovated old apartments, opened up bookshops and art galleries (Ergun 2004: 396–397). Coffee shops, restaurants and cultural events like the Istanbul Film Festival further re-invigorated the area. The particular neighbourhoods that became gentrified included Tünel and Galata at the southern end of the main boulevard of Istiklal Caddesi and Cihangir, previously a home to sexual minorities, especially the transgender/transsexual community who were partly driven out by police crackdown. Unsurprisingly, Beyoglu became a hot real-estate market: although population density has been decreasing in all neighbourhoods, middle- and upper-income groups have returned to Beyoglu, and prices for a building just on a side street rose more than ten times between 1996 and 2004 (Dokmeci et al. 2007).

In the debates over the form and direction of this renewal, Beyoglu became a highly symbolic space for the struggle over cultural hegemony, since Istanbul and especially Taksim/Beyoglu are being reinvented as the 'cultural capital of Turkey' and of Europe (in 2010). Beyoglu was articulated into and claimed for various political projects. While Western-oriented and outside commentators somewhat nostalgically promoted the restoration of Beyoglu's 'elegant', civilized and cosmopolitan past, it was seen as the source of urban problems and degeneration within the Islamist discourse and as a largely foreign heritage within Turkish nationalist secularist discourses (Bartu 1999). In the attempt to position Istanbul as a 'world city', notions of cleaning and purification took hold. For the first metropolitan mayor, Bedrettin Dalan (1984–1989), Beyoglu was to be cleared from traffic congestion, prostitution and drug trafficking (ibid. 35), a process that continues to this day with raids of gay bars and sanctions against members of the transgender/transsexual community who eke out a living through prostitution. Intense conflict arose around the construction of Tarlabasi highway in the 1980s, when the Chamber of Architects opposed the mayor's plan to demolish nineteenth-century buildings and relocate the local population.

As was mentioned before, when the Welfare Party led by Erdogan won the local elections in 1994, its success was partly based on addressing the negative effects of globalization. It criticized the consumption inequalities between the populations in the shantytowns and the wealthy neighbourhoods, who benefited from globalization. However, this critique fed into a general moralism against entertainment and fun (Bora 1999: 53). One of the first populist measures taken by Beyoglu's new mayor (after the Welfare Party gained local government) was to order the removal of tavern tables on streets and sidewalks and to make restaurant owners conceal their indoors with curtains. This was justified as making the streets more accessible to those who could not afford to eat out. However, the mayor's policy was overruled by the popularity of outdoor eating and drinking. After a few weeks, following a sit-in (or 'sit-out') organized by a group of secularists, the tables had to be allowed out again (Navaro-Yasin 1999: 72). Under Erdogan's metropolitan administration the concern with creating a clean, decent and 'Turkish' Beyoglu continued (Stokes 1999: 126). One of the most controversial debates emerged over Erdogan's proposal to build a mosque and Islamic cultural centre in Taksim Square right next to the Atatürk Cultural Centre, the marker of Turkish nationalist secularism, as a means of creating an 'Islamic' image of the city for tourists (Bartu 1999: 41). However, as these and other policy plans did not succeed in Beyoglu, the AK Parti modified its symbolic politics and re-valued Beyoglu as an opportunity to invoke the Ottoman model of coexisting different lifestyles (ibid. 40). The Ottoman tradition became a symbolic frame into which both Islamism as well as contemporary urban lifestyles of consumption, drinking and night-life entertainment could be articulated, making it possible to embrace these cultures in line with the party's religious conservatism.

However, despite this ideological suture, the night-time and entertainment economy in Beyoglu—unlike in London and other UK cities—has never been presented as a motor of economic growth let alone urban renewal by the local authorities. In explaining the council's policy, the local planning officer (Suayip 2007) oscillated between demonstrating a cosmopolitan acceptance of night-life entertainment culture defining it as part of an established tradition on the one hand, and casting it as a cause of decline on the other hand; in particular, he depicted the pavyons and gazinos as the reason for the flight of residents from Beyoglu. The policy of the district municipality is best described as a form of toleration due to the economic benefits and the popularity of the restaurant, café, bar and night-life culture. However, explicit promotion is avoided in order to prevent the impression of contradiction to the conservative Islamist ideology of the ruling government. Therefore, the development of night-time entertainment does not feature as an explicit goal in the overall planning policies for Beyoglu.[16] These rather define it as a quarter for tourism, leisure, commerce and retail. While the local tourism board does promote Beyoglu's night-life culture, the kind of tourism imagined by the AK Parti is mainly oriented towards a 'cultural-historical' tourism centred on the architectural heritage of the area. Yet, there seems to be awareness that tourists also expect and appreciate the existence of a vibrant social and entertainment infrastructure in the city centre. As Beyoglu already is an established centre of night life, the central government under the AK Parti aimed to concentrate and confine all entertainment in this area. However, due to public resistance and resistance by other district municipalities this model of a single entertainment zone could not be realized, and it remained in the scope of every district government (*Kaymakam*) to define entertainment zones within its area. That night-life entertainment tends to be associated with urban decline rather than regeneration is not specific for the Islamist AK Parti. Similar concerns exist in other districts, for example Besiktas, a largely residential area, which has been under the rule of the secularist CHP (Republican People's Party) since 2003. As one of the wealthiest areas in Istanbul and the whole country, located just north of Beyoglu, the licensing manager of Besiktas municipality likewise pointed out (Aksoy 2007) that the growth of night-time entertainment in an area would negatively affect real-estate prices, and thus the interests of residents, respectively local electorate, would be given greater priority in planning and licensing than the development of the night-time economy.

Overall, the regulation of night-life entertainment and alcohol consumption in Istanbul shows great variation throughout the city. While some municipalities such as Üsküdar and Sultanbeyli (under rule by the Islamic parties) do not allow the consumption of alcohol on the streets, others such as Besiktas (under rule of the CHP) give rather little consideration to the rule that certain distances, determined by the district municipality, have to be kept between entertainment and drinking venues and religious sites. The devolution process in Turkey brought similar changes to the licensing regime as in the UK. Several policy areas, amongst them licensing, which used to be administrated by the police, were devolved to the local authorities, consisting of the city administration (*Belediye*; subordinate to the metropolitan government) and the administrative body that is subordinate to the national

government (*Kaymakam*), causing struggles over competences and responsibilities. For example, regarding the governance of noise, two different
departments are in charge acting on the basis of different criteria. Similar
ambiguities exist in relation to the competence of these authorities and the
police. Licensing is based on the zoning policies defined in the local plans
of the district. Licenses for night-life venues can only be granted within the
zones dedicated for commercial and entertainment functions. In these zones,
licenses are usually granted if technical regulations are abided by. These are
permanent licenses that can also be inherited. However, several separate
licenses may have to be obtained for different purposes (e.g. sale of alcohol,
music, etc.). Similar techniques of responsibilization as in the UK have been
implemented in the Turkish licensing law such as the nomination of a person
on the premises who may be held accountable. If drugs are found on the
premises, charges can be pressed against this person.

What has become a particular issue in the governance of night life is the
conflict between residential and night-life entertainment functions culminating, similar to other contexts, on noise issues. Such conflicts occur especially in relation to open-air venues, for example in Beyoglu, where sound
emanates from bars and clubs on rooftop terraces; or along the Bosporus,
where the sea carries the beats from the large open-air venues in Ortaköy/
Besiktas to other parts of the city, e.g. to the wealthy areas along the Asian
shore. Conflicts have intensified due to the parallel growth of night-time
entertainment and the ongoing gentrification processes in the centre. Both
in Beyoglu as well as in Besiktas most visitors of the club and night-life
scenes come from outside the areas. As in London, these developments
have resulted in increasing demands of (mainly) wealthy and outspoken
residents for protection from night-life sound. In the past years, authorities
responded to this situation by limiting late-night opening of outdoor events
and terraced clubs to 2 a.m., by reconfiguring the boundaries between
residential and commercial areas, defining special 'protected' residential
areas and closing down entertainment and commercial venues in residential
areas. Obtaining a license for open-air venues has become more difficult.
In 2006, the police raided and issued a closure order for a number of clubs
in Ortaköy. Stricter surveillance of the adherence to technical standards
was introduced and venues were forced to upgrade their sound systems and
install noise insulation in order to circumvent fines and closure.

This account of the political, economic and cultural contexts of the evolving night-time entertainment and club scene in Istanbul demonstrated that
processes of de-industrialization—as in the case of other cities such as London—served and still serve as an important backdrop for the party and clubbing movement. Due to the high concentration of night-time entertainment
in the centre, planning and licensing authorities are faced with similar challenges as in London. Devolution has affected night-life governance in Istanbul in similar ways as local authorities have taken over licensing functions
from the police, however, with the police retaining and exercising significant

powers of control and closure. Gentrification processes have been taking hold in close proximity to areas densely occupied by night-life venues. This has led to increasing tension between night-life entertainment and residential functions, particularly over the issue of noise, which is particularly due to more typical local features such as open-air night life on the streets, in rooftop-terraced venues or in spaces located at the shore of the Bosporus. Another significant feature is the role of private sponsorship in the cultural sector also affecting to some extent clubbing spaces and music festivals, where the display of sponsors' brands is a crucial finance strategy. The saturation of the market, strong competition and stricter licensing conditions (e.g. noise prevention, safety measures etc.) increased the pressure for professional management and diversification, the demands for high-end technology and the need to provide distinctive, high-credibility events through music gigs, clubbing concepts and DJs from abroad. All of this, together with rising rents in the centre, has driven high the costs of club cultural production and consumption. Electronic dance music and clubbing has thus not become such a mainstream taste and widespread leisure activity within the youth population as in the UK.

Although culture-driven strategies of urban renewal have been adopted in Istanbul, the night-time economy played little or no role in these. Its growth over the past two decades occurred without its explicit endorsement in urban renewal strategies and in the context of Islamic parties in the central and local governments. How can this acquiescence of Western-style night-life culture be interpreted, especially in a highly symbolically charged area such as Beyoglu? As Bora asks,

> Is it the proud generosity of the victor, a pluralism theme park, a pragmatic tactical stand, or is it the seduction of the modern that attracts the Islamic politicians into the soft and accepting metropolis? . . . Can the profane aura of modernism be instrumentalized for purposes of representing the Islamic sacred? (1999: 54)

It may have been a mix of reasons that led the AK Parti to compromise on their Islamist policies in the centre of the city, but not in other areas. To some extent, Islamist policy-making is a relational effect of secularists' othering (Navaro-Yasin 1999: 74). Attempting to escape the pigeonholes they were put, Islamic parties made contradictory strategic moves, sometimes fulfilling, sometimes countering what was anticipated from them. Certain urban night-life styles have become so customary in Beyoglu that to implement Islamist policies regulating public space, alcohol and entertainment would have gone against the grain of the everyday experience of the people frequenting the centre. Pragmatism combined with economic considerations and the need to bargain with the local business elite (Bora 1999) may have led to a different strategy of using Beyoglu's night-life and entertainment culture as a means of demonstrating an Ottoman cosmopolitanism and cultural pluralism.

3   Club Cultural Production and the Night-Time Economy Market in the UK

Recent studies of cultural, symbolic or entertainment economies in cities (e.g. Zukin 1996, Hannigan 1998, Scott 2000) have paid little attention to the role of club and dance cultures in the night-time entertainment economy. Research on nightclubbing and dance cultures throughout the 1990s mainly focused on the consumption of clubbing until Paul Chatterton and Robert Hollands, in a series of publications and research reports on several UK cities (Bristol, Leeds, Newcastle), began to draw attention to the supply structure of night-life culture. They put forward the argument that the 'new' urban entertainment and night-life economy in 1990s Britain was increasingly dominated by large, partly multinational, corporations aided by entrepreneurial city councils in need of local investment. Further, they pointed out that ownership and control tended to become concentrated in publicly quoted companies, for which branding was imperative to increase shareholder value and the trust of potential investors. The rising significance of branding, standardization of urban centres, and market segmentation would entail a socially segregated night life mainly oriented towards cash-rich consumers, whilst displacing older or alternative modes of night-life culture and forcing small and local entrepreneurs out of the market (Hollands and Chatterton 2003, Chatterton 2002). Such arguments are reverberated by similar claims about the capitalist incorporation of countercultural forms and social movements through the cultural and entertainment economies capitalizing on the synergies between leisure, retail and night life (Scott 2000: 209–210, Talbot 2007: 7, Hannigan 1998). As far as the production of dance and night-life culture has become a focus of attention, it was strongly seen in the context of gentrification, corporatization and social fragmentation in the wake of the economic restructuring of cities and urban space. Political economy approaches tend to subsume the cultural under the economic, assuming that the profit and growth motive of (global) corporate investors eradicates (local) cultural styles and creativity. Tied into narratives of loss of a 'golden age', such arguments fail to acknowledge that gentrification and regeneration are more contested processes requiring a more nuanced understanding of the social relations, the particular practices, the meanings, identities and local differences through which such spaces are lived (Jayne et al. 2006). Chatterton and Hollands' arguments about the dominance of UK night life by (global) corporate power are premised on the brewery industry and the closely connected or annexed pub sector, the branded high-street fast-food, coffee-shop and restaurants chains, the growth of style bars and leisure/retail/night-life complexes in urban centres such as Star City in Birmingham or Heron City in Spain (Chatterton 2002: 38, Hollands and Chatterton 2003). At the turn of the millennium only three brewers dominated the supply of beer in Britain, and nearly 80 per cent of the pub market was owned by pub estate companies (Hollands and Chatterton 2003: 365, 370–372). Yet, if considering the overall ownership structure of pubs and bars, the picture is less clear. Although the number of independent enterprises in the pub/bar sector has been going down in the past few years, and managed and tenanted pubs/bars taken together exceed the turnover of the independent pub/bar sector, independent pubs and bars still make up more than half (51 per cent) of all enterprises active in the bar, pub and nightclub sector in the UK in 2006 (Source: ONS 2007; see also Graph 3.2). While tendencies of concentration are discernible in some respects, for example, the brewery industry and pub and bar sector, it would be misleading to claim that night-life entertainment in general is dominated by global corporate power. This argument also fails to take into account the nightclub sector, which as a whole is characterized by small and medium-sized independent operators in most European countries, including the UK; although most of the largest companies in this sector are based in the UK. As the demand for nightclubbing and dancing is more exposed to fashion cycles and musical trends and involves a high degree of risk-management in relation to security and legality, corporate investors tend to stay away from this market (Key Note 2005). Similarly, corporate control is much weaker in relation to the production of electronic dance music than in the music industry generally, where major companies are beginning to lose ground due to new production and distribution technologies (Saego 2004: 93–95). Just as cultural industry research tended to focus on larger, more established business segments, much less is known about small and micro-companies, which often escape from view as they do not 'register on established indicators' and are therefore more difficult to investigate (O'Connor 1999: 76–77).

Mapping the sector of club cultural production especially at international level—important as this may be—is indeed fraught with difficulty; as is measuring the size of cultural production generally. The production of nightclubbing closely intersects with other domains of cultural production and mediates the distribution of such commodities as music, fashion and interior design. For example, Crewe and Beaverstock (1998: 303) emphasized how night-time economies both 'feed into, and feed off, other related cultural activities, such that complex social and labour-market crossovers exist between local clothes designers, bar owners, club organizers and DJs. Club cultural production is frequently part of multimedia or organization companies who also engage in publishing, distribution of sound recordings, radio activities or event management. Despite these overlaps with activities usually counted as part of the creative industries, club cultures are usually counted to the entertainment and leisure industries.

The main sources to turn to when trying to gain an insight into the structure and size of club cultural economies are national statistics, which provide aggregate data on employment and the size of the sector by industry classification; further, market research and company databases.[1] The best source to determine the size and development of the night-life sector in Britain is the Annual Business Inquiry by the Office for National Statistics (ONS), which provides total figures on key variables such as number of enterprises,[2] total turnover, gross value added and employment down to five-digit subclass level of the Standard Industrial Classification (SIC). This elicits separate datasets for nightclubs, bars and pubs that can be broken down by regions and even postcodes showing the geographic distribution of these night-time economies. Market research offers more detailed information on market developments, demographic aspects and profiles of nightclub audiences. However, extensive market research only exists for the UK and the US; for example, the Mintel reports on the nightclub sector in the UK have been published every few years since the mid-1990s. They are mainly based on surveys and market size estimations calculated on average spend per head and estimated number of admissions. Company databases[3] are valuable sources of information, as they make available data about financial profiles, ownership structure, subsidiaries, and the main business activities. Yet, these sources pose several limitations for mapping the industry size and structure of nightclubbing. First, nightclub turnover is difficult to assess, because companies often hold a mixed portfolio of licensed venues or comprise a whole set of other activities (Mintel 2006: 23). They may be registered under several industry codes depending on their main activity. Although the UK industry classification (SIC 2003) has a separate subclass for licensed clubs,[4] many operators of nightclubs and discotheques also appear under other codes (e.g. sometimes they are categorized under dance halls and dance instructor services, which in theory explicitly excludes licensed clubs). Measuring the size of the sector by turnover and company number as well as by employment is therefore tricky. Due to the high degree of informal and casual work or self-employment by independent promoters and DJs, many of these activities do not appear in the statistics or databases at all. Difficulties in mapping the sector at international level arise because so far, little research has been carried out outside the UK. Databases covering international company data only include a certain range of (the largest) companies depending on the type of subscription by the database licensee. Complete company data are often only available in national databases. The comparison of aggregate data collected from national statistics is complicated by the fact that industry categorization varies in the different countries. Major steps towards harmonizing the codes have been made through the reforms of the NACE classification within the European Union between 1990 and 2008 with a major revision introduced on 1 January 2008 (NACE Rev. 2; see note 4). Yet, even the use of the same codes does not guarantee that businesses are, or indeed can be, classified in a standardized and correct way either because of local specificities or because the actual businesses, a lot more fast-moving than the industry codes, escape the statistical categories. For example, the Mintel reports include both nightclubs and discotheques, and they do not distinguish between these types of venues. While discotheques were included, hybrid bar-clubs or late-night bars with dance floors were only added in the latest survey (2006).[5] Another limitation for mapping the nightclubbing sector at the international scale arises from the fact that, unlike the British five-digit industry classification, the four-digit NACE scheme does not include a subclass for these specific activities, but puts them together with bars, pubs, discotheques, cafés or other beverage-serving premises. Given these limitations it is impossible to determine the exact size and value of the nightclubbing sector. But the data do allow for mapping general trends of the market and industry structure in the UK over the last decade and for broadly outlining how nightclub companies operate. The following discussion is structured into two parts. First, the key features of club cultural production systems shall be outlined including their strategies of market making through diversification, the formatting of genres and stars, and internationalization. Second, the development of the British night-life and clubbing markets shall be sketched out in terms of economic size, consumer profile, the supply side (company size, ownership structure, employment) and the role of branding and advertising. Finally, some of these features and trends are illustrated by the case of the Ministry of Sound company.

CLUB CULTURAL PRODUCTION

Just as cultural industries, club cultures too are involved 'in the production of social meaning' (Hesmondhalgh 2002: 11). Although they do not share all the distinctive features of cultural industries, they face similar problems and deploy similar strategies to come to terms with them. This includes unpredictable, unstable and faddish demand for the commodities on offer. Clubbing and night-life entertainment offer experiential, time- and space-based commodities with a short life span. Control over the quality and use-value for the audiences is limited, because these qualities—as in service spaces generally (Lash and Urry 1994: 193–222)—arise to a great extent from a co-construction of producers and consumers. Consumers themselves are an important part of the product consumed (e.g. 'atmosphere'). Nightclub companies use several strategies in order to handle the fickleness of product and audiences. One is spreading the risk by building a portfolio of goods, where hits offset misses (Hesmondhalgh 2002: 19-21; Miège 1987: 274); for example, a portfolio of different nightclub venues, different events and DJs, different brands and concepts tailored to particular groups of consumers. Another approach is vertical diversification into a repertoire of services as an attempt to optimize synergy-based cross-selling opportunities, e.g. nightclub operators acquire 'feeder' venues such as bars near the club; they offer a variety of entertainment activities on one site; they diversify into other areas such as hotels, restaurant, recording and music publishing, bowling or pool bars, health and sports clubs and promotion; or they hire out their venues for video clip and movie production, fashion shows, office parties, product launches or private functions (Mintel 2006: 25). Especially with the abolishment of statutory closing times for pubs and bars and the extension of late-night licenses in the UK through the Licensing Act 2003, nightclubs have lost their special status as the only place to go after 11pm. As a consequence, diversification into the bar and restaurant sector has become more important to fight competition from late-night bars that offer dance facilities. Overall, the boundaries between bars and nightclubs have become more blurred over the years since operators have also tried to bypass difficulties of gaining planning permission for nightclubs by developing 'chameleon-like ' venues with primary use as a restaurant during the day, with drinking and dancing defined as auxiliary uses especially at night. Diversification into the bar and restaurant sector was also encouraged by government policies (e.g. planning laws) that aimed to introduce more diversity in night-life hubs in order to minimize 'binge drinking'.

In contrast to other cultural industries, the degree of vertical integration is low and the nightclub industry is characterized by subcontracting relations and interfirm networks with each company specializing in a particular aspect of production. Security is mostly done by private security companies. Many, especially larger, branded clubs employ in-house promoters, but otherwise promotion and management functions are frequently separated out. Especially, but not exclusively, smaller venues hire out their premises to external, mostly self-employed promoters who take care of DJ hire, marketing and promotion in return for (a percentage of) the admission charge above the cost for hiring the venue, depending on the deal. A typical pattern is some kind of share between admissions charges ('promoter takes the door'), and drinks sales ('house takes the bar'). However, as the promoter of Club Hussy in London pointed out in an interview, venues sometimes define 'bar levels', i.e. a certain level of turnover on drinks to be met by the promoter, as a condition for hiring out the venue, ending the deal if such levels cannot be sustained (Lise 2007). These sales levels or number of drinking units per person are sometimes calculated on the basis of high-volume drinking at full people capacity of the venue or even above. Such pressure for growing profits is likely to be passed down either from the owners of the buildings and spaces, especially since bars and restaurants have also been affected by the dynamics of property development (Roberts, Turner, Greenfield, and Osborn 2006: 1108), or by the corporate management in case the venue belongs to a larger, listed company. Meeting the 'bar levels' is a frequent point of contention and gives rise to promoters' frustration with operators being 'in it for the money', leading to a high degree of fluctuation of independent promoters, who often have to change venues. Typical reasons are that the owners or managers wish to look for more profitable events; that the venue becomes too small; that it cannot get longer licenses or the licenses required for particular forms of entertainment; or that the owners get into trouble with the neighbours. Promoter-led club nights build a reputation at a smaller venue and then trade up, using local DJs who already have a loyal following (Mintel 2004: 25). Ownership of space is a big advantage for club promoters in order to create events and clubs that are sustainable in the long run.

As was pointed out before, the 'qualification' (Callon, Méadel, and Rabeharisoa 2004)[6] and market-making in club cultural production involves producers, processes of mediation and consumers' co-presence. Qualification, the process through which certain commodities are connected to certain qualities and achieve credibility in the market, happens through the club's promotion work, media coverage and word of mouth. Such symbolic or image work is crucial and comprises practices of formatting (music) genres, (DJ-)stars (in joint action with the music industry and the media) and new trends and fashions. The genre- and star-systems as well as the branding of club concepts are deployed to stabilize continuous, long-term demand, while the ongoing cycles of fashion created by the media simultaneously undermines it (Ryan 1992: 199, 229–230). As Miège explained, the star system creates two groups of producers, a minority of stars (e.g. big-name DJs) who 'benefit to an outrageous extent' (Miège 1987: 274) compared to a large 'reservoir of talent', who works under highly casualized conditions with blurred boundaries between work and leisure. A similar structure applies to clubbing scenes, where a few big-name DJs are able to cash in enormous royalties compared to less well known or only locally known DJs, who work for very little money or no money at all. Formatting is an attempt to frame audiences and to attach what managers and promoters perceive as the 'right' and detach the 'wrong' types of consumers from their venues. When the quality of a product, in this case a clubbing night, depends to a certain extent on consumers who are recognized as credible, then consumers in turn have to qualify for being part of that event. Goods and agents are thus inserted in a web of mutual legitimization and qualification. As other forms of cultural production, club cultures create artificial scarcity and exclusivity. In other words, credibility is partly achieved through social closure, a crucial mechanism of which is the boundary work at the door (see Chapter 4). As was shown at the example of the music industry and the fashion modelling business, cultural economies depend on a careful balancing of symbolic and economic capital as total market value is an economic and cultural aggregate (i.e. 'credibility' or reputation, and profit; see Entwistle 2002,

Ryan 1992: 194). The sole focus on increasing profits may serve detrimental to long-term interests, as it diminishes symbolic capital, which secures the attachment of high-status consumers in the first place through the distantiation from 'commercialism' and 'selling out'.[7] Balancing the need for symbolic and economic capital often leads to ambivalent processes of opening and closure, as times of low demand create weak boundaries, and times of high demand create strong boundaries around the good. Some club managers voluntarily reduce the capacity of their venue in order to appeal to upmarket crowds. To increase the scope for selective closure, club managements deploy other, more implicit strategies at the door (see Chapter 4). However, the attempt to frame and attract the desired customers is always at the risk of overflowing. Either new claims to membership emerge, or the target audience withdraws. Consumer attachment is highly unstable and unpredictable, especially in highly saturated clubbing markets.

The industry structure of club cultural production is similar to the cultural industries generally, which is characterized by concentration of relatively few large, integrated firms and a high number of independent, small and medium-sized companies often involving only one or a few venues. This also applies to the supply structure of nightclubbing in the UK, where nearly 90 per cent of the estimated 2,000 venues are run by small, independent operators (Mintel 2006: 27). Club cultural production therefore can involve high degrees of standardization in branded nightclub chains, but at the same time there are medium- to low- profit-making smaller companies as well as non- or low-profit oriented artistic or social-movement related initiatives seeking distinctive values by aiming for a high degree of innovation and responsiveness to local milieus, audiences and cultural symbologies (O'Connor 1999: 76–77, Power and Scott, 2004: 7). However, it should not be forgotten that even large, highly profit-oriented brand-driven companies have to show innovation and have to connect with local discourses of authenticity in order to remain competitive, especially in saturated markets.

Although the genre of electronic dance and club music has been adopted for distribution by major music companies, Saego argued that in distinction to pop genres, there is a 'relative lack of widespread US interest, involvement and participation in its development', as club culture is much less central to youth culture in the United States (Saego 2004: 101–102). Due to new technologies major companies can be bypassed more easily, as local vinyl pressing facilities can be used for production, and independent labels, record shops and club nights are used as distribution channels. Equally, digital technologies for recording, storage and distribution (e.g. selling via phones or the internet, audio streams, blogs, forums and MySpace pages) have opened up decentralized means of communication and exchange organized in networks of interdependent local scenes (ibid. 94–95).

As was outlined in the introductory chapter, club and dance culture has grown into a global cultural phenomenon that is difficult to make sense of, as origins, influences, cross-fertilizations, international links and relations of power cannot be pinned down so easily. While electronic dance music has been described as the most globalized cultural form, partly glorified as a democratic and accessible, rhizomic structure of mixing, sampling and fusing that results in fuzzy boundaries and uncertain authenticity (Saego 2004), the pessimistic picture emerging from Hollands and Chatterton's account of night-life entertainment suggests a clear-cut opposition between locally grounded entrepreneurs driven out of the market by global corporations and investors (Hollands and Chatterton 2003). While both these depictions capture a moment of truth, neither of them fully attends to the patterns of club cultural production. Hesmondhalgh provided a useful framework for considering different levels of internationalization with respect to cultural production and consumption. He distinguished between the internationalization of cultural texts—as audiences and symbol creators draw on, interpret and adapt texts from many other places; the internationalization of cultural businesses through companies making investments or distributing their cultural commodities in more than one country; and the emergence of complex, transnational cultural identities (Hesmondhalgh 2002: 178). Instead of a democratic mixing or a domination of the local by global corporate forces, the electronic dance music and clubbing scene is a product of more complex forms of exchange and global/local dialectics. Local independent companies especially in cities outside the UK sometimes cooperate with international organization and production companies. Rather than UK night life being dominated by (multinational) corporations, it is often UK-based companies who export their dance and clubbing brands, invest in foreign markets and influence local cultures/markets by selling, protecting and expanding their clubbing concepts. However, as later examples will show, there is no direct or full control by these companies over the local recreation of their global brand (see also Schroeder 2006: 15). Although these companies do not dominate particular local scenes let alone the global clubbing market in terms of market share, UK clubbing brands have grown into leading brands in the global market. However, the picture is more complex considering that the brand-owning companies, their holding companies, investors or shareholders may not be from the UK, but may have international investors and shareholders, including those countries to where the brands are exported. There are, therefore, no easy or straightforward answers to questions of cultural and economic power and domination. (Club) cultural economies are highly place-specific (Scott 2000). Local traditions, norms and sensibilities as well as politics and forms of governance shape the final outcomes of production/consumption. Even though large corporations do have high bargaining power in entrepreneurial cities eager to attract investment, cities most likely prefer restaurant, café, hotel, leisure or retail brands to bar and nightclub chains. Despite all tendencies towards standardization, no clubbing and night-life scene in any one city resembles that of another.

NIGHTCLUBBING IN THE CONTEXT OF THE
BRITISH LEISURE AND RECREATION MARKET

As the licensing data and market research suggest, the British night-time economy has seen a massive upsurge especially in the late 1980s and the 1990s. Despite the significant and visible rise of the night-life sector in many cities, however, going out to pubs, bars and clubs remained a rather marginal leisure activity in terms of consumer spending on leisure and recreation more generally. Even in the UK, which has one of the most thriving nightclubbing scenes, eating and drinking out, home viewing, DIY/gardening and gambling take by far the largest share of consumer spending on leisure and recreation,[8] which was estimated at 11.5 per cent (or £83,93 billion) of all consumer expenditure in 2004 (see Table 3.1).

By comparison, admission to nightclubs was estimated at £700 million by Key Note market review a few years ago (Key Note 2005). Although nightclubbing seems of minor significance when compared to eating and drinking out, it is quite remarkable that expenditure on nightclub admission (not including drinks) has almost reached the same level as cinema consumption. These figures do not include beverages, which are a major source of income for nightclubs accounting for more than two-thirds of the sales (Mintel 1996: 12). Therefore, if measured by admissions and drinks, the UK nightclub and bar industry by far outweighs cinema-going with an annual turnover of £bn 2 (according to market research by Mintel) or even more than £3.3 billion according to the Annual Business Inquiry (ONS 2007). Yet, watching television, video or DVDs is still the dominant leisure activity at weekends and evenings. In addition, clubbing has carved out a small segment of about 5 per cent of the total holiday market. The value of the clubbing holiday market in 2002 was estimated at £1.8 billion (Mintel 2003: 15). However, in view of the estimated changes in consumer expenditure on leisure activities between 2000 and 2005 (Table 3.2), the nightclubbing market clearly deviates from other sectors that have increased quite substantially.

Table 3.1   Consumer Expenditure on Leisure Recreation by Market (£m, £bn and % change), 2000 to 2004.

	£bn, £m	*% 2000–2004*
Home viewing	13,075	38.0
DIY and gardening	10,870	30.9
Eating and drinking out	27,250	8.1
Cinema	770	34.4

Sources: Consumer Trends/Family Spending/Cinema Advertising Association. Crown Copyright material; adapted by Key Note: Leisure & Recreation Market, Market Review October 2005.

Table 3.2   Expenditure on Selected Leisure Activities in £m, 2000 and 2005.

	2000	2005	% change
Cinemas	827	1,135	+37.2
Health, fitness	1,433	2,164	+51
Nightclubs and discotheques	1,830	1,825	-0.3
Tenpin bowling	219	269	+22.8
Theme parks	232	286	+23.3
Eating out	22,230	27,563	+24

Source: Mintel 2006: 17.

Research also shows that there are significant divisions in leisure lifestyles especially by age group. While nightclubbing is a rather small segment in the overall leisure and recreation market—even if an estimated quarter of adults in the UK use nightclubs, and 10 per cent of adults visit once a month or more (Mintel 2006: 10)—it has become a major leisure activity in the youth market. Nightclubbing strongly appeals to a very tight age group of predominantly 18- to 24-year-olds of whom 29 per cent go out to a nightclub at least once a week, and a further 29 per cent who go at least once a month, an age group that will continue to rise by 6.6 per cent between 2004 and 2009 (Mintel 2004: 7, 27). According to the Key Note review (2005), roughly 50 per cent of the 15- to 19-year-olds and 75 per cent of the 20- to 24-year-olds are consumers of nightclubs in the UK.[9] Visiting of nightclubs drops off to occasional visits at age 25, and becomes less frequent with marrying or co-habiting. Older age groups and educated professionals prefer going out to bars rather than nightclubs. In sum, nightclubbing has a strong foothold among the young population; yet, its (economic) significance when compared with other leisure activities and the general population should not be overestimated. This demographic profile of nightclub audiences in Britain has remained quite constant over the years. On average, club-goers in Britain visit a nightclub once a month and spend around ten pounds a night, which has also roughly stayed the same throughout the years (Mintel 2004: 12). The frequent club visitors are drawn from middle-income groups; but, as mentioned previously, the nightclub sector has benefited a lot from the increase in student numbers in further and higher education. Particularly full-time undergraduates (roughly a third of the 18- to 24-year-olds), although low on disposable income, are considered important audiences for mid-week events.

The night-time entertainment sector in the UK, i.e. in this case, bars, pubs and nightclubs taken together, has increased fairly steadily since the late 1990s in terms of turnover and, more moderately, in the number of enterprises (Graphs 3.1 and 3.2). In 2006 licensed clubs amounted to 15 per cent of the bars sector (SIC 55.4) in total, both in terms of turnover and the number of companies. In terms of value added the clubbing sector looks rather moderate (Graph 3.3), and if calculated on 2006 prices, the turnover of the nightclubbing market even shrank between 2001 and 2006. This development is also indicated by the slump in admissions (Graph 3.4) since the early 2000s, with admission numbers in 2007 lower than in 2001. By contrast, between 1991 and 1996 nightclub admissions in the UK had risen by 26 per cent peaking in 1998 (Mintel 1996: 3, Mintel 2000a: 14). This development fed into new investments in larger, high-capacity clubs outdoing each other with the latest state-of-the-art technical equipment in the mid-1990s. One such example was Home, a club that opened up in central London in the late 1990s spanning seven storeys and three dance levels, various bars, a private members club and a restaurant. However, since 2000 and 2001 the market fell and stagnated ever since, mainly because of increased competition from late-night bars and summer music festivals, superstar DJs who priced themselves out of the market, negative publicity on binge drinking and new legislation that had great impact on the industry such as the Private Security Industry Act 2001, the Licensing Act 2003, the introduction of the Alcohol Harm Reduction Strategy in 2004, the 2005 amendments to Use Classes Order of 1987 and the smoking ban that came into effect in July 2007 (see the discussion in Chapter 2).[10] Forecasts expected the nightclubbing market to recover slowly in the next few years (Mintel 2004: 43–44); however, in the light of the recent financial and economic crisis such expectations may no longer be realistic. With the number of total visitors and admissions going down, but admissions per visitors going up, it seems that the nightclub audience contracts to more dedicated clubbers, who go out more frequently. Possible after-effects are that nightclub operators either aim for a wider consumer base by offering more varied venues that allow for a mix of activities, or that they preserve their distinctive values through refurbishing and rebranding, creating large destination venues for dedicated, regular clubbers (Mintel 2006: 3).

Considering the regional significance of the night-time economy (bars, pubs, nightclubs) for the various regions of the UK, it is more evenly distributed geographically than the hotels and restaurants sector (Section H, SIC 2003) on the whole. Similar to the creative industries, which are strongly concentrated in Greater London and the South East (roughly half of employment in this sector is believed to be located in these regions; Pratt 2004: 26; Bassett et al. 2005: 144), London, quite obviously, also plays an important role for the night-life sector accounting for 15 per cent of the overall turnover of the industry, but turnover is almost as high in the South East (including cities such as Brighton), the West Midlands (e.g. Birmingham) and the North West (Manchester, Liverpool). On the measure of turnover between 1998 and 2005, the growth of the bars sector was particularly marked in the West Midlands, London and the South East (see Graphs 3.5 and 3.6).

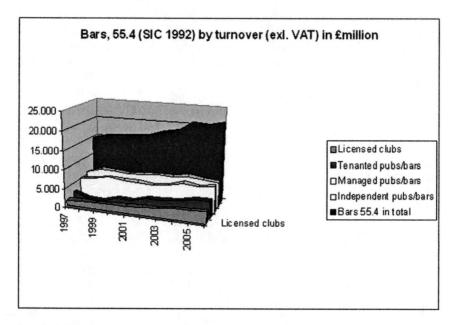

Graph 3.1 Source: ONS, Annual Business Inquiry: Section H—Hotels and restaurants 1995–2006

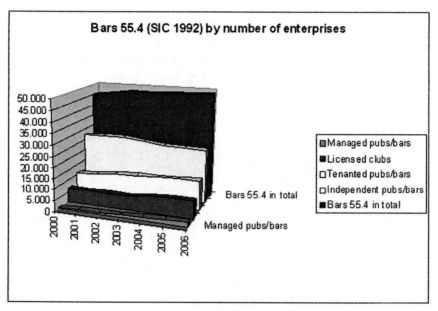

Graph 3.2 Source: ONS, Annual Business Inquiry: Section H—Hotels and restaurants 1995–2006

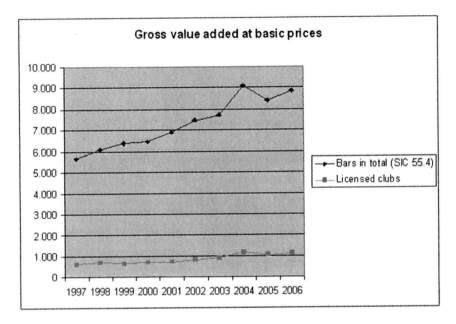

Graph 3.3 Source: ONS, Annual Business Inquiry: Section H—Hotels and restaurants 1995–2006

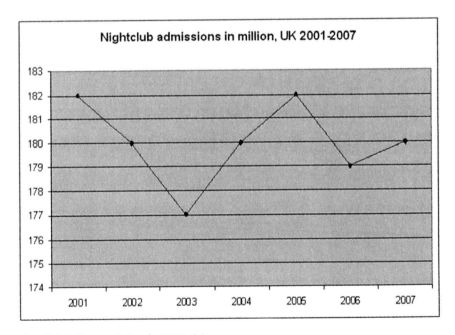

Graph 3.4 Source: Mintel: 2006: 24

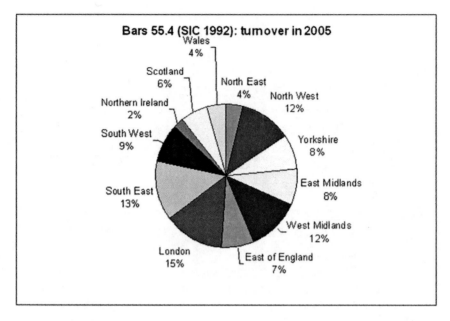

Graph 3.5 Source: ONS, Annual Business Inquiry: Section H, Regional Standard Extract 1998–2005

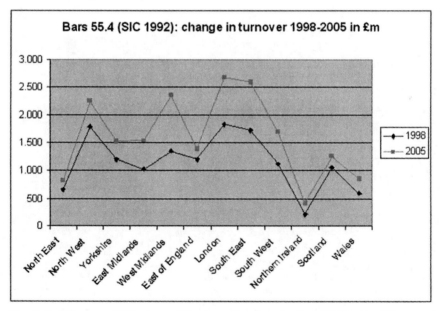

Graph 3.6 Source: ONS, Annual Business Inquiry: Section H, Regional Standard Extract 1998–2005

At the end of the 1990s it was estimated that around 830,000 people were employed in the British night-time industry either directly or indirectly (according to the Brewers and Licensed Retailers Association 1999, as quoted in Chatterton 2002: 39). Cultural industries in general have a high proportion of casual, irregular or self-employment although full-time weekly wages can be considerably higher than the regional averages (Pratt 2004: 27–28). The former also applies to the bars sector (i.e. pubs, bars and nightclubs), where almost two-thirds of the employees are employed part-time. The rate of full-time employment is highest in managed pubs (44 per cent) and lowest in licensed clubs with the large majority of staff (74 per cent) working on part-time contracts (ONS 2007). A large share (40 per cent) of employees is paid below the minimum wage (Chatterton 2002: 39), and employees have to put up with long hours and hard working conditions. As was argued by several authors (Hobbs, Hadfield, Lister, Winlow, and Waddington 2003: 23; McRobbie 1999a: 18), the night-time economy offers those excluded from the classic Fordist employment model the possibilities of flexible and casual work and incomes temporary or supplementary to a day job. As the night-time economy is a highly informal business, money can be earned at the side. But it seems that this comes at the cost of easy exploitation. As Bianchini has pointedly stated, compared to the licensing regime the sphere of work in the night-time economy is under-regulated. The night can be 'the time of exploitation, a time ghetto for low-paid workers' (Bianchini 1995: 125).

As pointed out above, the supply side of nightclubbing in the UK is dominated by a majority of small or medium-sized businesses (i.e. either single-site operators or those with fewer than five sites) and a few large companies. However, no single company has a significant share of the market, and thus, local competition is quite strong (Mintel 2006, Key Note 2005). The number of clubs, bar-clubs and discotheques in the UK has been estimated between 1,700 and 2,000 (Mintel 2006, Key Note 2005); however, numbers are likely to be higher as the number of enterprises running licensed clubs (which includes social clubs) by far exceeds this number (ONS 2007; see also Hobbs et al. 2003: 25, who estimate the number of licensed clubs at 3,800). Almost 90 per cent of the premises are operated by small companies as defined above. Despite a growing trend towards concentration at the level of larger enterprises, the independent sector even increased its share since 2004. Between the late 1990s and the early 2000s established operators disappeared from the market (e.g. First Leisure, which was the biggest company in 1996) or changed hands. Luminar became by far the largest operator in 2000 owning 174 outlets and accruing 20.3 million admissions (that is 11.4 per cent of all admissions, Mintel 2000a: 5; see also Hollands and Chatterton 2003: 374). Its market share has gone down in the past few years (see Table 3.3); yet, with 110 venues in its portfolio in 2006, Luminar still has a clear lead over the second largest company. Luminar is followed by about six medium to large companies operating up to thirty venues, and two medium-sized companies owning up to ten venues. Due to the limitations posed by the company databases, the average size of the majority of smaller companies is hard to establish, yet it can be assumed that a substantial share of these are single-site operators.

As said before, companies active in the nightclubbing sector often diversify by building portfolios of related products and services, which is why precise measures of the nightclubbing market are impossible to make. For example, Luminar Leisure, CanDu Entertainment and other companies not only operate licensed clubs, but also restaurants, pubs or bars. While Luminar achieved a turnover of about £204 million in 2007, medium to large companies owning between ten and thirty venues have a turnover in the range of £30 million to £80 million. Notably, Ministry of Sound Holdings, parent to a number of subsidiaries, also has a turnover around £30 million and more, mainly accrued by its subsidiary recordings firm. Five of the above companies have national or international investment or pension funds or banks as ultimate owners (Luminar, CanDu, Novus, Eclectic Bars/previously Barclub and Nexum Leisure). Novus Leisure has probably the largest portion of international shareholders although its main owner is Novus Acquisition Limited based in the UK. In several of the other companies (Table 3.3) the shares are held by the company directors or other, mostly UK-based individuals plus, in some cases, a capital investment group.

Table 3.3   Supply Structure of Nightclub Operators in the UK.

Operator	Nightclub venues 2004	% of total venues 2004	Nightclub venues 2006	% of total venues 2006
Luminar Leisure	176	9.0	110	5.5
CanDu Entertainment	—	—	25	1.3
Novus Leisure Ltd	—	—	22	1.1
Urbium	25	1.3	—	—
Po Na Na/Barvest	23	1.2	—	—
The Nightclub Company Ltd	19	1.0	—	—
Barclub Ltd	—	—	15	0.8
Nexum Leisure	14	0.7	12	0.6
G1 Group PLC	—	—	11	0.6
Summit Clubs	—	—	11	0.6
Vimac Leisure	—	—	8	0.4
Utopian	—	—	6	0.3
Other	1,693	86.8	1780	88.8
Total	**1,950**	**100**	**2000**	**100**

Sources: Mintel 2004: 17; Mintel 2006: 27.

With the increasing importance of shareholder capital in nightclub economies, marketing, advertising and branding have become crucial techniques for acquiring credibility and value (a 'publicity surplus', Ryan 1992: 66). In particular large companies listed at the stock exchange depend on the trust of stock exchange investors. Brand reputation strengthens beliefs in expected future profits (Ryan 1992: 187, Lash and Lury 2007: 6). Accordingly, promotion and marketing techniques differ markedly from the mid-1990s rave and clubbing scene, which tried to appear as independent, unique and secretive as possible ('underground'). For example, it was a well-kept secret that Heaven nightclub in London, which was an important place for the Ibiza-influenced house-music scene in the early 1990s, was owned by Sir Richard Branson's Virgin Company. Apart from refurbishment, technological upgrading and product differentiation, branding became a central strategy for tighter niche-marketing, diversification and for entering new markets. Brands are meant to stabilize sales patterns by generating consumer loyalty (Ryan 1992: 185–187). A typical strategy pursued by a number of companies concentrating on devoted clubbing audiences (e.g. Ministry of Sound, Miss Moneypenny's, Gatecrasher) is to create a brand around a flagship club or event, establish a record label, and set up residencies, branches, franchises or tours abroad, especially in the clubbing holiday destinations. Miss Moneypenny's, founded in 1986, operates a flagship club in Birmingham, which was relaunched in 2003/2004, runs several residencies in the Mediterranean and established its own record label in 2004. It planned to open up similar venues in the UK and Europe (Edinburgh, Dublin, Manchester, Paris, and Barcelona; Mintel 2004: 24). Another international dance-music brand is Gatecrasher, which also refurbished its flagship club in Sheffield in 2003, runs its own dance label and branches in Leeds and Nottingham and operates tours and events abroad, especially in the Mediterranean (Mintel 2004: 24). While back in 2000 most of its outlets were still branded individually, Luminar Leisure diversified into several brands. It runs venues as Oceana, a multi-million pound, multi-room venue brand that typically incorporates two nightclubs and several bars, restaurants, roof terraces, private suites and themed rooms such as New York Disco, Venetian Grand Ballroom or Parisian Boudoir. Liquid's branded venues are more geared towards the mass-market, while the Lava & Ignite brand offers various music genres for more 'sophisticated' clubbers. In addition, the Life brand was created as a bar and club concept for smaller town, traditional bars during the week with club nights on weekends (Mintel 2006: 31).

With fiercer competition on the market, soaring prices for big-name DJs, and the necessity to invest in advanced technologies (e.g. sound systems, security, measures against noise pollution), the production costs of clubbing have gone up. Apart from shareholder capital and branding, advertising has become an ever-more crucial funding strategy. Retail companies and advertisers have discovered club audiences as a crucial gateway to the youth market and have begun to use clubbing and party layouts for advertising campaigns. Music and clubbing festival organizers especially seek funding through advertising. Typical sponsors seen at festivals are TV-channels, radio stations, beverage or tobacco brands. But also nightclubs increasingly open up their spaces to outright sales promotion. While the logos of the main (non-)alcoholic beverage or tobacco brands have been commonplace inventory of many bar and club spaces for some time, more obtrusive techniques have found their way into some clubs. For example, a manager of an upmarket club in Istanbul named at least ten companies, amongst them a bank, a mobile phone company, designer labels and beverage brands, each spending between US $5,000 and $15,000 on advertisements in the club per season. The venue displayed logos or products such as glass cases with fashion and jewellery and even a car, as well as screens for commercials. Roughly estimated, the income accrued from these sponsors amounted to at least a quarter of the turnover per season.[11] This being a more extreme example, the majority of clubs in Istanbul do sponsorship either by selling sponsored drinks, displaying logos or putting on special nights for certain brands; or by direct funding in response to a share from the admission charge. Due to a more common role of private sponsorship in the cultural sector, sponsorship also seems to be more widespread and has a visible presence in the club cultural scene.

The growing significance of and crossover to advertising and promotion might suggest that clubs are becoming mere formats and pretexts *designed* for advertising and for composing and selling ideal target audiences to advertisers (Miège 1987: 277–278); however, this reasoning would be overly economistic. If this were the case, products would lose their aura of authenticity. Without a distinct quality of the product itself neither the club-consumers, nor, as a consequence, would advertisers be interested. But it is clear that advertising imperatives enter directly into, or at least affect, operation and management by prompting the matching between advertisers' ideal target groups and the club audience. If a substantial portion of income is derived from advertising, advertisers are likely to invest in those companies that draw the target audiences preferred by the advertisers. Vice versa, nightclubs can attract potential financial sponsors if they can convincingly show that they catch the favoured audiences. In the example given above, where sponsorship had an exceptionally significant role, this resulted in a highly exclusivist setting with a selective door policy and a strong orientation towards attracting celebrities, who in turn would draw high-status consumers.

Several UK clubbing brands have ventured into the clubbing holiday business in the Mediterranean resorts and/or have opened up clubs in other metropoles (e.g. Home in Sydney, Ministry of Sound in Bangkok). This export of British club culture already goes back to the mid-1990s when the UK clubs Cream and Ministry started up party nights and organized trips for British clubbers to go to Ibiza (Mintel 2003: 13). Companies such as Global Underground, Renaissance, Gods' Kitchen, Gatecrasher and Ministry of Sound have multiple affiliations and partnership agreements in different locations across the globe. Asian metropoles have been popular targets of such expansion because of the large proportion of an increasingly affluent youth population whose interest in Western fashion and lifestyles could be easily aroused.

Ministry of Sound, in particular, led the way for global expansion. It was founded in 1991 by the Old Etonian entrepreneur James Palumbo with £250,000 he had earned as a bond trader in the city (Eimer 2006: 25). The company grew rapidly in the 1990s. When it opened, it was modelled on New York's 'dry' dance clubs like the Sound Factory, as it only had an entertainment license for all-night dancing, but not an all-night liquor license (Swindells 2005: 120). Ministry of Sound was one of the first night-club companies to diversify into a number of related areas and to pursue a strategy of branding. It set up a radio show that was broadcast in thirty-five countries, a monthly music and clubbing magazine (*Ministry*; see also Chapter 7), established its own music label and grew into Europe's largest independent record company (Ministry of Sound Recordings) selling about 2 million dance compilation albums a year and achieving a turnover of £28 million and more (Sherwin 2006: 38). Ministry of Sound is sometimes taken as the epitome of the corporatization of night-life entertainment (Hollands and Chatterton 2003: 361), mainly because of its ambitious expansion and diversification, resulting in a company that had more than twenty subsidiaries at some points. Despite the successful establishment of a global brand, since late 2002 profits were outpaced by investments. Severe cutbacks had to be made including the reduction of staff, the closure of international offices, the shutdown of the magazine and several record labels (Eimer 2006, Howorth 2003). The company was eventually reorganized into three core subsidiaries (Recordings, Limited, International) and a holding company. In 2003 the London club was refurbished to attract older, higher-spending clubbers. In 2006 Ministry of Sound acquired the successful Hed Kandi record label, around which it planned to create a broader lifestyle brand, part of which was the launch of branded cosmetics and beauty products (Goodman 2007). As turnover figures suggest and the operating manager confirmed, the primary business of the company is CD sales (Eimer 2006). To some extent, therefore, the (national and international) nightclub operation has become a promotional means to increase CD sales. The first time the club concept of Ministry of Sound was brought to China was in 1997. The company's move into Asian markets was a result of the downturn since the late 1990s and early 2000s and a 'way of reviving the company on the cheap' (ibid. 25). A Ministry of Sound branch was set up in Bangkok in 2001 but closed 2 ½ years later because the Thaksin government, as part of a 'social order' campaign, had imposed a general closing hour at 1am except in the newly created entertainment zones (Gampell 2006). New branches were eventually opened in Singapore, Taipei, Beijing and Egypt (Chee 2005). According to media reports, the company makes about $300 million worldwide every year by franchise settlements. These require local owners to pay a fee to Ministry of Sound for the right to use its brand and DJs. However, such franchise agreements do not always run smoothly as a recent lawsuit filed by Ministry of Sound against its Singapore partner demonstrates. A 15-year contract was signed in 2005, but disputes occurred around the payment of royalties and the management of the club. The licensee was accused of not adhering to the Ministry of Sound guidelines on music and door policy, service and crowd control and of promoting its own nightclubs in the area (Sujin 2006, 2007).

Clearly, such types of international franchise agreements as arranged by Ministry of Sound and other UK clubbing brands feature a form of co-operation that centres on the marketing of British brands and club cultural products rather than on cultural exchange. As a media report describes the promotion of British clubbing in China:

> They all have English names such as Cargo, Angel and Babyface, and are expensive to run. They use top British and European DJs such as Paul Oakenfold (who charge up to Pounds 60,000 a night), who are flown over first class. (Eimer 2006: 25)

Nevertheless, as the above example shows, this one-directional cultural flow is not an even process of domination, but meets local resistances and adaptations, thereby escaping full control by the companies owning the brand.

CONCLUSION

In sum, this chapter demonstrated that despite the overall rise of the bar, pub and nightclub industry in the last two decades and the pivotal role club cultures play for young consumers, the economic significance of just the nightclub sector is considerable, but not extraordinary. Compared to other leisure activities such as home viewing, eating out or health and fitness, going out clubbing does not appear to have reached such a central status as is sometimes ascribed to it. Nightclubbing economies in Britain are less dominated by corporate power than suggested by previous research into the night-life entertainment sector more generally, which pointed to the power of big corporations, processes of standardization, market segmentation and social fragmentation (Hollands and Chatterton 2003, Chatterton 2002, Chatterton and Hollands 2003). Although strong tendencies of ownership concentration are manifest within the alcohol and beverage industries and to an increasing extent in the pub sector, the nightclub sector is structured by a few, large companies and a majority of small and independent companies with no single company having a substantial market share. It is also characterized by a low degree of vertical integration and a high degree of subcontracting relations as well as by highly casualized and informalized employment relations. Club cultural production shares several features of the cultural industries, for example, similar strategies of market making such as the formatting of stars, styles and brands and the 'hits offset misses' approach of dealing with risk. These attempts to stabilize demand in the long-term depend on the help of scene-relevant media, but are at the same time undermined by the ongoing cycles of fashion hyped by them.

Overall, the pub, bar and nightclubbing market in the UK showed a fairly steady growth over the past decade, and tenanted and managed pubs and bars especially profited from this development. Nightclubs, by contrast, were faced with stagnating markets and decreasing profits in the context of legal changes that eroded their competitive advantages over pubs and bars or that entailed rising costs (e.g. Private Security Industry Act 2001, Licensing Act 2003, changes to the Use Classes Order in 2005 and the smoking ban in 2007). The dynamics of the property and stock markets also affected the night-time economy in terms of growing pressures for profit exerted by property owners, landlords or shareholders of listed companies. If, at the extreme, profit margins are calculated on the basis of high-volume drinking at full venue capacity and geared towards speeding-up turnover of the audience, then it is hardly surprising that together with overcrowding and shortness of transport resources, problems such as binge drinking, disorder or violence are intensified.

In order to come to terms with fiercer competition on the market, many companies diversified into related services in the bar, restaurant or hotel sector, the leisure or cultural industries. Boundaries between late-night bars and clubs have become less clear as venues increasingly offer facilities for a range of activities. This raises the question as to whether or not clubbing will remain a separate concept or become one of several aspects of multi-functional leisure venues responding more flexibly to the needs of the audiences (Mintel 2006: 23). In addition, club cultural economies have developed interfaces with other fields of practice. In particular, clubbing has also become a medium for social or business networking, especially in the cultural sector, as well as for advertising and other promotional purposes, with formats sometimes blurring and the functions blending into each other. Other typical strategies to adapt to fluctuating or stagnating markets are branding and internationalization through international cooperation in event organization, branches or business ventures via franchising. The complex constellations between the local base of branded club-concepts, shareholders and investors of brand-owning companies do not allow a general, straightforward answer about relations of power in these international exchanges and networks of club cultural production. They call for more research and case studies of international dimensions of club cultural production in order to establish how particular places are integrated into these relations. Clearly, brands created in the UK scenes count to the leading international clubbing brands. However, larger brand-holding companies often are in multinational ownership. As the examples illustrated, branded club-concepts are prone to some degree of adaptation to place-specific circumstances and to appropriation by local strategies.

4 Sensing and Meaning the Body
The Local Organization of Clubbing Practices

Popular and academic representations of clubbing are strongly infused with images of 'otherness'. The dance club is often regarded as an atmosphere of ecstatic feelings, collective bliss and rapture, and as an 'other-worldly environment' (Thornton 1995: 21), where the structures of everyday life are temporarily suspended through thresholds that separate the visitors from daily routines, education, work and family commitments; where social identities are undone and new identifications and roles are taken up and played with; where social boundaries between groups dissolve and where participants act out transgressive, carnivalesque bodies. In popular discourses such as magazines, fanzines or websites, clubbing appears as an icon of pleasure and fun. Images of liminality and transgression shape a morality of pleasure and the justificatory discourse that underpins cultures of clubbing. These images of liminality are 'built in to the promotion of night-time products' (Talbot 2007: 19) and frames visitors' expectations of, and scripts for, a 'good' night out.

This chapter delves into the question as to how the broader cultural values and images of clubbing are transformed into situated practices and experiences in the dance club. The realization of emotional and experiential scripts is mediated, facilitated, but also partly impeded by the institutional and spatial arrangements of clubbing. It is actively worked at through certain types and combinations of practices that involve cultural and social competence; and it is aided by certain technologies and rituals of passage. A key feature of the organization of practice in the dance club is the tension between routinization on the one hand and the construction of special and extraordinary moments on the other hand. Hobbs et al. referred in this respect to the 'routinization of liminal practices' in night-time pleasure zones (Hobbs, Lister, Hadfield, Winlow, and Hall 2000: 711). Central to clubbing practices are aesthetic and prosthetic forms of embodiment, which help generate a liminoid atmosphere[1] and a state of 'otherness'. Yet, dance clubs do not always deliver on this promise. While the messy, chaotic character of a large gathering of people provides for spontaneous and unforeseen events and encounters, the local management of crowds geared towards preserving security, order and safety tends to turn nightclubs into sanitized and controlled environments for de-control (1991: 24). In the following parts, this chapter first situates clubbing in the context of contemporary body cultures before discussing some typical elements of the organization of practices in dance clubs. It shall be emphasized that this offers a contextualized account that draws on ethnographic fieldwork and interviews relating to specific settings (i.e. mainly clubbing environments in London and the UK; on methodology and the field of study see the introductory chapter). Nevertheless, it aims to distil some general aspects that are common to, and relevant for, varied club environments in different geographical contexts of clubbing—even if they are interpreted in locally distinct ways. Almost any club nowadays has certain routines of controlling admission. Clubs also shape particular modes of sociality and types of social organization mediating between individuality and group ethos, for example, in conventions of dance. In the second half of the chapter, the aesthetic and prosthetic forms of embodiment shall be theorized more thoroughly. These involve sensory stimulation and simulative, playful acting 'as-if', which afford certain qualities of experience and experiential styles. The discussion explores as to how these affect classification practices and give rise to interpretive devices that reframe notions of authenticity and mould performative understandings of identity. The final part of the chapter introduces the concepts of boundary work and narrative identity that inform the empirical analyses of the following chapters.

CLUBBING IN THE CONTEXT OF CONTEMPORARY BODY CULTURES

It was argued that contemporary body cultures partly have evolved as a response to the distantiation from the body that characterized the civilizing process and the Cartesian body–mind dualism of Western modernity. Drew Leder pointed to the paradox that the body, whilst being an 'inescapable presence', is essentially characterized by experiential absence (Leder 1990: 1). Although it is the ground of experience and is always a field of lived sensation, it ordinarily fades and recedes from our awareness when engaged in purposeful actions and daily routines. Contemporary societies offer a number of occasions (e.g. in sport, massage, alternative medicine and body therapy), where the body is made a thematic object of attention and is turned into an active presence of '*Erlebnis*' and a medium for authenticating identity (Rittner 1983). The dance club clearly is an institution that provides opportunities for body-related and body-focused experiential consumption, although this is not necessarily framed by the quest for authenticity. First, the body can be enacted and experienced in different ways than are typical of everyday life. The club emphasizes expressive and mimetic practices such as dancing, dressing up and body decoration. This includes the carnivalesque construction of masks and the staging of beautiful and erotic bodies. It also offers the possibility of creating bodies-out-of-control through intoxication and sensual excitement spurred by auditory, visual and tactile stimuli or by stimulants absorbed into the body such as drugs and alcohol. Second, the experiential commodity of clubbing encompasses particular forms of sociality, of relating to friends and strangers. This includes a greater degree of bodily proximity as well as haptic experiences between strangers normally avoided or merely tolerated as an inescapable feature of public life in cities. Participants draw from the energy and excitement, the affective ambience of a collective event. In Durkheim's terminology (1995), clubs try to produce a state of collective effervescence fostering emotional bonds and attachment to a moral community which seems to affirm values that differ from the ones dominating the spheres of work, education and urban public life: self-control, productive efficiency, competition.

None of these elements is specific to clubbing spaces alone. Other types of leisure environments too emphasize the quest for excitement (Elias and Dunning 1986) through absorbing sensual stimulation and the collective nature of the event, which encourages expressivity and spontaneity. Similar to theme-parks, shopping malls, certain kinds of holidaying, urban spectacles, sport events, music festivals and concerts, casinos or gambling halls, they fashion, in varying degrees, 'fantasy worlds' (Hannigan 1998). These are based on the distantiation from, or transcendence of, the everyday facilitated, for example, by techniques of simulation (as in themed nights). As Hannigan pointed out in his book *Fantasy City*, such leisure sites constitute a solipsistic 'world in itself' with its own rules, meanings and spatio-temporal organizations, existing in physical, economical and cultural isolation from the real world (ibid. 4). Immersion in these spaces is based on the distantiation from potentially disturbing experiences, in connection with, for example, urban poverty and homelessness, conflict, violence or else.[2] Clubbing and dancing also share elements with certain types of sports as they are both linked to motility, sociability and mimesis. Enjoyment is gained from special types of movement, playful interaction and the strong affects generated in mimetic acting (Elias and Dunning 1986, Shilling 2005: 115). Even though fitness gyms, for example, cultivate rather different body practices and are underpinned by different cultural values than clubbing, both the dance club as well as the fitness studio fashion environments where deep involvement in the ongoing practice is a strongly valued element, if not normative requirement, of the setting; calling upon participants to appear entirely engrossed in the practice and to surrender either to the 'dictates of dance abandon' (Thornton 1995: 21) or to the dictates of the trainer or machine (Sassatelli 1999: 233). Unlike the fitness studio of course, the night-time economy does not idealize, or only partly idealizes, the fit and disciplined body, but propagates an unhampered hedonism, intoxication and even unruly behaviour (Hobbs et al. 2000: 705).[3] In sum, clubbing is one of several sites that are characterized by body-focused, experiential consumption through the immersion in solipsistic worlds. What is specific to it is perhaps only how various elements are combined to create a particular type of activity in particular types of spatial-temporal settings.

As mentioned at the start of this chapter, a certain stream of thought is predominant in discourses on dance and club cultures: these tend to be imagined as back regions and spheres of play outside, or on the peripheries, of everyday life, where routines, commitments and norms temporarily cease to be in force and where emotional distance can be gained from the stresses and strains of everyday life.[4] However, clubbing is not simply detached from, but operates both within and against the structures of everyday life (Grossberg 1990: 115). Despite its image as an 'elsewhere' (Pini 2001), everyday norms, values and routines also reach into the sphere of clubbing. In their modes of operation, their methods of organizing, managing and regulating crowds and space, clubbing spheres appear ordinary and similar to, rather than different from, everyday contexts and service spaces. Although dance clubs allow for alternative kinds of bodily expression, they are also sites for cultural body and emotion work (Shilling 2005) that forms a central part of identity at least for certain segments of the population. Such emotion work involves the control of one's body appearance and presentation through impression management, and the display or alteration of feelings in line with the ideals and expectations of particular fields of action, particularly at workplaces. Clubbing inverses the ideal of the productive capacity and efficiency of the lean, emotionally managed body (Shilling 2005: 87) into an ideal of unproductive excess and transgression. Yet, it also affirms the importance of youthful attractiveness, creativity, fitness and fun. Emotion work is also present in club settings as participants aim to realize the organizationally prescribed emotional scripts, not merely as a surface performance, but by turning them into deep acting and actual experience. The production of 'ecstatic' bodies is connected to certain technologies of self, in which potential risks and obstacles are carefully managed through ongoing self-monitoring (see in more detail Pini 2001). Thus, many of the technologies and practices in clubbing can be seen as an expression or perhaps mere enhancement of the ways in which bodies are lived in everyday life, work and consumer culture. Sound and music have become central to people's daily activities, especially of the young. Music accompanies the move through shopping and leisure spaces. It is used to stimulate emotions, atmosphere and sociality, to affect the length of stay in service spaces, and it prompts people to latch their movement practices onto it (Shilling 2005). Likewise, the use of chemical stimulants, such as tranquillizers, painkillers, sleeping pills, antidepressants and more has become a normality (Shilling 2005: 113) and provides the backdrop to the chemical enhancement of bodies in contexts of clubbing through illegal substances.

All this indicates that dance clubs do not simply transcend the structures of everyday life, but remain implicated in the latter whilst trying to offer refuge and transcendence. This point is not to be misconstrued as concurring with the functionalist arguments weaved through Horkheimer and Adorno's critique of the cultural industries as mere compensatory escape realities, which prolong the alienating character of capitalist labour

(Horkheimer and Adorno 1969). By emphasizing the intricate linkage between club cultures and structures of everyday life, no (d)evaluation of the practices and experiences of participants is intended, for example, that such cultures would only offer inauthentic, pre-patterned experiences. Similarly, other versions of functionalism as implied in Elias and Dunning's argument that the excitement gained in institutions of leisure makes highly rationalized society tolerable through a temporary transcendence and release from mundane routine (Elias and Dunning 1986) would be too simplistic. Even though this contains a kernel of truth, it is necessary to account for the different modes in which people participate in club cultures and for the multifaceted experiences they get out of it. Eric Cohen's typology of tourist experiences (Cohen 1979; see Hetherington 1998: 117) offers a useful scheme of different orientations and degrees of commitment that also helps highlight people's varied relations and approaches to clubbing. Escapism may be only one among several orientations. For example, going out to bars and clubs may be seen more as a form of recreation in settings that are considered part of, rather than separate from, everyday life. Escaping into an 'other-worldly' environment may be quite secondary to preserving a strong attachment to everyday commitments, roles and identities. By contrast, instead of mere escapism and diversion, other participants may see club cultures as spheres that enable them to search for more authentic and meaningful experiences than everyday life offers them. Some may take this further and come to reject beliefs and values of everyday life, identifying more fully with a clubbing lifestyle. At the end of the spectrum there may be participants who exile from their 'ordinary' everyday life and come to regard the club scene as part of a permanent alternative to the former.[5] The different ways in which people view the relation between everyday life and the sphere of clubbing and the significance of clubbing within biographical contexts will be the focus of attention in the following chapters (5, 6).

THE LOCAL ORGANIZATION OF PRACTICES IN DANCE CLUBS IN LONDON

Queuing and Admission: Rituals of Separation and Passing

There are manifold ways in which people frame their practices of going out clubbing. While some take a more instrumental approach, tying in their daytime practices and routes through the city with night-life entertainment in order to minimize effort, others engage in time-consuming rituals of preparation, which help mark 'the night out' as a special event. Practices of dressing up, having drinks with friends, listening to music and travelling to the club together by cab, car or public transport are part of getting ready for the night. However, this process of distantiation is not always straightforward as experiences and impressions that interfere with the creation of the right mood have to be warded off. Clubs are sometimes located in remote areas and backstreets which, when they have to be walked through, can involve feelings of unease about potential risks and dangers. Of course, a large number of clubs and night-time venues are situated in central areas and entertainment hubs, yet in these too, a *blasé* mode may have to be adopted as a shield against disturbing impressions arising, for example, from the close proximity of entertainment to poverty, conflict or even violence.

In contrast to the rave scenes of the late 1980s and early 1990s, a typical institutional feature and a key routine of nightclubs in Britain and elsewhere is the supervised admission of visitors at the entrance. Using Turner's terms, nightclubs are liminoid spaces whose exclusivist nature generates a rite of passage (Turner 1982). The preparation rituals, the travel to the club and the organization of people into queues, which mark off and enclose a collective body of potential club visitors from other passers-by, all contribute to the separation from the everyday. The queue subjects the visitors to disciplinary power of partitioning, ranking and surveillance, for example, through electronic screens and body searches. In an environment supposed to create fun and pleasure, these routines are sometimes experienced as alienating. They may thwart the separation from the everyday. But the queue and entrance of the club can also turn into a stage for the presentation of spectacular costumes and outfits claiming attention and star-like status. Such queues are created to make sure the numbers of people admitted to the venue do not exceed its capacity as well as to prepare an ordered security check. Moreover, this routine is part of a series of mechanisms to compose the audience of the club. The social mixture of the crowd is a central element of the atmosphere and the image of the club (night). Although club promoters and managers do not have full control over it and only have limited legal or legitimate means of exclusion at hand, the composition of the crowd is managed through a range of indirect instruments (such as music policy, promotion or advertising directed to particular target audiences), of which the controlled admission at the door is the final step. Yet, the selection of audiences contradicts a general expectation that, apart from more accepted reasons for exclusion such as age limits for younger customers, service spaces should in principle be open to everyone. In the case of licensed premises too, visitors are well aware that the doors of a nightclub are filters to a commercial space and a protected good reserved to a limited number of people at the time. But nightclub audiences frequently want to see these spaces either as public territories with access being allowed to everyone or as community spaces reserved to members of a particular community. Especially in gay and lesbian night-life contexts tensions occur between the frames of service and community space affecting the procedures of opening and closure and the perceived entitlements to these spaces (see Chapter 8). In recent years, however, exclusivity and elitism have been more explicitly endorsed by some club managements in order to appeal to upmarket crowds and to create a long-term following via membership schemes (see Chapter 3). For example, a London club, which aims to provide environments mainly for women to explore their sexuality, freely admits to being 'very elitist' and 'not ashamed to discriminate on age, looks or charisma' (Sommerville, 2008).[6] Admission to its parties at secret, partly private sites is reserved to members only. As a club for the 'world's sexual elite' it strives for a diverse yet elite crowd by selecting members via applications, which must be accompanied by a detailed self-description and photograph. On the basis of aesthetics, charisma, interests and success, young, attractive and successful professionals aged 20 to 45 are filtered out (ibid.).

The regulation and control of people's access to clubs via queues represents a 'turn' in Goffman's sense, involving certain decision-rules as to who is admitted, when and on what terms (for example, regarding admission fees).[7] On the basis of these decision-rules, participants are arranged and ranked according to certain categories. In many cases, however, the most important principle of organization in queues ('first come, first served') is overruled by the fact that nightclub managements divert people into several queues for different categories of visitors who enjoy different conditions of admission (time, fee). For example, in addition to a queue for people intending to buy a ticket at the club, most clubs have a guest list queue and sometimes special queues for people with pre-paid, 'queue jump' or 'late-night entry advanced' tickets handed out as flyers on the streets or in bars, or sold in advance. Most clubs announce a code of practice in order to render their practices of admission accountable to their audiences and to avoid confusion. Commonly referred to as 'door policy', this term, however, is fairly misleading as the admission to club spaces is often (also) guided by more implicit or vague decision-rules or by covert principles of selection. Typical official rules include, for instance, sexual policies in the case of gay or mixed dance clubs; or explicit dress codes if it is a themed night ('school uniform', 'fetish', or else). Advertisements in listing magazines, websites or flyers usually set out expected style and behaviour codes rather than clear-cut rules of admission.[8] Style codes are often upgraded and used to 'price out' or 'design out' unwelcome customers even before they turn up at the club (Monaghan 2002: 415) or to encourage 'self-regulation through customer identification with the ethos of the premise' (Chatterton 2002: 45). Inappropriate clothing may be used as an excuse to refuse entry to undesirable groups (Monaghan 2002: 415). Arguably, to some extent, the official, explicit rules and codes are used to legitimize decisions based on implicit, informal or covert principles of selection. In between the official and the covert rules of admission lie semi-official rules which are not necessarily published, but common knowledge. This includes, amongst others, gender ratios, 'no single men' or 'group of men' policies that operators deploy to equalize the number of men and women in the club.[9] Strategic vagueness and tactical improvisation are part of such rules in order to be able to respond flexibly to the actual situation (Monaghan 2002: 421). For example, the conditions for entrance via the guest list may be redefined in the course of a night depending on the number of ordinary visitors who pay full admission.

Having a position in the queue does not guarantee admission to the club as it may have filled up to full capacity by the time one reaches the top of the queue. Hence, some clubs even sell special guaranteed-entry tickets valid at certain or all times, also as a measure to spread out demand or attract audiences in periods of low demand. The queue creates a liminal condition, at which the outcome—whether or not one passes into the club—is uncertain. While the type of queue and the position one has in the queue define when the club can be entered, the final decision as to who is admitted or not depends on personal perusal by the staff at the door. This micro-management of admission[10] activates disciplinary power, surveillance and purification based on a life-world 'epistemology' of reading, typifying and evaluating bodies according to explicit or implicit criteria. Forms of behaviour are anticipated from certain modes of appearance. This encounter also opens up loopholes and space for negotiation depending on the type of boundary work activated. While 'informal' procedures may allow for the negotiation of access through community and networks of trust, others take a more 'rational' approach based on a strict typing of visitors, or implement 'hyper-selective' door cultures with subtle and exclusive rules of access (Chatterton 2002: 37).[11] Especially when potential visitors outnumber the capacity of a venue, as is the case in popular clubs or on weekend nights, but also when visitors face a possible refusal of admission, negotiations open up, in which claims for membership are staked out, sometimes by disclaiming the suitability of other people in the queue or by strategic impression management in order to conform to official rules. In such credibility contests, participants may assume transitional identities when challenging ascribed typifications and pretending to be who they are not in order to pass, for example, age regulations, sexual codifications, 'no single men' policies or else. This liminal condition can be specified by using Glaser and Strauss' typology of 'awareness context', which highlights the knowledge that interactants have in a situation about the identity of the other(s) based on certain signs of status (Glaser and Strauss 1964, 1967: 83–85). In the course of the negotiations between club visitors and door staff, closed awareness contexts on the part of the door staff are transformed either into open awareness contexts, where the parties are fully aware of the other's identity; or into suspicion or pretense awareness contexts, in which the visitor's 'true' identity is not known, but is suspected to be different from the one claimed, or in which both parties know, but pretend not to be aware of it. For example, when at a nightclub in central London door supervisors had announced that single men would not get in, several male visitors started to chat up women in the queue, faking female company, a strategy that was pretended not to be noticed by the door managers. Likewise the decisions and justifications of door staff frequently give rise to suspicions by participants as to the true motives or covert rules informing the management of admission. Mutual suspicions about either the manipulation of signs on the part of visitors or the use of implicit rules on the part of door managers lead to a game of tactics and counter-tactics where verbal status claims are often treated as secondary to behavioural signs or clothing style or where verbal justifications for certain decisions are not taken at face value. As a female club-goer recalled in the interview, she used to pass the door of a club despite being underage until she and her friend turned down an invitation of the door supervisors to go out with them:[12]

> The bouncers had been on our case to go out with us and we just weren't having it. We went to go in there the following week, they wouldn't let us in. They were like 'oh, have you got any ID?' . . . They wouldn't let us in and we were just like 'What?' (Sally 2000: 11)

On the part of club-goers in the UK and certainly also elsewhere, this ritual of passage sets the tone for the night. It is constructed as an encounter with authorities, to whose power of evaluation and decision-making one normally has to surrender, which can be influenced through strategic politeness or impression management, or which can be challenged and negotiated. Some justifications of exclusion are more easily accepted than others. The exclusion on the grounds of inappropriate clothing, by contrast, often meets resistance and conflict over classifications. The entrance of a dance club constitutes a significant point where the demand of visitors for recognition as a suitable member of the space is either affirmed or rejected, provoking concern amongst club visitors, who frequently feel intimidated and hassled by the door staff and body searches as previous surveys and studies suggest (Mintel 2000a: 8; Measham, Parker, and Aldridge 2001: 165–167). But at the same time the door supervisors are exposed to status threat, disrespect and problematic situations including physical aggression from visitors. The super-ordinate role of door staff is frequently accomplished by deflating the status of potential problem customers or by physical means if all else fails (Monaghan 2002: 408). It is a point of potential conflict due to contradictory expectations of the interacting parties. But it is also imagined by club visitors as a boundary that can become a first site of transgression, for example, by deceiving and outwitting the authorities at the door. The attempt to regulate bodies that prepare for liminal, carnivalesque enactments may provoke (ironic) distantiation from the docile body the visitor becomes at the door. Even aggravating experiences at the entrance can be integrated ex post into storylines that reinterpret these experiences as fun, special, memorable moments reconciling them with the emotional script of clubbing.

Moments of Entry: Modalities of Adjustment

After passing the door, the logistic ordering of bodies and practices continues inside. Visitors are directed to queues for the cash desk (and the cloak rooms) before being released into the centres of the club. Architectural design and spatial layout provide for particular modalities of passage either directly onto the dance floors or into more remote sections of the club such as bars, seating or chill-out areas. While the latter allow for a slower acclimatization to the space and a more contained, reflexive way of 'getting into it', the former may expose participants to spaces dominated by sound and movement inciting a mimetic adaptation and instant immersion in dance and movement. Such sensual intensity and stimulation, created through music and a dancing crowd, may almost impose a new type of movement, especially if space for other types of movement such as standing, walking or sitting is restricted. The confinement of the visual field (through darkness, dry-ice fog or the dissolution of static backgrounds) intensifies the effect of auditory stimuli, reduces the scope for detachment and reflection by destructuring the sense of temporality.[13] Particular technological features too, such as body-sonic floors, may help increase the impact on the senses.

Clubs are structured into different zones of bodily and sensual involvement and detachment with more or less fluid boundaries between them. Dance and non-dance spaces, just as auditory space, have no fixed boundaries, but are, if at all, demarcated by bodies and their movement or stillness. Corridors, galleries, balconies, corners, bars, chill-out and seating areas provide for different kind of practices and partly more remote involvement for socializing and chatting, for resting or watching other participants. Different codes of behaviour apply in the various zones and areas. People engaging in practices that differ from those dominating in their immediate surroundings, such as standing still and observing in the centre of a dancing crowd, may be perceived as out of place. The dance floor is not a place to rest and step back. Likewise, people who engage in types of expressive and artistic dance performance in the middle of the crowd may be seen to break the group ethos. A great number of clubs, especially larger ones, offer several dance floors and bars with different music policies or themes in order to cater for the tastes of diverse audiences and social groups. Although this enables the visitors to move between these spaces, it does not automatically entail that groups intermingle; sometimes it even has the contrary effect of maintaining the lines of separation between people with different social backgrounds, ages, ethnicities, sexual orientations or aesthetic tastes.

Sociality and Social Conventions

Clubbing is usually seen as a social activity in the sense that its key aspect—just as in other youth dance cultures—is the co-presence of people dancing to music together, even though the type of dance they engage in need not necessarily involve much interaction with other dancers. Music is a key element that coordinates people's practices, e.g. by orienting their movements to a particular rhythm. This is a co-presence of people most of whom—depending on the size of the club or the scene—are strangers to each other or where parts of the crowd know each other vaguely as regular visitors of the club or the night-life scene. It is commonly assumed that people go out clubbing with friends and acquaintances. In most cases, the audience of a dance club consists of smaller or larger groups of friends more or less unacquainted with the other groups. These groups and circles of people may be close cliques of friends just as well as rather coincidental gatherings of loose acquaintances who met in a bar or another social event beforehand. Even though a dance club is a sphere of sociality, this is not of the kind that it can always be joined in easily. Social boundaries are not automatically suspended and may preclude the sharing of emotional space. Rather than a unified emotional community, it can be described as a sociality of tribes and groups characterized by 'communion and reserve, attraction and repulsion' (Maffesoli 1995: 160). Many interpretations of dance and club cultures that are based on Maffesoli's neo-tribe thesis tend to overemphasize shared sentiment and collective identification and pay little attention to the struggle for membership and belonging, to processes of social closure, or to the different factions within club crowds. Following St John's (1999: 224) analysis of an Australian alternative-lifestyle festival, clubbing contexts too are more aptly depicted as 'contested communities', entailing a unity in diversity with tendencies towards massification and tribalism, homogeneity and heterogeneity, inclusivity and exclusivity.

Instead of the predominance of collective identification and shared sentiment, sociality in the dance club involves and mediates between values of individuality and group ethos (Douglas and Isherwood 1979). Such articulation of individuality is sometimes overlooked in accounts that stress the importance of collective identification and the 'unshackling' of individuality and identity in dance culture (Malbon 1999: 154). From the viewpoint of Douglas' grid-group model, the mode of sociality in dance clubs has many features of an individualist environment, in which individuals face little constraint by the group or by conventions and rules (low grid/low group).[14] Even though there are rules, they are open to challenge and negotiation. The club crowd is—despite the boundary represented at the door— normally not a strongly bounded group. It requires little commitment or altruistic sacrifice from its members to the group as a whole, but rather consists of small groups of like-minded souls. Overall, insulations between individuals are relatively weak as there is a general expectation of openness towards strangers. These environments are egalitarian in principle, but still involve status competition and differences, which may lead to the formation of small enclaves and exclusivist in-groups (e.g. VIP areas). Dance clubs are contexts in which individuality may be articulated and expressed in a variety of ways; yet, it tends to be mediated with, partly mitigated and circumscribed by the ethos of collective solidarity.

In a way, one's 'sociality' has to be brought into the club. As interviewee Valerie pointed out:

> Clubbing is nice to do with a big group of people who you know reasonably well, so that if you go to a club, you've got a base. And then you kind of go wandering off, and you can make your friends, and you can kind of buzz around, and then you can sort of go back to the nucleus. (Valerie 2000: 7)

Normally, it is expected that people already have a social base when joining a club or meet acquaintances inside; all else would be seen as rather unconventional or even strange. Although clubs do provide for anonymity as well as sociality, people are not expected to be out clubbing alone. Being on one's own is felt to be less enjoyable, and people may feel more self-conscious or even embarrassed when recognized as being alone. A male interviewee in his late twenties explained:

> You don't expect people in clubs totally on their own. You think it's a bit strange, if there is somebody in a club, dancing on their own all night . . . If somebody is dancing on their own, you start to think you stick out a bit. (Lennie 1999: 19)

This quote indicates that people who are out on their own only catch others' eye when they do not appear to be socially involved. Club visitors are expected to participate and interact, to be open to spontaneous communication with strangers as part of the spirit of clubbing. Despite these expectations, co-presence in clubs also preserves a moment of civil inattention and indifference towards others as in other public contexts.

For some participants more than others, clubbing may involve the quest, and sometimes the competition, for status. Instead of clear rules of membership, access and belonging to the space are established through tests of 'fitness'; not in the literal sense of bodily fitness, but through the assessment of suitability and capability according to particular notions of purity. As elaborated earlier on, these rest on codes of fashion, style and behaviour, which are evaluated at the entrance. Depending on visitor frequency, these tests imply a broader or narrower conception of purity. As interviewee accounts indicate (see particularly Chapter 8), tests of 'fitness' are not only carried out by the door supervisors, but by participants themselves when staking out claims for status and belonging against other members. Belonging, therefore, is negotiated in the social practices inside the club and involves the search for individual recognition or even recognition as a group, for getting noticed in a positive way and singled out as a significant figure or group of the crowd.

One way in which individuality is constructed in dance clubs is through fashion or costume. When club managements announce aesthetic styles ('casual', 'street-wear') or more rigid dress codes (e.g. 'fetish outfits'), these codes allow for and even require being accomplished in individual ways.[15] Apart from being stylish or fashionable, what is more significant in the carnivalesque value-scheme of clubbing is the creation of a persona through special outfits and costumes. Popular storylines in participants' accounts of this study centred on the characters they embodied and the responses these provoked from other people. Special outfits and costumes help become a significant member of the club and help constitute special moments set apart from everyday routines of appearance. Another way of gaining recognition is linked to spatial positionings in zones more explicitly coded for performance, for instance, stages, podiums or illuminated spots that mark out certain individuals from the crowd. Podiums and stages, normally reserved for professional performers and dancers employed by the club, can be used by members of the crowd outside performance times. In the following example, this was couched as a symbolic act of transgression and almost 'collective revolution' as the space was reclaimed for collective action of the crowd overturning the difference between professional dancers and 'ordinary' visitors:

> They had these podiums, they were set up on the dance floor, and when the dancers had fucked off of the podium, all these people got on the podiums, and I am now on the podium fucking giving it loads, sniffing the poppers out of my edge. It was great, absolutely great. (Sally 2000: 11; see also Buckland 2002: 118)

In a similar manner, another interviewee described dancing on a podium as part of a *collective* act of letting go of the *self* allowing for a certain degree of individual posing framed within, and subordinate to, the group ethos.

> You just get up and start dancing, actually what it is, you feel part of the crowd then, yeah we are all here together, and everyone is letting themselves go a bit, and it's not just one or two people just showing off, I think it's a group thing . . . People are loosing their ambitions a bit, getting up and dancing, maybe posing a bit, but not to the extent 'I am' sort of thing, people mostly would get up on the podium for a laugh. (Lennie 1999: 18–19)

Dancing appears as the focal point and the central activity in a club, so much so that an interviewee commented that she 'never understood people who go to clubs and don't dance' (Clare 2000a: 3). In many depictions of club culture, dancing is associated with the 'loss of self', with letting go from self-discipline, the breaking free of body from mind, with sensual pleasure and transgressive bodies, with absorption in movement, music and collective bliss as part of the distantiation from the world outside. Yet, dancing and letting go are embedded in the routinization of practice and sometimes linked to a great deal of reflexivity, self-control and awareness of oneself in relation to other people. There may be barriers to becoming immersed in movement (e.g. if the dance floor is empty), experiences of inhibition (e.g. because of mutual observation of participants), or an alteration of involvement and detachment.

Meanings of ecstatic dancing, fun, pleasure or transgressive play are shaped in specific contexts and interpreted in locally prescribed ways. Apart from being associated with becoming part of a collective body, dancing is also connected to the expression of individuality, identity and the search for recognition. Symbolic rewards, for example, of being noticed and looked at, were a significant component of the pleasures described by participants.[16]

Dance clubs allow for postures or movements that would be perceived as weird or even indecent in other public or semi-public places; yet certain codes of practice circumscribe what styles of dance are deemed appropriate or out of place in particular contexts, what forms of movement and bodily comportment would or would not gain positive recognition. When trying to abide by these mostly unwritten rules, members rely on their practical, embodied understanding and mimetic faculties. These codes of how to comport oneself also depend on the musical genres played, on the particular local setting and the audience of the night. As these codes are implicit, there is no agreement, little degree of regulation and hardly any sanction, except that security intervenes against participants whose behaviour poses risks to others or breaks the rules laid down in the operation schedule and licensing conditions (e.g. open drug consumption). Gender roles and sexuality also mediate what types of dance or body practices are believed to find acceptance and recognition.

The following examples demonstrate how varied the semantics of dance and transgression can be. Lennie, a heterosexual male in his late twenties, described his fairly controlled and reflexive way of getting into dancing. After entering the club with his friends, they would get a drink, stand a bit, walk around 'just to see who was in the club', making comments and then, 'we'd say, "when are we gonna hit the dance floor?"' (Lennie 1999: 17). This is carefully planned in terms of the time and the spot where to start. Spatial scenarios and territories are assessed for potential trouble, for example,

> You wander around, you assess where you're gonna stand . . . and if there is maybe three or four lads, you don't necessarily wanna get into them, you don't wanna get close to them, because you feel you might be infringing their space. (ibid.)

This mode of involvement was framed by the motivation to meet women, without, however, violating the 'territory' of other competitors on the dance floor. In a similar way a gay male interviewee in his late twenties linked dancing not only to flirting and meeting sexual partners, but more generally to gaining attention and recognition of his aesthetic and erotic desirability:

> . . . to be outstanding to the rest of the people around me, I want to be the better dancer, so people actually look at me, which I achieve. And I think the more people look at me, the better I feel. (Erik 2000: 13–14)

The unmitigated endorsement of such individualistic search for recognition may in part reflect its greater acceptance in gay clubbing cultures (Buckland 2002: 101). Unlike participants, who carefully consider other people's territories on the dance floor, a trained female dancer in her early twenties casts the expansion of her territory and the extension of the dancing into non-dance space as transgressive and enjoyable. Her understanding of dance as an artistic practice of performance also shaped her favourite way of dancing in clubs, in which she wanted to break certain codes of movement and spatial ordering, for example, by rolling around on the floor. Nevertheless, what another interviewee described as the individual type of interpretive or expressive dance may be perceived as out of place by others. Using the dance floor as a stage for performance and showing off may not only break the group ethos, but also codes of cool resulting in the opposite, the 'ruining' of oneself on the dance floor (Gary 2000: 20–22). While the trained dancer alluded to the artistic dancing body, other interviewees sought recognition for an intoxicated, 'grotesque' body out of control.[17] The loss of control through excessive intoxication is often constructed as a sign of conspicuous consumption and is invoked with some self-irony for earning prestige and 'notoriety' (Falk 1994: 121): Alex, a gay male interviewee in his early forties, recounted how he fell asleep on top of some speakers under heavy influence of drugs (Alex 2000: 4). Self-irony moderates the emphasis on individuality: 'My fantastic usual way of getting noticed is getting absolutely shit-faced, usually falling, falling downstairs' (Gary 2000: 22).

As this discussion demonstrated, individuality and group ethos are mediated in various ways. Meanings of ecstatic dancing, fun and transgressive play are not only shaped in specific contexts and interpreted in locally codified ways, but social positionings of participants also inform particular scripts of practice and their narrative representation.

AESTHETIC REFLEXIVITY, BOUNDARIES, AND IDENTITIES

Central to clubbing practice are aesthetic and prosthetic forms of embodiment. As outlined in the previous part, this involves the presentation of self in compliance to aesthetic style codes; attempts to appear fashionable, attractive and erotic; the use of special outfits, carnivalesque costumes, make-up, hairstyle, movements, gestures and verbal communication to create a persona; the (self-ironic) distantiation from roles and the play with pretense identities; mimetic practices in dance, and the use of certain technologies such as chemical stimulants in order to enhance the body's capacity for sensation, to loosen up, or to increase bodily stamina. In such a context of co-presence, which centres on collective dance and movement more than—or at least as much as—on verbal communication; intuitive, embodied understanding, kinesthetic awareness and empathy play an important role for the coordination of practices.

Previous studies of clubbing and dancing emphasized the significance of play-forms of sociality and stressed the playful, autotelic quality of dance (Malbon 1999: 149), the distance from the normativity of everyday life and the 'transcendence of body as oppressed object of power' (Buckland 2002: 126). Play creates such distance by providing an alternate ordering with its own rules (Malbon 1999: 137) and by opening up an imaginary sphere: 'dance is therefore about using the body to conjure up "virtual", "as-if" worlds by configuring alternative ways of being through play' (Thrift 1997: 147). Probing imaginative possibilities of 'as-if' involves subjunctive consciousness, which is about imagining or 'fashioning' the self through a 'better' or different kind of reality (Buckland 2002: 36, 125–126; Radley 1995: 12; Turner 1986).[18] In contrast to the view that play is linked to unreality, inauthenticity or insincerity set apart from 'real reality' (Bauman 1993: 170), Malbon suggested that the experience of an imaginary world of play may create authentic feelings of relief from tensions of everyday life (Malbon 1999: 144). Similarly, the metaphor of carnival and Turner's notion of liminality were used to describe how multiple identifications and new modes of subjectivity may emerge in contemporary shopping sites such as malls (Shields 1992: 16). In a less optimistic tone, however, writers on postmodern shopping worlds and urban entertainment, especially in the US context, demurred the inauthenticity of places and cities which would only allow for programmed, surrogate experiences (e.g. Hannigan 1998). Hannigan described the blurring boundaries between authenticity and illusion and how consumers can revel in a simulated experience at the same time as being able to step back and see through the constructed character of it (1998: 69; see also Lash and Lury 1994: 58 and Grossberg 1992: 224). The liminal quality of such sites may support the search for new lifestyles and performative identities; yet, these are not automatically emancipatory, but may reinforce restrictive identities and power relations.

This part of the chapter builds on and further develops these perspectives, aiming to theorize the forms of social practice in club and dance cultures and the effects on modes of experience and the construction of identity more thoroughly. The basic question is as to how dance clubs, which primarily rest on the technological stimulation of the sensual apparatus of the body and the imaginative play with styles and roles, may become sites of experience. What does the prosthetic and playful nature of such practices entail for the 'grounding' and authentication, or dis-authentication, of experience and self? How, if at all, does the body emerge as a corpo*reality*? What forms of reflexivity and what sensibilities do arise in such contexts and practices? How do participants evaluate the authenticity of their sensations, emotions and desires, or gauge the realness or play-character of the performative practices of others and of the social encounters they make? Drawing on debates on aestheticization and prosthetic culture (Featherstone 1991, Lash 1993, Lury 1998, Welsch 1997), ethnomethodology (Pollner 1987) and on the notion of boundary within cultural sociology (Lamont and Molnár

2002), I shall develop heuristic tools for analysing how social actors deal with processes of virtualization in club culture, and how this affects modes of constructing reality and experience and the negotiation of identity and difference (e.g. class, gender, sexuality, ethnicity). In the final part of the chapter, this is related to the concept of narrative identity (Ricoeur 1992), which informs the narrative analysis of the following chapters.

Aestheticization and Prosthetic Culture

It was the British sociologist Mike Featherstone who, in the context of his book *Consumer Culture and Postmodernism*, coined the term 'aestheticization' in order to highlight the saturation of consumer society with images, signs and simulations leading to a 'loss of stable meaning' (Featherstone 1991: 15). The starting points of this theme can be found in Walter Benjamin and Georg Simmel's works, who both reflected upon the new experiences afforded by modern urban life and consumerism in the early twentieth century (Benjamin 1955, Simmel 1995). Benjamin deliberated on the dream images; associations and illusions conjured up by the 'phantasmagoria' of commodities and characterized these kaleidoscopic fragments as allegories. In contrast to the traditional notion of allegory as double-coded message, these allegories have no coherent meaning (Benjamin 1982: 54, Featherstone 1991: 23). Such flow of images has also been described as a figural rather than discursive form of signification evoking desire and sensual, bodily involvement instead of meaning and contemplative distance from the object (Lash 1990). The saturation with signs and images is also a central theme in Wolfgang Welsch's writings on aestheticization. He distinguished the immaterial aestheticization of consciousness from the material dimensions in the world of objects, media and technologies (Welsch 1997: 5). According to Welsch, the virtualization of reality through immaterial or 'epistemological' aestheticization reaches deeper than the former and is of profound significance at a cognitive level. While Featherstone mainly concentrated on the domain of lifestyle and practice, Welsch's approach is more akin to a sociology of cognition and knowledge. Following Kant, Nietzsche and philosophers of science such as Paul Feyerabend, Welsch pointed to the metaphorical, poetic and fictional means as the 'protoaesthetic' foundation of cognition (Welsch 1997: 20). Further, he argued that the 'awareness of the foundational aesthetic character of our cognition, our reality and our forms of understanding is today asserting itself right through to everyday understanding' (ibid. 46). This suggests that everyday modes of reasoning increasingly involve an awareness of the contingent and constructed character of 'reality'. Aestheticization in this sense occurs not only within consumer culture or the media, but is also built into the creation and the use of technological tools, for example, into (computer-) simulation techniques in the productive domain. In relation to subjectivity, aestheticization becomes manifest in the perfection and 'styling of body, soul and mind' and the substitution of moral standards by aesthetic competence (ibid. 6–7). According to Welsch, aestheticization cultivates a new 'role model' called the *homo aestheticus*, which is characterized by its 'sense of possibility' (ibid. 15). In sum, Welsch referred to the proliferation of aesthetic objects, of life-styling, and of mediation and virtualization. This raises the question in what sense these different phenomena can be subsumed under the term 'aesthetic'. Whilst keeping the polysemy of the concept of aesthetic,[19] Welsch described sensation and perception as the two key dimensions of *aisthesis,* locating the aesthetic faculty between the cognitive and the emotive level (ibid. 62–63).

The affective and sensual dimensions of *aisthesis* were also highlighted by Scott Lash and John Urry (Lash 1993, 1994; Lash and Urry 1994). Their concept of aesthetic reflexivity aimed to counterbalance the 'cognitive bias' in reflexive modernization theory (Beck 1992, Giddens 1991). Pointing to the aesthetic, sensual and embodied forms of reflexivity, Lash and Urry argued that these are as central to modern self-identity as the cognitive self-monitoring highlighted by Giddens. Aesthetic reflexivity was to stress the aesthetic side of modernity and its significance as a moral source of the modern self (Taylor 1989). According to Lash, this legacy increases its importance as social structures are being replaced by information and communication structures, rendering more crucial the accumulation of cultural capital, self-monitoring and self-interpretation through aesthetic expert systems (Lash 1993: 19). Post-industrial economies increasingly depend on the flow of signs at the level of production, distribution and consumption. These signs can either have a cognitive (informational) or aesthetic (expressive-symbolic) content (Lash and Urry 1994: 4). Following Kant's notion of aesthetic judgement, Lash and Urry cast aesthetic reflex-ivity as a pre-judgement that involves the subsumption of particulars by particulars, while cognitive and moral judgements rest on the subsumption of particulars by universals (ibid. 47). Pre-judgement suggests that aes-thetic reflexivity is embodied in the background assumptions and in the pre-cognitive classifications generated in the natural attitude. But aesthetic reflexivity oscillates between a natural attitude and a reflective attitude. It is not a monitoring through reflective distance (a meta-reflexivity), but closer to the mimetic faculties that inform practice and being-in-the-world (reflexivity as practical consciousness). An example would be symboliza-tion (the representation of sense impressions through symbolic or meta-phorical language) or association (the correlation of sensuous experience with particular situations or emotions) (Rodaway 1994: 146). The classi-fiers in aesthetic reflexivity are concrete particulars, rooted in the life-world (e.g. visual signs, objects, sounds, movements as mimetic symbols), while the classifiers in cognitive reflexivity are more abstract, conceptual catego-ries. Drawing on Taylor (1989), Lash and Urry distinguished between two modes of aesthetic reflexivity, symbol and allegory (Lash and Urry 1994: 52–54). As in Benjamin's use of the term, allegory privileges the signifier over, or is at least uncoupled from, the signified. It is one of many representations and involves the revelling in the constructedness of the experience instead of the search for the authentic (Lash and Urry 1994: 58). By contrast, the symbol rests on a unity of signifier and signified and expresses some invisible essence (Taylor 1989: 421). While Featherstone discussed aestheticization foremost as an effect of the merging of art and everyday life with the advent of postmodernism, the notion of aesthetic reflexivity draws attention to the role of implicit, embodied forms of understanding as well as to mimetic practices, imagination and intuition that are essential to social interaction.[20] In this sense, aesthetic reflexivity can be seen as a key element of (face-to-face) interaction and not only as an upshot of (post-) modernism or post-industrialism.

The problematization of knowledge, authenticity and self-identity through processes of virtualization is also a pivotal issue in the analysis of technology and the media. Photography, television and, more recently, the new information and communication technologies have prompted much reflection on their cognitive and social implications (e.g. Lury 1998, Slater 1998, Turkle 1996, Žižek 1997a). Prosthetic technologies more generally alter the perception of space and time, 'self' and 'other' as well as modes of relating to, and interacting with, others. As has been pointed out extensively in various places, e.g. in the debate on cyborgs, prosthetic technologies have expanded from mere substitution of the organic towards the extension and optimization of the body. The fusing of the organic and inorganic into hybrid configurations destabilizes and blurs traditional boundaries between human or inhuman, natural or artificial, internal or external, subject or object. It creates border zones, where boundaries can only be defined on a case-by-case basis rather than by general principles (Schneider 2005: 373). This is thought to have changed the concepts of individuality and selfhood. In her analysis of the prosthetic in photography, Lury, for example, explored how visual technologies have reconfigured the Western concept of the possessive individual as an individual, who frames the 'self' as the proprietor of a unique body and interiority (MacPherson 1962). Prosthetic culture[21] refers to a new technique of self by means of experimentation, through which aspects previously deemed immutable, fixed and automatic are brought into the realm of volition, conscious calculation and intentional modification. While this seems to resonate with reflexive modernization theorists' assumption that self-identity is increasingly achieved through reflexive self-monitoring, the experimental individualism of prosthetic culture is more about self-*extension* and self-transformation through perceptual or mechanical means (Lury 1998: 3). Similar to the 'sense of possibility' of the *homo aestheticus,* prosthesis involves the transfer into otherness through any kind of enabling resources that extend or change the capacities of the body and its senses. The experimental individual of prosthetic culture 'is an individual who in looking in the mirror of the technological order no longer sees a reflection, but looks through the mirror to what he or she could be' (Lury 1998: 23)—or should be: Enabling technologies can render any body as potentially imperfect and in need of improvement, turning prosthetic optimization into a normative programme and obligation of individuals (Schneider 2005: 387–390).

The Problematization of Reality and Experience Through Aestheticization

Processes of aestheticization disrupt the construction of reality and intervene into the experiential paradigm of the possessive individual. According to Baudrillard, the saturation of everyday life with images and signs, for example, in simulated leisure and media worlds, enmeshes every aspect of reality with the production and circulation of signs to such an extent that it becomes impossible to distinguish between what is real and what is a sign or image of the real. In Baudrillard's view, (hyper-)reality is nothing but an 'aesthetic hallucination' (1983: 148). Similarly, the enhancement of our sense organs and perceptual, cognitive system through prosthetic technologies is usually seen to transform and redefine not only 'what constitutes "reality"', but also how we constitute reality' (Rodaway 1994: 145). As Simmel pointed out, technologies such as the telescope and microscope help fashion new objects, involve different ways of working and operating on these objects thereby constituted and may lead to different conceptions of time and space (1971: 356).

Before following up the question as to how processes of aestheticization and prosthetic technologies in club cultures affect people's modes of experience, I shall focus in more detail on the notion of experience in phenomenological sociology (Schütz) and ethnomethodological conceptions of the construction of reality (Pollner 1987). Following William James (1952), Alfred Schütz elaborated on the problem of reality in terms of multiple realities whereby he suggested that there are various orders of reality characterized by specific cognitive or experiential styles, a specific tension of consciousness, time-perspective and mode of sociality (Schütz 1971: 230). Crucially, a phenomenological approach to reality presupposes that 'it is the meaning of our experiences and not the ontological structure of the objects which constitutes reality' (ibid.). Therefore, such orders of reality were termed 'finite provinces of meaning'. Schütz' notion of experience figures a possessive individual defined by interiority and continuity of consciousness. Experience is constituted in the individual consciousness and is premised upon a unique body. It derives its uniqueness from a set origin and continuity in time and space and from clear boundaries against other entities. In his book *Phenomenology of the Social World*, Alfred Schütz linked experience and the continuity of consciousness to time-consciousness (Schütz 1967). In this very basic sense, subjective meaning originates in the stream of consciousness of lived experiences (*Erlebnisse*). However, these have no discrete identity and meaning; only the act of turning-toward

(*Zuwendung*) marks off elements from the flow of duration. By bringing some elements into the foreground and relegating others to the background, this marking-off involves relations of similarity and difference. Meaning therefore is always a retrospective and reflexive act of turning-toward (i.e. reflecting upon and remembering)[22]. This marking-off of meaning is not arbitrary, but depends on pragmatic interests in the intersubjective sphere, which determine what type of reflective attention the socially located ego will adopt (e.g. judgement, will, belief, valuation, pleasure, etc. Lash 1999: 143). In addition, the specific meanings are constituted through insertion into the total stock of experience at hand at any one moment (Schütz 1967: 78). For example, judgements or classifications refer back to previous, similar classifications or are clouded by expectations according to past experiences. The ordering of lived experiences through subsuming it under particular interpretive schemes therefore, is a 'synthesis of recognition' that coincides with the moment of perception (ibid. 79–83). This ordering occurs in varying degrees of reflective glance, e.g. as reasoning, as a problem-solving operation, as emotion, in a flash or in habitual recognition (ibid. 84). Synthetic recognition connects the signifier with the signified and constitutes the point where the (pre-)judgement of cognitive or aesthetic reflexivity sets in, unless novel lived experiences fail to connect with, and call into question, the interpretive schemes and classifiers. Usually, this is the starting point for a sociology of cognition, which takes as its object of investigation the social foundations of the interpretive repertoires and cognitive schemes. This includes social conventions of 'interpreting, focusing, categorizing, associating, and remembering' (Zerubavel 1999: 22), social classification systems as well as discourses of authenticity.

Recognition also involves the subsumption of experience under a particular order of reality (e.g. dream, fantasy and hallucination, play, etc.). As Schütz pointed out, everyday life (and the state of wide-awakeness) forms our paramount reality: it is the world of the senses and physical things, whose existence is taken for granted; it is governed by pragmatic motives and projects of working/acting upon the state of affairs through bodily movements and operations; it is an intersubjective sphere of communication constituted around specific forms of sociality, of experiencing one's self and specific time perspectives (Schütz 1971: 230). This cognitive style of paramount reality—in Pollner's term (1987: Chapter 2), mundane reason—rests on a network of background assumptions or 'mundane idealizations'. First, mundane reason posits a dichotomy between an external objective reality and an inner subjective world ('I'), which is regarded as the central feature of being and individuality. Second, it assumes that objects, events and processes in the outer world are determinate, coherent and non-contradictory[23] and that other persons share the same background assumptions (Pollner 1987: 26). Paramount reality therefore is an intersubjective domain with common procedures for constructing reality. Nevertheless, subjective accounts do not always (or hardly ever) overlap leading in many cases to discrepancies ('reality disjunctures') and contests over what accounts represent the 'real'. In this process some accounts are authorized and others discredited as representations of reality. Power and conflict structure the validation and invalidation of experiences and accounts (in Laing's terms [1967], this is called the 'politics of experience'). This is embedded in a web of norms and discourses that circumscribe particular social positions, roles or practices. Reality disjunctures may also occur within the individual's experiences; especially, as we shall see, when moving between different orders of reality. Such discrepancies are often resolved by 'ironicizing' or dismissing certain experiences as delusion, fantasy or else.[24]

Paramount reality may become a quasi-reality at times when one is immersed in other orders of reality such as dream or fantasy, which imply different cognitive or experiential styles. For example, the world of fantasy (comprising day-dreams, play, fiction, myths, jokes, 'as-if' realities) lacks pragmatic motives and purposes and is not confined by the standard temporal order. It makes possible the suspension of inhibitions or particular moral imperatives. Like fantasy, ecstatic states also involve a transcendence of paramount reality and a turn towards another, extraordinary realm of reality (Schütz and Luckmann 2003: 622). The construction of such states is conscious, partly planned and may be linked to certain (body) techniques. Ecstatic states may not only constitute a cursory reality, but may also stay pre-eminent after returning to paramount reality, challenging the relevance structures and the pragmatic motive of everyday life. Memories of these states can be taken to paramount reality and translated into language and symbols (ibid. 622–623).

As was suggested with Cohen's typology of tourist experience (1979) in the first part of the chapter, people's modes of relation vary in terms of the degrees and forms in which layers of paramount reality are bracketed and relevances of everyday life are questioned or left behind. For example, intoxication through drugs or alcohol intervenes in the specific tension of consciousness and can accentuate a reality which is no longer compatible with the province of everyday reality (e.g. as the next chapter will show, from the viewpoint of a drug-induced state certain things seem to be real, while they are not in the state of wide-awakeness). Like a dream reality that reaches into everyday reality, the finite provinces of meaning may clash and produce disjunctures regarding the realness of particular experiences. Yet, in other cases the world of the club may be part of everyday reality and its particular cognitive style. Even if people engage in playful practices, their belief into the existence of paramount reality is not necessarily suspended. Play does not always entail identification and deep involvement, but can go along with pragmatic motives at the level of paramount reality. Therefore, play and paramount reality are not necessarily clearly demarcated from each other. Play contains elements of everyday reality and vice versa, everyday reality is permeated by playful, mimetic elements (Gebauer and Wulf 1998: 189). Play can be regarded as a kind of social action which interactants frame as 'play' through meta-communicative signals, agreeing to take their practices and encounters not for 'real'. Within such a frame the action paradoxically is and is not what it represents: it is true in play, but not true in reality (Gebauer and Wulf 1998: 193–194, Bateson 1972). The belief in the sincerity and authenticity, not in the existence, of the actions is thereby suspended.[25] The boundary between play and reality is therefore unstable and indeterminate and depends on the participants' framing and interpretation of their actions.

In view of this conceptualization of experience and reality, aestheticization and aesthetic practice can be seen to constitute a finite province of meaning similar to the world of fantasy and play described by Schütz. As pointed out before, one can move between these worlds by adopting particular cognitive and experiential styles of framing. From a somewhat different viewpoint, debates on aestheticization emphasize that these orders of reality become increasingly merged (presupposing that they once were more clearly demarcated). As Welsch (1997) pointed out, processes of virtualization reach right into everyday understanding in such a way that the boundary between real and virtual may be unclear, unstable or even impossible to draw. On the one hand, participation in an 'as-if' world need not go along with the suspension of the belief in paramount reality (one may see through the constructed character of simulated worlds); or, on the other hand, as critics of simulation would argue, the simulated worlds become 'paramount' and produce a fundamental state of de-realization. In comparing the experiential paradigm to the experimental individualism of prosthetic self-extension, it can be noted that experience involves the distinction between subjective and objective domains on the grounds of a subject–object dualism and a unique body. It is grounded in a metaphysics of depth (Tseëlon 1992) and a separation between inside and outside reflecting a particular model of self based on the Cartesian body–mind dualism. Bodily appearance and expression do not necessarily coincide with the inner, deeper reality of the subjective world. The notion of authenticity captures the possibility of insincerity, deception and concealment of the 'true self'. But the logic of authenticity is paradoxical. Whilst taking the body as a symbolic-expressive signpost of the self, it also assumes its capacity for dissimulation.

By contrast, self-extension highlights bodily transformation and a body whose boundaries (between the internal and external) can no longer be defined so easily. Immersion in technologically produced sensual intensity disrupts time-consciousness, the construction of experience and the logic of authenticity.

Aesthetic and Prosthetic Forms of Being in Clubbing Culture

Aestheticization affects the construction of experience and reality by opening up spaces for (imaginary) transformation. As Zerubavel pointed out, 'stretching the conventional boundaries of the self by essentially transforming oneself into somebody else is also a major feature of ludic environments' (1999: 60). The following focuses on the particular modes of aestheticization that inform the transcendence of everyday reality within club and dance cultures. These can be loosely categorized into two basic moments correlating with the dimensions of perception and sensation in *aesthesis*.[26] One sways towards a subjunctive type of acting 'as-if' and embraces stylization and performative, mimetic practices. The second can be thought of as a more direct intervention in the nervous system of the body and its time-consciousness.[27] It comprises the search for excitement (e.g. through intoxication) and the fabrication of particular sensual conditions through the (technological) stimulation of auditory, visual and haptic senses. The following parts will elaborate on these two dimensions as stylization and sensation respectively.

Stylization and Acting 'as-if'

All acting that involves the body (movement, posture, gestures) and is not mere mental deliberation is performative and is a form of acting 'as-if' insofar as it mimetically re-enacts previous actions following certain models of how to comport the body and how to perform social roles.[28] Movements are based on techniques of the body learned through mimesis. As theorists of mimesis argue, many social processes involve not only the body, but also a mimetic, i.e. aesthetic (sense-based) orientation towards others (Gebauer and Wulf 1998).[29] Taking this viewpoint, can stylization be circumscribed as a special form of acting? From a mundane perspective, stylization embraces practices of decorating or masquerading the body through fashion, dress, outfit, make-up, hairstyle, costumes and more. This also extends to body action, the 'decoration' of the body with gestures, postures and movements as in dance, which has been described as the creation of imaginary, 'as-if' spheres (Radley 1995). Stylization occurs on social and cultural stages and is modelled on knowledge about certain objectified conventions and styles. Stylization 'contains a note of generality' (a general law of form); it represents not a specific individual reality, but the general character of something (Simmel 1997a: 212). As Simmel noted about fashion, it always remains somewhat external to the individual as its ephemerality and mutability are in tension to the sense of self as a continuous, enduring entity. Fashion therefore, is at the 'periphery of the personality', as it helps keep personal feelings invisible by using it as a kind of mask (Simmel 1997b: 198). In this way, fashion can preserve inner freedom by 'sacrificing the external' to compliance with social conventions (ibid. 198–200). This alludes to the possible gap between the outer appearance and what is believed to exist as the 'inner core' of a person. Likewise, in his reflections on style and adornment, Simmel defined the essence of style as 'the unburdening and concealment of the personal', the 'toning down of this acute personality to a generality and its law', to 'a more typical' or 'stylized costume' (ibid. 216). However, stylization does not only create superficial masks or imaginary characters understood as 'less real' or 'unreal', but can also accentuate personality and a certain self-image. It does not simply imply inauthenticity and artificiality, but circumscribes a border zone which provides for shifting and temporary framings of 'play' or 'reality'. Thinking of an outfit, which is encoded/decoded as a mask and not as an expression of someone's identity, involves a tacit agreement upon a frame of play, within which not to take the mask for real, but for a signal. Within this frame of play social actors refrain from inferring essences of the person who is wearing that mask, but take it as a simulation of the character that it represents: this mask does not represent what the character, which it stands for, would represent (Bateson 1972). But play may become entangled with reality, once the interactive exchange becomes an instrument for purposive contents (Simmel 1950: 49, 1997a: 125). In addition, interactants might misunderstand each other, disagree on the frame of their encounter or enter into a more complex game whose frame is unclear altogether ('Is this a game or is this real?').

The play with masks, styles or virtual roles can be understood as an identificatory practice of acting 'as-if' (Žižek 1997a: 137–139). In discussing the adoption of virtual identities in cyberspace, Žižek pointed to two different modes of identification, based on Lacanian theory: imaginary or projection–identification on the one hand, and symbolic identification on the other hand. Imaginary identification is a play with what one considers to be false images of the self. Symbolic identification may work like an acceptance through disavowal by passing off less acceptable, publicly non-acknowledged facets and fantasies as a game. The boundary between play and reality is fuzzy, vague and dynamic, because the 'self' is fundamentally decentred and indeterminable and at best objectified provisionally and temporarily. Self-objectification is never complete. As Žižek explains, 'decentrement thus first designates the ambiguity, the oscillation between symbolic and imaginary identification—the undecidability as to where my true point is, in my "real" self or in my external mask, with the possible implication that my symbolic mask can be "more true" than what it conceals, the "true face" behind it' (Žižek 1997a: 141). Stylization thus conceived is a mode of identification and acting 'as-if' comparable to what Turner called the 'subjunctive mood of culture' in liminality—the maybe, might-be, fantasy and conjecture (1986: 42). It can accentuate the becoming into the desired other (idealization), the staging as other (dissimulation), or the miming of other (simulation). These modes of identification slide into each other. They constitute a phantasmatic, virtual hypertext—a horizon of possibilities—against which notions of reality/authenticity can temporarily be marked off (Žižek 1997a: 143). The hyphenated term 'play-reality' might best capture the unstable boundary between play and reality and the indeterminate nature of the 'real'. Play-reality highlights the simultaneity of, or the oscillation between, real and not real. Instead of a Cartesian conception of self, this suggests a surface model of a 'transient self which is situationally and interactively defined' (Tseëlon 1992: 121) rendering the distinction between external appearance and inner reality, the evaluation of 'true' and 'false', 'real and imaginary' irrelevant and stressing 'the fluid, plastic nature of identity' (Zerubavel 1999: 60). These two levels of reality can be compared to Deleuze's reflections on the actual and the virtual (Deleuze 2000: 68–71). The relation between the actual and the virtual is reversible, and they presuppose each other. The virtual can turn into the actual and vice versa. For example, in the process of acting, an actor makes the virtual image of a role actual, while the actual image of the actor becomes opaque. The notion of play-reality can be seen as such a continuum or spectrum embracing the actual and the virtual as two poles relative to each other. Nevertheless, the reversibility between the two poles also implies that time-consciousness or reflective judgement may temporarily determine what is virtual or actual (and vice versa): 'Each world *whilst it is attended to* is real after its own fashion; only the reality lapses with the attention' (James 1952: 643; see also the discussion in Schütz 1971: 207). Returning to the question if stylization can be distinguished from social action as a special form of simulative acting, the answer can only be that this depends on how these modes of action and identification are understood by the participants through the meta-communicative frame(s) of their encounters.

Sensation

Alteration of the body's sensuous state is another means of creating a sense of transcendence of everyday reality, in particular, of the corpo*reality* of the everyday. This involves changes and disruptions to the sensuous states and bodily feelings that characterize everyday life, for example, through particular (technological) interventions into the body's nervous system and time-consciousness. In the context of clubbing, intense sight- and soundscapes, the energy of a dancing crowd and the physical proximity of people as well as drugs and alcohol contribute to sensual excitement and (over-) stimulation, altering emotive states and the perceptual and cognitive style that frames a certain order of reality.

As debates on media and communication technologies showed, certain prosthetic resources reconfigure the sensual and perceptual apparatus of the body and its boundaries. Any kind of enabling resource can be seen as a prosthetic technology; fashion, costumes, masks too are prostheses. Unlike these exogenous techniques, the consumption of drugs, for example, can be seen as a prosthetic alteration of the body's sensuous state through 'endocolonization' (Turkle 1996), i.e. the absorption of the prosthetic resource into the body. Žižek's reflections help specify the reconfiguration of bodily boundaries through endocolonization. He suggested that this led to a blurred boundary between the inside and the outside of the body (Žižek 1997a: 134). This affects not only the perception of one's own body, but also the hermeneutic attitude towards the bodies of others. Spelling out three different dimensions of this indeterminate zone, Žižek noted first, the destabilization of the boundary between true life and its simulation (through technobiology), second, between objective reality and our illusory perception (through media simulation) and third, between fleeting affects and the 'hard core' of self (as in the play with virtual identities and masks in cyberspace, Žižek 1997a: 133). Even though cyber technologies neither completely transform our bodily grounding in the life-world nor entirely fuse human and machine (Shilling 2005: 185, 196), the hermeneutic horizon of everyday experience is nevertheless altered or affected in varying degrees.

Other commentators on technology and prosthetic culture (Lury 1998, Strathern 1992, Haraway 1991) drew attention to the wider implications of the blurring of these boundaries for the conceptions of individuality and identity. The anthropologist Marilyn Strathern coined the term 'merographic capacity' (1992). This refers to the way in which entities are made up and related to each other through partial analogies of similarities and differences. For example, the individual is defined by means of partial analogy to society and nature: by being more and less than, similar to and different from or limited by society or nature. Likewise, difference between people is perceived though relations of similarity and difference that make up certain genres or types (Lury 1998: 12–16). Following Strathern, Lury suggested that this kind of relationality in the sense of 'calibrating similarity and difference' is being cancelled in prosthetic culture. Relating parts to wholes (e.g. individuals to society, to nature or to other categories such as gender or age), is being troubled by the fact that there no longer are clear-cut relations of similarity and difference. For example, what is the age of a person with transplanted organs from various other persons? Instead of a shift in the merographic relations (in the sense of parts being disassembled from nature and reassembled under culture; see Schneider 2005: 392), the category 'age' itself becomes disassembled into various parts and reconstituted as an effect of prosthesis.

Club and dance cultures provide environments for constructing sensuous excitement helped by technological means, either exogenous technologies such as auditory and visual stimuli, or by substances absorbed into the body. These interventions partly disrupt, although do not completely deactivate, time-consciousness. Bodily sensations are not separated from awareness and retrospective reflection but may be translated and symbolized into meaning by being embedded in the horizon of previous experiences. The familiarity with the body's habits and responses as well as with symbolic systems and knowledge at hand provides a backdrop for the symbolization and classification of current sensations and emotive states, for instance, as new or well known, as 'natural' and/ or as 'artificial' (caused by intoxication), or else. This embodied knowledge or memory makes the body's reactions to certain stimuli somewhat predictable and understandable, but also provides for the possibility of being deeply surprised by new states and processes that disrupt the familiar repertory of stimuli–response circuits (Pollner 1987: 161).[30] New sensations, provided they are pleasurable, are prone to repetition, routinization and to symbolization.[31] However, the modification of the sensuous state, especially when intensified by the prosthetic endocolonization of the body through drugs, may disrupt (time-)consciousness and memory as well as the way in which the effects of these prostheses are symbolized and classified and (dis-)authenticated as part of the 'self'. It may not be possible to classify them as either one or the other, as either 'real' or 'simulated', 'natural' or 'artificial', but may fashion new modes of making sense of such experiences.

Aestheticization, Boundary Work and Identity

Club cultures provide structures for the advent into otherness through aesthetic and prosthetic forms of being. Otherness suggests transformation through playful identification or through the construction of certain sensuous states. As was emphasized, by fashioning an experimental individual oriented towards possible becoming and self-extension, contemporary prosthetic culture reconfigures the possessive individual defined by the continuity of the body, consciousness and memory into an individual who lacks—at its extreme—'the narrative continuity of memory . . . interiority and depth' (Lury 1998: 5). The following chapters analyse how transcendence and liminality are fabricated in nightclubbing through aesthetic and prosthetic means and what this entails for the construction of experience and identity. How are classification practices, boundary work and the negotiation of identity affected by such aesthetic and prosthetic transformation and experimentation? What interpretive devices do social actors employ to make sense of processes of virtualization? Do they substitute the logic of authenticity and the surface–depth model of self for a pure surface model, or do they deploy new ways of defining authenticity?

Different viewpoints on this issue shall be noted briefly. On the one hand, it has been argued that a postmodern sensibility is eroding the logic of authenticity (Grossberg 1992: 224–233; Massumi 1992: 136); on the other hand, the increasing significance of an ethic of authenticity has been emphasized (Eder 1993, Hetherington 1998, Rose 1999a), partly as a counter-effect of aestheticization (Welsch 1997: 183). In reflecting upon cultural practices (of popular music), Grossberg, for example, spoke of 'authentic inauthenticity'. This (ironic) nihilism 'renounces both its claim to represent reality and its place in a representational economy' (1992: 224). It recalls insincerity, deception, role-distance and disaffection. In a similar way, Massumi described the 'structural cynicism' arising from the fact that a concurrence between interiority (thought–feeling) and exteriority (speech–action) is no longer expected as one does not have to believe, or invest affect, in the simulation of official identity categories (Massumi 1992: 136). While many studies of youth (sub-)cultures emphasized the centrality of notions of authenticity for the construction of membership and credibility (Widdicombe and Wooffitt 1990; Widdicombe 1993, 1995; Thornton 1995), clubbing was regarded as the ultimate postmodern sphere for 'promiscuous' style cruising, 'deliberate inauthenticity' and for the 'disappearance of a culture of meaning' (Polhemus 1996: 91–98). On the other hand, Rose argued that the logic of authenticity lay at the heart of the 'ethicalization of existence', which he saw as a response to disintegrating external moralities (Rose 1999a: 264–267, 271–272). Similarly, other authors suggested that the quest for authenticity and narratives of liberation and self-realization are central in contemporary expressive and neo-romantic life-forms in the legacy of the counter-cultural tradition (Hetherington 1998: 8, 69, 76–77; Eder 1993). Instead of a simple 'either/or', these sensibilities are entwined with each other ranging at the extremes from a depthless virtualism on one end to a deep expressivism on the other end (Hetherington 1998).

The following chapters investigate these sensibilities at the example of the classification practices and the symbolic boundary work manifest in experiential accounts of clubbing. Symbolic boundaries are the 'conceptual distinctions made by social actors to categorize objects, people, practices', which create group boundaries or feelings of membership and which are 'an essential medium' for status acquisition and the maintaining or contesting of social boundaries (Lamont and Molnár 2002: 168).[32] Before turning to questions of membership, group boundaries and identity more specifically (Chapter 8), the subsequent analyses explore how participants frame various orders of reality and how they resolve possible disjunctures between them by validating or invalidating experiences. Of particular interest is how these classification and framing practices are mediated by social positionings of gender, class and sexuality. In the literature, symbolic boundaries are mostly understood in terms of distinctly bounded categories or binary oppositions (e.g. play *or* reality, female *or* male). However, as Zerubavel highlighted, in addition to such purist 'either/or' boundaries, certain cultures or social contexts such as art and play emphasize what he calls 'fuzzy-mindedness', that is, an aversion to boundaries; or 'flexible-mindedness', a fluid mind-set characterized by a 'both/and' logic of classification encouraging ambiguity rather than clear-cut categorization (Zerubavel 1999: 57). Similarly, aesthetic and prosthetic practices in clubbing propel forms of boundary work that do not centre on binary oppositions (*either* real *or* not real, authentic *or* artificial) but on a logic of 'both/and' (simultaneously real *and* not real). This does not imply that 'either/or' boundaries are irrelevant; rather they are complemented by 'both/and' boundaries which prompt temporary and reversible modes of authentication.

The notion of identity, too, has been circumscribed in terms of relations of sameness and difference resting on binary boundaries of 'either/or' (A or non-A; Sampson 1989: 12). Identity is always a provisional, a wobbly fixing and, in the case of personal identity, a centring of the subject which is fundamentally decentred, non-transparent and never fully intelligible. Nevertheless, as Foucault suggested, modern subjectivity is tied in with a hermeneutic of the self in the name of truth (Rabinow 1997: 87–92) sought in the body (and sexuality) and in the continuity of consciousness and memory. At the core of personal identity is the search for permanence and self-sameness in time (Ricoeur 1992: 116–118); but this is essentially intertwined with otherness as time is a 'factor of dissemblance, divergence and difference' (ibid. 117).[33] Identity always involves the 'dialectic of *self* and the *other than self*' (Ricoeur 1992: 3), which means that otherness is constitutive of selfhood.[34] In Ricoeur's philosophical-linguistic conceptualization of selfhood, narrative weaves together concordance and discordance (ibid. 147–148). Sameness (*idem*) and otherness evoke four different components. First, there is the numerical sense of identity. This is identity as oneness: two occurrences are recognized or identified as one and the same thing. Here identity or sameness is opposed to *plurality*. The second dimension is a qualitative sense of identity. This is identity as extreme resemblance of two things. Identity then is opposed to *difference*. In a third sense, identity may refer to the uninterrupted continuity of the same individual beyond the changes over time that might have destabilized similitude. Identity then becomes the reverse of *discontinuity*. But change is only conceivable on the basis of the fourth principle of identity, which is permanence in time. This is identity as an immutable, invariant structure that remains despite changes and that overlaps with selfhood (*ipse*) (Ricoeur 1991: 189–191).

In its accentuation of transformation and mutability, the practices of aestheticization outlined before disturb, on the one hand, the construction of sameness-identity. For example, the creation of masks disrupts similitude; in extreme cases sensation or intoxication may disrupt the sense of continuity; prosthesis challenges the sense of oneness or the calibration of sameness and difference as such. On the other hand, stylization and sensation may also be constructed as expression and enhancement of sameness-identity: ' . . . ecstatic sensations can actually be about an extraordinary and, for many, unparalleled and extremely precious experience of *their own identity*,' as Malbon stressed (1999: 127). As we shall see, there are manifold ways in which participants integrate their clubbing experiences into their narrative synthesis of self and other. But—as this chapter meant to propose—instead of only binary oppositions and relations of similarity and difference (identity vs. abject otherness), identities are also articulated in relation to a horizon of virtuality and imaginary visions of *possible* becoming (identity vs. virtual otherness).[35] Rather than a clear-cut boundary to difference, the latter suggests a more fluid and ambiguous boundary between same and other involving the logic of 'both/and'.

The next chapter explores first, how participants frame the 'reality' of the club sphere in relation to paramount reality, particularly when making sense of drug-induced experiences; and second, how disjunctures arising from the different layers of reality affect narrative configurations of identity and agency. This is followed by an analysis of the role that notions of self-experimentation and transformation play within autobiographical narratives. The final two chapters consider how performative understandings of identity (i.e. identity as a result of stylistic and prosthetic resources) affect common-sense notions of the categories of gender and sexuality and the negotiation of identities and membership through the embodied interactions in club contexts.

5 Thresholds of Reality
Clubbing, Drugs and Agency

There's this strange sort of seductive kind of you could, I mean, I—I felt over the summer like 'Don't get too carried away with this', you know, because, it's not really, it's not reality. It's great to go and do it and for five or six hours just, it's, you know, you're in a completely different world almost, you're not doing any of those things you'd have to do everyday, which is, sort of, I suppose, escapism, escapism, is kind of, I find that quite attractive. (Kay 1999: 7)

I can see both sides of the two worlds and I choose to stay in between, because the world we live in today is an amazing world as well, the big cities, the technology, the communication. It has a lot of bad shit happening, but that's life and at the same time you do your work to live in this world, when you have to, you go to this other world, this underground world of dancing. (Yong 2001: 8)

These two accounts both sketch the dance world as an other world. Yong describes the dance world as an 'underground', but equally valid reality as everyday life. The two worlds, not only calling to mind the sacred and the profane, but also dualistic principles of religious ontology, seem to complement rather than oppose one another. The city, technology and communication on the one hand, and dancing on the other hand, constitute two spheres and modes of being, between which Yong moves back and forth, depending on his needs. Kay, by contrast, sketches a hierarchical relationship between the two worlds, one that is more, and another that is less real and valid. It conjures up Platonic philosophy and its dualism of the true realm of ideas and the less reliable sensual realm of the body. The lack of validity of the dance reality prompts an ethical self-reflection: Whilst delightful, the 'underworld' of dance is depicted as a sensual sphere of temptation and seduction distracting the protagonist from her everyday commitments.

These examples demonstrate that different meanings and values are attributed to the sphere of clubbing. The main focus of this chapter is to investigate different ways of accounting for the 'reality'[1] of the club world and how these demarcate particular notions of agency and ethical concerns. The first part of the chapter explores how interviewees framed and authenticated or dis-authenticated the 'reality' of the club sphere in general, while the second part concentrates on how drug consumption was narrated as a temporary transcendence of everyday reality and identity in the club-world. Drug-induced states were embedded into discourses of pleasure and excess, but also evoked responsibility and control. In discussing examples of how these notions are weaved into narratives of drug experiences, gender aspects shall be highlighted in the framing of agency, excess and the problematization of drug use.

OTHER REALITIES AND OTHER 'SELVES'

Andreas Huyssen once remarked, 'the lure of mass culture, after all has traditionally been described as the threat of losing oneself in dreams and delusions and merely consuming rather than producing' (Huyssen 1986: 55). This discourse continues to influence critical views of outside observers and commentators, and, as Kay's quote above illustrated, also affects how participants themselves make sense of their experiences of the club world. Notions of delusion and disillusion are frequently called up in resolving discordances that arise from the move between different orders of reality. By framing the club sphere within a particular order of reality, participants at the same time classify and evaluate the practices and experiences of clubbing, validating the extent to which they can be seen as authentic parts of the self. In other words, the subsumption of experiences under a certain order of reality reflects back on the narrative configuration of identity and agency. The 'other reality' of the dance and club world also constitutes a notion of an 'other self', which is either made concordant with identity (*idem*; see Chapter 4), for example, through narratives of transformation, or remains relegated to a status of 'other' as in narratives of delusion and disillusion. The latter often problematize the emotional connections, friendships and relationships forged in the club and serve as a form of distantiation. Such invalidation and distantiation, it seems, is more pronounced in women's narratives. To some extent, this may reflect the genderedness of the high- and mass-culture dichotomy, which linked women's identification with, and participation in, 'mass culture' to their possible immoralization.[2] In some cases, however, the boundaries between real and not real, authentic and inauthentic are blurred and prevent the narrative closure of sameness-identity keeping a balance of both, same and other.

Alluding to the falseness of the simulacrum, Kay, an art graduate in her mid-twenties, stated that the dance world is not to be taken for real. While she did not offer a clear reason for this viewpoint, her reference to everyday commitments or routines suggests that the artificiality of the club context stems from the fact that the ways of being and modes of practice it engenders cannot be sustained forever, but just temporarily. After a couple of hours they would give way to the demands of the everyday again. Kay's prescriptive self-appeal 'don't get too carried away with this' reflects the anxiety of losing control. This is probably why she passed off the dance world as a pleasurable, but escapist, temporary and illusory reality. By contrast, the notion of underground reality used by Yong, a Korean media student, is clearly marked off from the world of work and technology. His account conjures up a pragmatic attitude of being in control of moving from one sphere to the other. Wandering between these worlds does not seem to cause confusion between these orders of reality. Kay's assessment of the dance world also correlated with how she viewed herself as a participant. She framed her role and participation in clubs as insincere, cynical and disaffected partaking, which was not to be taken seriously. Yong, by contrast, derived symbolic value from his involvement as a DJ, which he charted as part of his identity project as a significant cultural producer.[3] The way he described his work—in terms of communicating with people and intervening into sensual states of bodies by mastering music technology—suggests that the dance world is not so different from his depiction of the everyday world after all.

> It's like this space-ship, people are dancing, you're taking the space-ship, taking them on a voyage, you start with a slower, let's say, a 135bpm, duv-duv-duv, minimal, you start more minimal, simpler and then gradually you start taking up the speed, you start taking more elements into, and more noises and then around midnight, you start getting full on and you see the people, because you put the track, you put it in, you hear it on your headphone, then you put the fader up and it's like, it's a bit like having sex, you do your move, you do what you know you can do and you see the people just reacting to it, jumping, screaming. (Yong 2001: 18)

These examples of Yong and Kay staged, on the one hand, a 'pragmatic' self in control of technology, moving easily between the club and everyday world, and on the other hand, a 'seduced' self who, fearing the loss of control, devalued the club sphere as unreal. Turning to a different example, Costa, a Greek gay student in his mid-twenties, evaluated the authenticity of the club sphere at two levels. One was from the viewpoint of a tourist in search of the authentic origin of clubbing. Before coming to live in London he had been going out clubbing in Greece and Spain, but the clubs he had visited there had only tried to 'imitate' or 'follow' London. By contrast, London clubs were credited a status of place. They expressed local experiences and history (Augé 1995: 77), in Costa's words, the 'real thing'. In his view, clubbing was an 'English movement'; it was 'originally born here' (Costa 1999: 2). Therefore, when going out in London, you don't feel like you're in a London like club, you *are* in London, you experience the main thing, you are going to clubs that have been running for nine years so far, and it is so nice knowing that you are in a club that changed so much throughout all these nine years, and so many different people had been in that club, the same dance floor that you are dancing, so many DJs have changed . . . that is exciting for me being a foreigner and coming to London, it's the thing, you enter in a club scene, where everything is so, not updated, it's so the real thing, it's not following London, you *are* in London. (Costa 1999: 1–2)

While London clubs figured as the authentic origin of club culture, the very setting of clubbing itself is characterized as an constructed environment. This resembles Kay's notion of a simulated escape world, except Costa did not describe the practice of clubbing as escapism. The constructed, illusory ambience of the club was marked off from reality and the 'self' constituted as 'other'. Yet, Costa adopted a more neutral position on the qualities of this 'other self':

It's a club, it's an illusion, you are not the same person, you can't be the same person, even if you are natural, on a natural high, without any drugs, you may be a bit pissed as well, so you are not the same anyway. Or even when you are not drunk as well, you are not the same anyway, because it's dark, and it can't show, so you are different, physically or emotionally, you are different. I mean nothing is real in a club, from the way you dress, you may be dressed more glamorous . . . your mental state is not the same, you are much more relaxed, not that frustrated . . . nothing is real, you are another person, better or worse, you are another person, and that's why it's nice going to the clubs as well. (Costa 1999: 3)

Costa's account seems to imply a simultaneity of 'both/and', real and not real, referred to as play-reality in Chapter 4. Yet, to be precise, in both instances he came to a clear judgement regarding the reality-status of the clubbing context and of the 'self' in a club. In one sense the clubs were the real thing as opposed to the copy, and in another sense they were less real than everyday reality. Like Yong he drew symbolic value from clubbing. Taking part in the authentic experience of clubbing in London was highlighted as an important component of his cultural assimilation and integration as a foreigner. At the same time his reflections on the non-real aspects of the club were tied to the notion that attempts of reading others were bound to fail and that the symbolic reading of gestures or body style was estimation at best. The 'other reality' of the club in this case was paired with a 'deluded' self. Yet, instead of disapproving of the inauthenticity of clubbing participants, this was externalized as a normal element of a club setting one had to anticipate when making social encounters in clubs. This explanatory device also served as a form of emotional distantiation in cases of disappointment by diminishing the hopes and desires invested in clubbing and by relieving from the responsibility for choices and acts.

> Most of the time, you go to a nightclub trying to find a boyfriend, but you end up finding a one-night stand, which is really normal as well. Whether it makes you sad after that or happy, that's it, when you go to a club you can't expect anything more, because you can't analyse the character of anybody there, you just see the body language, the movements, the gestures, the style, way of dressing, that's it. So you just go guess, so you go there, you sleep with somebody, and then you realize that it wasn't the way you thought it would be. (Costa 1999: 3)

Delusion and disillusionment about relationships or friendships formed in clubbing contexts were frequent themes in interviewees' accounts. On the one hand, new connections with people in clubs were represented as an experience out of the ordinary. On the other hand, the authenticity of these new links was often questioned later on. While the emotional bond seemed real in the club, it appeared false in retrospect. Hailey, an Australian student in her early twenties, had a more pronounced view, deploying an 'ethics of authenticity' as a yardstick for evaluating people in a club. Again, this staged a 'deluded' self, but in this case disappointment was articulated more explicitly and resulted in the moral not to trust friendships built through clubbing.

> You do feel very connected to a lot of people, and you meet people, and everyone is quite friendly ah and then ah, and then suddenly I found myself surrounded with a couple of people who were really negative and they weren't very nice people . . . and I dropped back a bit and went 'These people aren't real', you know, 'these people are messed up'. (Hailey 2000a: 2)

> People are being personal and the next day you think back—maybe not even the next day, maybe the next week, the next month, when that person isn't in your life anymore—you sit back and think, 'how, how true is all that?' . . . I don't think it's a healthy place to form friendships mostly by going out clubbing. (Hailey 2000a: 5, 7–8)

In all the examples discussed so far clubbing spaces and participants were highlighted as either 'real' or not 'real'. By contrast, the two extracts following below framed club sociality as a play-reality, simultaneously authentic and inauthentic even though different emphasis was put on one or the other. While Clare, like Costa, addressed the artificiality of the club environment, she nevertheless emphasized the realness of the feelings she experienced in a club. Hailey, as before, tended to disavow the realness of clubbing, which remoulded the Cartesian dichotomy of mind and body but maintained the related opposition of knowing and feeling. Hailey did not externalize the illusory character to the club as such, but referred to the body(–brain) as a source of deception that would cloud her 'feelings' against better 'knowledge'.

> It's not real in a club, it's not, it's a constructed environment, totally artificial, but the feelings that you get are very genuine and true feelings of joy and happiness. (Clare 2000a: 22)

> When you go out with people and you meet people, you sort of feel it's real . . . you feel, I can have this connection with everyone, which isn't real and *you know* at the time that it's not real, *but you, something inside your brain feels* like it is. (Hailey 2000a: 5; emphasis by S.R.)

Both Costa as well as Hailey used the device of illusion and disillusion. In Costa's narrative this was part of him reflecting upon dance spaces in terms of finding a boyfriend or sexual partner. He accepted the symbolic way of reading others as an approximation that was likely to be delusive. Hailey, by contrast, assessed other participants in clubs in terms of their authenticity, which made her wary of disappointments ensuing from the involvement with other people in clubs. In her view, the artificial sociality in clubs was a result of the manipulation of the body through drugs. Two other interviewees held similar values of authenticity. They disapproved of the artificiality in women's, respectively lesbian, clubs. In these cases, the inauthenticity was not put down to drug consumption, but to the expectation to perform lesbian identity cues and codes of cool. Aniela, for example, a lesbian woman age thirty, criticized the play with styles and the put-on of 'attitude' and instead preferred people who were 'themselves'. Nevertheless, once in a while she also enjoyed taking part in the role-playing game. Expressing an 'other' side of herself also constituted a pleasurable experience. Overall, in Aniela's account dance spaces provided for both the disruption of identity, as well as the dis-alienating, authentic articulation of identity—when she danced and felt that she did not 'have to play anything' (Aniela 2000a: 8).[4]

These accounts designed different types of narrative synthesis of self and other, either ironicizing[5] clubbing experiences as a dimension of otherness within the self, or affirming them as an expression of identity. While clubbing appeared as a realization of the 'good life' in several respects, it was considered detrimental to the pursuit of other goals (e.g. forming friendships and relationships). Such ethical ambivalence was also echoed in the narratives about drug experiences, which calls into question the thesis that drug use has become normalized in Britain (Parker, Measham, and Aldridge 1995; Parker et al. 1998; Measham et al. 2001). In the following part, this thesis shall be outlined briefly before reflecting on the configuration of sameness and otherness in discourses on drugs. This serves as a backdrop for analysing the framing of reality and identity in the interviewee narratives of clubbing and drugs.

NORMALIZATION OF DRUG-USE IN CLUBBING

A decade ago a comparative survey carried out in ten European countries suggested that the UK hosts the most drug-experienced young adult population (Griffiths et al. 1997; Measham et al. 2001: 1). Britain had life-time and past-year rates[6] of drug use over twice as high as the next placed country (quoted from Measham et al. 2001: 11). The apparent prevalence of drug use, particularly for recreational purposes, was considered to indicate a process of normalization, insinuating that the use of illicit drugs had not only become more widespread, but also more acceptable and tolerable. At the core of the thesis of normalization was the claim that 'for many young people taking drugs has become the norm' and that over the coming years in urban areas at least 'non-drug trying adolescents will be the minority group' (Parker et al. 1995: 22, 26, as quoted in Pearson 2001: 168). The popularization of recreational drug use in rave and dance culture served as the key evidence for these arguments.

Indeed, clubbing culture is a very significant leisure sphere for consuming drugs. Although many of the substances consumed (except alcohol) are illegal, drug consumption is underpinned by the promotion of liminality in night-time entertainment, which is connected to body-focused experiential and conspicuous consumption (see also Chapter 4). Drug use of clubbers was found to be 'wider in repertoire and greater in frequency and quantity' than of the overall adolescent and adult population (e.g. Measham 2004: 339, Release 1997). Field research in three nightclubs in a city in northwest England in the late 1990s found that two-thirds of a club crowd had usually taken, or were planning to take, an illicit drug that night (Measham et al. 2001: 96, 107).[7] The most widely used drugs in these clubs were cannabis, ecstasy and amphetamines; however, the selection and use of drugs differed by the genre and music policy of the dance club. People in techno clubs tended to use a wider range of drugs (cannabis, ecstasy, amphetamine, LSD, ketamine) than, for example, the clientele of garage clubs, where alcohol and cocaine were more common (O'Hagan 1999). Further, clubbers often differentiated between 'drinking clubs' and 'drug clubs' (Moore 2003b). Over the years, some drugs have become less and others more popular. The decrease in the use of ecstasy, LSD and amphetamines was accompanied by a rise in the use of cocaine powder especially since the second half of the 1990s, or GHB[8], which has become fashionable on, but not only on, certain parts of the gay club scene. In addition to the claim that 'dancing on drugs' was common among club-goers, Measham et al. (2001: 69) also asserted that drug consumers in clubs are regular users; regular being defined as either weekly, fortnightly, monthly or at least once every three months.

The popularity and the centrality of drug consumption within clubbing culture were confirmed by most research studies. Nevertheless, different criticisms were raised against the thesis of normalization, with respect to both the general as well as the younger populations (Shiner and Newburn 1999). The findings of the British Crime Survey, a large-scale household survey that includes a self-completion module on drug use, suggest that speaking of a normalization of drug use may indeed be exaggerated. Apart from the unanswered question as to what level of consumption would be indicative of normalization, a tendency of normalization applies, if at all, foremost to the use of cannabis.[9] Even though the British Crime Survey does not warrant to speak of the normalization of illicit drug use among the general young and adult population, the surveys and field research focusing on nightclub audiences demonstrated that clubbers' drug taking exceeds the consumption levels of the general population. This, however, is not necessarily representative of the club scene generally due to its differentiation into various scenes and genres.

Drug use may have become 'normal' or even a 'normative' situational requirement within certain spheres and audiences of clubbing, but it is still embedded within a normative context that defines such practices as illegal and thus puts them under risk of criminalization. The ambiguity of the prevalence yet prohibition of drug consumption in clubs means that drugs remain a symbol of transgression and otherness by being relegated to a more or less necessary status of secrecy. Venue owners and managers are in the awkward and often hypocritical position of offering a space for audiences who wish to engage in partly illicit practices whilst having to comply with legal regulations and licensing obligations.[10] To some extent, even authorities acknowledge the impossibility of keeping clubs drug-free as drugs may simply be taken before entering the premises.

Normalization is hard to imagine within such a context, particularly if it is not merely defined as a statistical norm, but as a cultural process of normalization, which involves more than the dimensions of quantity, frequency and distribution of use. Normalization would imply that drug consumption has lost its status and image of being extraordinary and transgressive, special, illicit, ethically and morally wrong and associated with guilt feelings; that the belief takes hold that drug consumption can be made compatible with everyday activities, commitments and identities (Measham et al. 2001: 12) and that it can become a more or less regular, openly carried out and routinized activity that goes unremarked rather than being marked as special, frowned upon or criminalized. Some of these points were emphasized by Nigel South, who argued that drugs indeed have become such taken for granted facts of everyday life:

> . . . in just over twenty years, experimentation with or use of drugs has become so closely woven into the experiential and cultural fabric of 'ordinary' everyday life in Western society. Drug use may still represent a route to 'unreality' and a means to slip away from the constraints of routine, but today, in many more different ways for many more different people, drug use is actually a part of the 'paramount reality' of everyday life. (South 1999a: 4)

SAMENESS AND OTHERNESS: DRUGS AND OTHER REALITIES

If drug use, in the context of clubbing at least, has become a part of paramount reality, to what extent is it still considered as a route to other orders of reality, and how is this otherness made sense of? Have traditional images of the ethically and morally problematic otherness of drugs disappeared so that the consumption of drugs is considered a normal, routine practice that goes unremarked? As elaborated in the previous part, drugs are widely accepted in clubbing. To some extent, albeit not in all contexts, they have become normal and normative situational requirements signifying the 'authentic clubber': 'I'm a clubber, I take drugs', Hailey self-ironically remarked (2000: 27) whilst reflecting on the significance of drug use for being a 'real clubber'. She ridiculed the normal and partly normative status of drug use in dance clubs that is built on the endorsement of an illicit and transgressive practice. Similarly, Kay hinted at the almost normative dimension of drug taking in clubs and the sense of exclusion created when abstaining from drug consumption (Kay 1999: 3).

The research discussed above provided insights into the scale and patterns of drug use in dance culture, yet it did not offer much depth in relation to the subjective meanings of drug use and how these mediate normality and otherness. Shiner and Newburn criticized the normalization thesis for paying inadequate attention to the meanings and perception of drug use and the normative context by young people themselves (Shiner and Newburn 1997: 526). The investigation as to how drugs are integrated into experience and narratives was not given much attention in the early days of research on rave and club culture despite the classic outline of Howard Becker (1967) and the works he inspired (e.g. Willis 1976).[11] Their common point was that a drug experience is not only determined by the pharmacological properties of a drug, but also depends on the meanings individuals ascribe to a drug by drawing on symbolic systems at hand, such as the meanings and knowledge circulating in peer groups.

Discourses of drugs, for example, literary narratives, are heavily inscribed with images of other reality. The meanings ascribed to this other reality are various depending on the type of drug; and so are the ways of validating or invalidating these realities as more or less true or artificial, as illusory self transformation or as a liberating, dis-alienating experience of a more 'real' self. In tracing drugs in cultural and literary history, Sadie Plant (1999) provided useful insights into different notions of other reality. Literary discourse configured drugs as a technology that alters the body's sensations and ways of perception, rendering the corporeal condition contingent and variable (Ricoeur 1992: 150–151).[12] In nineteenth-century Romantic poetry and fiction, for example, opium was praised for its inspiring qualities of assisting the faculty of dreaming, spurring creativity by creating a wealth of imagination and new insights into lost memories. The power and agency ascribed to opium was such that it was seen to seriously confuse and blur the different realities and even to annihilate agency and accountability (S. Plant 1999: 21, 24; see also Ricoeur 1992: 151). Cannabis was not seen to be as extreme, but was also associated with a reconfiguration of the senses and an increased sensitivity and capacity of perception through synaesthetic effects that opened the depths of an otherwise superficial and increasingly speeded-up world (S. Plant 1999: 33–36). By contrast, cocaine was considered to bring about a boost of energy, euphoria and erotic agility rather than access to a world of dreams and fantasies (ibid. 59–77). Cocaine narratives also evoked a sense of split identity by sketching an alter ego previously secreted within everyday identities. Narratives of LSD and other hallucinogens tended to stage a metamorphosis into a different species such as the transmutation into an animal. The 'trip' is a temporary annulment of identity, but also tells of a transformative experience of an 'other reality' (ibid. 108).

The dance-drug ecstasy added new dimensions to these notions of otherness. Like cocaine it was interpreted as an amplifier—of emotional and psychic states, of bodily sensations and of the desire and capability to connect with people. Ecstasy was less regarded to trigger a hallucinatory immersion into an imaginary reality rather than sensual pleasures of increased body involvement. It was seen to enhance the bodily awareness of the here and now; as a turning outwards rather than a turning inwards; the body becoming sound and rhythm, fusing the inside and the outside. Echoing the interpretations of 1990s dance culture, Plant suggested that the engineering of bodily sensations through ecstasy 'steals identity away' (S. Plant 1999: 168), that it 'possesses and entrances' the dancers and blurs the boundaries between interiority and exteriority. But ecstasy not only figured as the emblem of a sense-based 'rush culture', it also remained attached to transcendentalist, psychedelic discourses (Reynolds 1998: xix–xx). Reynolds spoke of a double coding in relation to ecstasy. On the one hand, he referred to the use of the drug as 'consciousness-*razing*' stimulant in tandem with amphetamines in a 'working-class weekender lifestyle'; on the other hand, combined with LSD or other hallucinogens it would run along the lines of the 'middle-class bohemian' or counter-cultural project of 'consciousness-raising' (ibid. 405–407). While the association with class-inflected lifestyles may be too general and far-fetched, it nonetheless points to different forms of using and experiencing the drug. Given that the increased capacity to perceive does not necessarily generate a hallucinated reality, but intensifies the awareness of paramount reality, what kind of narrative configurations of reality and identity did ecstasy give rise to? Popular discourses on ecstasy called up metaphors of change and transformation rather than transgression, for instance, the therapeutic transformation of personality. Central was the notion that the drug could enhance a person's capacity to love and relate to others and help overcome inhibitions. Moreover, ecstasy fuelled a fantasy of rebirth, often depicted as an estrangement of the body and as a configuration of new bodily experiences one had to come to terms with.[13]

The variety of meanings of 'other reality' within discourses on drugs demonstrates that drug experiences cannot be simply generalized as a form of escape or 'getting away from reality'. Notions of other reality go along with constrained agency and accountability, but also with enhanced agency. Apart from being represented as keys to positively connoted, other dimensions of reality, drugs, drug consumption and drug users, however, also became associated with a negatively connoted otherness of deviance, addiction and criminality. To what extent these markings have disappeared, as the thesis of normalization claimed, shall be explored in the following discussion of interviewee accounts.

Gendered Meanings of Excess, Agency and Otherness

Feminist critiques of drug discourses and research drew attention to the fact that female drug-taking in particular carries connotations of problematic otherness. Two main discursive threads were identified in relation to women who consume drugs: on the one hand, their victimization, on the other hand, their immoralization. While the first stressed the increased vulnerability of, and the threats to, women's safety, the second referred to the abuse and undermining of women's 'nature' epitomized in their reproductive capacity. Hence, by virtue of the coding of women as body and nature, the choice to take drugs came to be seen as an unethical, 'unfeminine' act (Henderson 1999: 37; Ettorre 1992: 10; Measham et al. 2001: 36–37). As assumed by the normalization thesis as well as indicated by research on clubbing, such negative images have been increasingly neutralized, especially in this particular context. Studies focusing on women in clubbing scenes emphasized that female drug-taking and 'being out of it' has become more socially acceptable and is no longer so heavily associated with personal pathology (e.g. Pini 2001: 12–13, Hutton 2006). Other quantitative and qualitative research has found little difference in the drug practices of men and women in clubs, except for some variances in the quantity and frequency of use. Both women and men take the same types of drugs. Yet, gender differences were noted in terms of the effects sought after. Females were reported to attach more importance to physical stimulation and increase in energy by using amphetamines, whereas males were slightly more inclined towards hallucinatory experiences and perceptual distortions achieved with stimulants such as LSD (Boys et al. 2000: 37–38; Release 1997: 12). Measham et al. found that fewer women than men took illicit drugs in clubs (2001: 109), and women more frequently reported negative physical side- or after-effects such as nausea or headaches (ibid. 129; see also Release 1997: 22–24).

The following analysis of interviewees' narratives of drug consumption in the context of clubbing demonstrates that drug taking, even by participants who were regular users of drugs over certain periods, was still construed as ethically ambivalent. This calls into question that drug use within club culture, despite higher than average rates of consumption, has become *fully* normalized. Heavy consumption may instigate consumers even more to reflect on and to problematize their practices of taking drugs. The extent to which drug use has become normalized cannot be measured by quantity and regularity of drug consumption alone. One way in which the ethical ambivalence became manifest was through notions of excess, which served as a metaphor of transgressive pleasure on the one hand, and signified the potential loss of freedom and control on the other hand. As Rose (1999a: 266) argued, the contemporary regime of freedom is characterized by two 'pathologies' or moral limits: one is non-consensual conduct; the second, which is more relevant in this context, is excessive conduct. Both limits tend to be represented as a lack of exercise of will and choice.[14] Similarly, in the narratives explored here, 'excessive' drug taking appeared as a vehicle of immersion into another 'reality', but tended to tip over into a problematic or pathological state (e.g. symbolized in the fear of dependency) that called for mastery in order to affirm willpower and self-responsibility. This does not mean to suggest that these interviewees were excessive users of drugs; rather, the image of excess emerged as a central cipher in the configuration of transgression and transformation, agency and ethics—in particular, of the ethical boundaries between the 'good life' and problematic otherness. Such ethical ambivalence was manifest in most narratives; nevertheless, gender differences could be noted in the story-types, the representation of agency and in the emphasis of problematic aspects of ('excessive') drug taking.

A slight majority, fifteen of the twenty-three interviewees of this study, were regular users of drugs for a certain period in their lives. Most had experiences with more than one drug. The others had either abstained from or had tried drugs without becoming regular users. The main drugs referred to were cannabis, ecstasy, amphetamines and LSD. Other drugs, more rarely mentioned, were cocaine, magic mushrooms, poppers, ketamine, Rohypnol and GHB. None of the interviewees spoke of experiences with heroin. Some general patterns became manifest in these drug narratives.

First, drug consumption tended to be narrated from a *retrospective* point of view, whereby the most intensive period of clubbing and drug taking was assigned to the past. The narrated present was often designed as a reorientation towards slowing down and stopping, which highlights the ethical theme of mastery and control. Certainly, to some extent the narrative genre itself provokes ethical reflection, and the fact of sharing drug experiences with an academic researcher may have emphasized this. Yet, the interviewees were not asked directly, but in most cases themselves chose to bring up the topic. Secondly, while interviewees compared and contrasted the effects and experiences of different drugs at some point, they tended to generalize their experiences without always differentiating between the types of drugs, implicitly privileging the experience of a particular drug, or singling out particular effects of a drug. A third point relates to the role and significance of drugs in the overall narrative. Usually, clubbing and drug taking were embedded in general plotlines of biographical change and progress. In some cases, however, clubbing and drugs assumed a cardinal role[15] in the narrative: they were made to account for significant changes in the life history and thereby acquired biographical meaning. The drug history then moulded the general plot structure of the narrative, marking off three phases. It involved first, a period of initiation (the 'honeymoon'); second, a period of acclimatization and intensification ('excess'), in which excessive drug consumption was in danger of tipping over into compulsion; and third, a period of reorientation (the 'comedown'; see also Collin 1997: 8–9).[16]

Both men as well as women shared this general plot structure and employed similar story-types ascribing a considerable degree of power and agency to drugs, which in some cases enhanced the agency of the protagonist and in others constrained it. The strengthening of emotional bonds in romantic relationships or friendships was one way of sketching the enhancement of agency through drugs. But stimulation through drugs was also linked to an illusioned, intoxicated and therefore less accountable self. While all interviewees endorsed the pleasures of drug taking and emphasized the great times of being 'totally off it', women's accounts tended to allude more clearly to the immorality of excess and to the discourse of victimization. Victimization, understood generally as constrained agency and accountability, could also serve to mitigate excess. Men's stories, by contrast, more explicitly framed excess and being out of control in terms of risk and adventure. Men also had a strong leaning towards stressing the transformative potential of drugs, clinging on to discourses of 'consciousness-raising' and emphasizing the change and advancement of personality. Metaphors of transformation in women's narratives were strongly tied to romance and sexuality (this, however, should not suggest that sexuality and romance were not touched upon in men's narratives). However, in none of the narratives did images of excessive drug-consumption only connote a positive otherness. Excess connoted the danger of getting out of hand and of possibly leading to compulsive drug taking. Conversion stories of the withdrawal from drugs highlighted health concerns and commitments in education and work life. Frequently, the experience of significant others, such as good friends whose drug taking had led to breakdowns and severe problems, served as a reason for re-orientation. Despite these similarities, women tended to accentuate health problems (e.g. 'bad trip' stories) and the disillusionment about relationships and friendships. Quite often they referred to their responsibility for family and respectability. Men were more inclined to highlight their responsibility for work and career. If they had not withdrawn from drugs, excess was usually framed within the self-controlling reflection on boundaries and limits.[17]

A significant dimension of 'other reality' for women was constituted when they felt obliged to conceal their drug taking not only from the authorities of dance clubs, but also from parents or family members who disapproved of and worried about the drug consumption of their kin. The consignment of drug practices to a secreted realm of life opened up a 'transgressive' and not normalized space. To a significant extent this transgressive realm of drug taking was closely linked to sexuality.[18] Sally, for instance, a young mother in her early twenties living in South London at the time, related how clubbing and drug taking enabled her to experiment with sexual practices that deviated from the model of the heterosexual, monogamous relationship. From Pini's (2001) viewpoint, this might appear as an articulation of 'new modes of femininity'. In Sally's case and also in other cases, however, this was tied in with conventional orientations towards romance and relationships. Drugs fostered emotional bonds even where they had not existed before. Sally fell in love with a man she had always disliked, a fact that she attributed to their drug taking.

> Then there was this guy that I used to go to school with called R. We were sort of friends in school, but I never really liked him because he used to treat girls like shit and just shit all over them, and anyway . . . As soon as he came out with us and we got on so well, I mean we were both off our heads like on pills and ah, we got on so well, and we ended up going out together. (Sally 2000: 2)

In this example, ecstasy appeared as quite a forceful disruption of identity. It not only carved out a temporary other reality in the club, but also brought on the way a more profound transformation. Ecstasy, and drugs in general, became metaphors for a significant change in her life:

> And I ended up staying with him . . . and having the child with him. It's just quite bizarre really, and I think, to be honest with you, I put that all down to drugs really, because I found it sort of quite bizarre, because, ah, I think, if it hadn't been for drugs, then we would never have got together, and then I would never have my daughter, which is quite a weird thing. (Sally 2000: 2)

However, the relationship terminated after two and a half years. In retrospect this relationship that had been instigated by the powerful impact of drugs was dismissed as illusory reality and self-deception. Drug taking—or the withdrawal from it—came to substitute for other explanations of the failed relationship with the child's father.

> We never actually got on, really. The only, the only reason we stayed together—we got on fine until I was pregnant, because when I was pregnant, obviously I stopped taking drugs and you see people in a different light . . . I think they really discolour your judgment of people, I think they really do. (Sally 2000: 3)

Correspondingly, Sally reinterpreted the drug-induced sexual adventures through the disillusionment device. In retrospect she came to realize that she had partly been used as a sexual object (victimization). This ironicization of experience, whereby drug intoxication was storied as disabling, counterbalanced her emphasis on the enabling role of drugs. However, all these disillusions were superseded by the climax of Sally's story, a new romantic love relationship that had sparked off in a club context and that had led to her engagement. Apart from mentioning that she had brought her drug consumption to a halt during pregnancy, Sally did not moralize about drug taking and parenthood, which could be seen as an indication of the normalization of drug use. The withdrawal from drug consumption was sketched almost as a beneficial side-effect of her becoming a mother. Nevertheless, her evaluation below illustrates the rather more implicit ethical considerations in relation to drug use. In speculating on the potential impact drugs could have had on her, she stated:

> Maybe I'd be totally fucked up on drugs now from doing too much clubbing and being burned out, if it hadn't been for me like having her, because, you know, it's only really 'cause I had her that I, you know, you chill out a bit and you mellow up. (Sally 2000: 12)

Clare, a heterosexual female in her mid-twenties, like Sally, described the enabling and disabling effect that drugs had on her sexual roles and practices. Again drugs and the drug ecstasy in particular were wedded to the construction of romance and the enhancement of heterosexual agency. But they were also linked to the disruption of the conventional heteronormative model. Drugs were part of her lifestyle as a professional dancer on the club scene. Clare performed in fetish clubs on the one hand and in table-dancing clubs on the other hand, both of which she portrayed as unconventional. For example, as a fetish dancer she performed bisexual roles. The plot structure of Clare's narration suggested that at the beginning, drugs supported her agency and enabled her to experiment with what she identified as a 'secreted side of her personality'. But in the long run drugs seemed to undermine her agency. Clare assessed her drug use as almost addictive behaviour. In her clubbing past, she reported, she sometimes felt like she 'had failed', if she 'didn't have something to take in the course of the night' (Clare 2000: 7). This reflection on the possibly addictive nature of drug taking mainly referred to her job as a table dancer, which propelled her intake of cocaine. She described this dependency much like a 'process-addictive behaviour' (see Schaef and Fassel 1988) relating to the whole action context of table dancing, which made her feel like 'being sucked in'.[19] This is where the third element of the plot structure set in: overcoming excess and the withdrawal from drugs. Her general evaluation of her clubbing history converged on this change, from 'taking huge amounts of drugs to nothing' (Clare 2000: 13). In this regard, Clare mingled a 'love story' with a 'mastery story' (see the analysis of these story types in Hänninen and Koski-Jännes 1999). The retrieval of agency and control was brought on the way by a new relationship, which made her give up the job as a table dancer and reduce her drug intake. Again, drugs were assigned a cardinal function for the beginning of this heterosexual relationship. The drug GHB enhanced her sexual agency and helped her seduce her later boyfriend.

> So you know, if it hadn't been, you know, if it hadn't been for the fact that I was wearing a rubber bikini and I had taken this drug, I don't think we would have got together. (Clare 2000a: 13)

In relation to the experimentation with bisexual roles, the role of drugs was more ambiguous. While drugs enabled her to act out a bisexual role in her fetish dancing, drug intoxication seemed to diminish her sense of control in relation to homosexual experiences. In relation to these she presented herself as a victim of predatory sexual advances. On the one hand, drugs opened up spheres of 'transgression' and experimentation; on the other hand, drug taking tended to slide into 'excess' and 'addiction', undermining her agency and accountability. If enhancing her agency, drugs did not appear to set aside her responsibility, but still left her responsible and accountable for her acts, for example, for having made a good 'choice'. Clare also talked about her drug experiences in relation to friendships. In the passage quoted in the first section of the chapter Clare reflected on the artificiality of the club environment, but still classified the feelings in clubs as authentic. However, with regards to friendships evolving from drug-induced states she also employed the disillusion device. With the drugs wearing off, the close emotional connection with strangers wore off, too. The authenticity of these connections was questioned in retrospect. In contrast to Hailey or Sally, however, Clare's withdrawal from drugs did not lead to a complete disauthentication of the drug-induced experiences.

By contrast, Alex, a gay clubber age forty, in narrating his initiation into drugs via ecstasy, modelled a similar experience of friendship and love. Like the female interviewees quoted before, Alex was aware of the artificial amplification of the emotions, yet, he underscored the realness of this emotional connection rather than dis-authenticating it.

> So we all did it [= the drug ecstasy, S.R.] together and it was just like 'wow', when I did it with like mates. And it was like fucking hell, because like I love these two people, like genuinely love them, but I don't think I would ever say it, but all of a sudden it was like, I felt it big time. And I was telling them, and they were telling me, and we really meant it. And we knew it was drugs, but we also knew it was true. That's the big thing about the friendship thing, when you're on it it's like, you *know* that you're on drugs and you *know* that you're sort of everything is heightened and it's all sort of like, 'Oh I love you' and blah blah, you know it's a bit sort of wishy-washy like that, but at the same time you know it's true, you, I mean, I—I do genuinely feel like I know it's true. (Alex 2000: 17)

Male interviewees tended to evaluate drug-induced states as life changing and transformative and less often deployed the disillusionment device, in particular, with respect to relationships or friendships. Instead, more emphasis was put on integrating the discordant elements of 'other reality' into a narrative of progress, for example, through the notion that drugs helped amplify, strengthen and liberate the 'real' self. This was linked to spiritual insight, fine-tuned perception, a special connection with oneself and the enhancement or clarification of feelings. Alex referred to ecstasy as the 'truth drug', alluding to the use of ecstasy in therapeutic contexts.[20] He accounted for a nervous breakdown that he had had by reasoning that the regular use of ecstasy might have revealed and magnified his 'baggage' of negative feelings, which eventually erupted and caused the breakdown.[21] Despite this severe disruption, he did not dismiss the drug, but evaluated it quite positively as having enabled him to deal with, and eventually to overcome, his problems.

A different dimension of 'self-realization' was highlighted by Yong, the Korean media student and DJ. Having explored a range of drugs, he described his heightened awareness and how cannabis, in particular, had improved his artistic agency and creativity:

> Your mind is stimulated and you start thinking things. It's like there is this invisible flow of inspiration and because you are under the effect of this hash, you just grab inspiration. If you start drawing, the drawings become much more artistic. I write a lot of poetry when I smoke this, poetry just comes out really beautifully. (Yong 2001: 10)

Far from blocking out the awareness of reality, drugs would lift the barriers that usually prevented people from receiving and processing sense impressions with all their information and meanings. This clings on to psychedelic discourses of the late 1960s, which celebrated drugs, in particular LSD, as an intensification of the capacity to perceive internal or external reality. In Yong's narrative the drug-induced protagonist was depicted as 'more real', 'whole' and 'connected' than the non-drug induced one, whose ability to grasp the depths of the world was constrained by the routines of everyday life.

> The human brain is made in a certain way that you block out certain information and so, that's the world that we see, that we hear, that we smell. But if we were to be able to receive all the information that there is around the world, our brain would have to be this size. So taking these drugs just works parts of your brain that aren't worked usual. Why, because you get up in the morning, you go sleep at that night, we go work, we do certain things—that don't—block —it's a good life like that, it's just a certain kind of life, so LSD, what I think LSD does, is, it just connects you. (Yong 2001: 29)

While all the women, who spoke about drugs in relation to family or relatives, referred to silence, taboo, guilt feelings or lack of understanding, Yong problematized family in a different way. Cannabis affirmed his agency and strengthened his will. The daily joint-smoking ritual in his youth made him meditate and 'see through' his life (Yong 2001: 12), giving him the courage to break through the tradition of obedience and to object to his parents' educational plans. Yong convinced them of his plan to study media in order to become a film director. Apart from these positive transformations, Yong also described how excessive drug intake exposed him to the risk of losing control over life. Like Clare, Yong sketched a period when he was afraid of 'being sucked in' by the increasing intensity of the drug and dance lifestyle. He began to reconsider his drug consumption. This was partly instigated by a significant other, a friend who had 'gone crazy' as a result of 'having taken too many drugs.' When Yong was on the verge of 'dropping out and going off travelling', his parents dissuaded him from his plans. This did not lead to a withdrawal from drug consumption altogether, but prompted a 'controlled', more pragmatic approach to drug taking that enabled him to stay in 'both worlds'.

Going off travelling was what Chuck did, a male design teacher in his late thirties. A year after his initiation into rave and ecstasy culture in 1989, he decided to terminate his 'yuppie lifestyle' and to go to Australia. He described, modelled on the ecstasy-rebirth myth, a significant relation between drugs and sexuality. The experience of his first 'E' was narrated as a severe disruption of sameness-identity, as a disorienting experience of homoeroticism. Coming to terms with it, he tried to separate the inside and outside and to determine 'whether it's me and only me or whatever' (Chuck 2001: 33). Eventually, the homosexual desire was not, as in Clare's case, externalized and attributed to the drug, but led to the redefinition of his sexual identity as bisexual. In retrospect, therefore, ecstasy seemed to have propelled the 'coming-out' of his 'real' homosexual desire. As in the cases of Clare and Sally, drugs also accompanied his exploration of different sexual roles and practices enhancing his agency and opening up a dimension of positive, transgressive and transformative otherness. Chuck also evoked the image of heightened awareness. In two stories in particular, he depicted an encounter with the police. In one instance he thought to have identified undercover police at a dance event and concluded

> You sometimes feel that you get extra sensory perception when you are on drugs and when I'd been on drugs I felt that, when I've taken E, I felt that, when I've taken trips I felt that. (Chuck 2001: 27)[22]

In the second story the protagonist was stopped and searched on the street in relation to a robbery that had taken place. The police failed to recognize that he 'was tripping off' his 'skull' (ibid. 28). Due to his increased sensitivity and faculty of imagination, he managed to make up all sorts of stories in order to conceal his status as an illegal immigrant in Australia. Thereby he outwitted the police. In contrast to these stories, Chuck also recalled situations where drugs had not enhanced his agency, but had led to a complete loss of control. One time he climbed on top of a lorry after having done two 'Es'. On another occasion, he woke up underneath a standing train after having taken Rohypnol. Anecdotes of losing control in women's accounts were often related to body and health and were couched in terms of risk. They came to explain a withdrawal from, or change of drug-taking habits. On the contrary, losing control after excessive drug intake in the men's narratives often conveyed a sense of fun and adventure, featuring a tragic–comic hero. Men referred to bodily translocation or 'being out of place' (when high on acid); whereas women's accounts of hallucinatory experiences on acid carved out the metamorphosis of the protagonist, or the socially shared metamorphosis of reality. For example, Clare recounted how she turned into a cat in the mirror; Sheila, a woman in her early twenties, recalled how she and her friends perceived a light spinning out of a cup. Similar to others, Chuck drew a dichotomy of two worlds, a hedonistic sphere of clubbing, drugs, sexuality and night life and an everyday sphere of work and routine. Unlike Kay, Chuck ranked the night life over the day life.

> I remember a couple of times coming out of clubs at five or six o'clock in the morning and just watching people going about their daily lives, you know the street cleaners, the newspaper deliverers, the vans stocking up the shop, the bus-drivers, you know the early morning people that are around at about, people going off to work early; and you think 'I am so far away from this and I don't want anything to do with it, you know. What is their life, what is this business of getting up in the morning? The morning, I am going home, I'm gonna spend a day in the sunshine.' (Chuck 2001: 29)

However, unlike Yong, who had decided to stay in both worlds and make them compatible, Chuck eventually decided to return to the 'normal' way of life, fuelled by the decision to stop taking drugs. Like Clare and Sally he sketched his disillusionment and reversed the hierarchy of these worlds. The sphere of dance and night life again became the other, less valid and ethically somewhat problematic reality and was subordinated to the ethical values and (material) needs of work and day life.

> You know it's very hedonistic, it's extremely in that way, it's self—ah yeah, it's self-indulgent, it's knocked from reality, but you know it's another kind of reality that would be lovely if it was possible (laughs); and for a while it was possible, and for a while I believed it was gonna be possible forever, but well, I mean I can't keep on taking drugs forever. And when you stop, you stop believing it, because you start believing other things as well, that you need to work and you need to go and get an education and a job and pay into the system. (Chuck 2001: 29)

Part of this conversion story was another disillusionment, which happened to have coincided with his 'best' experience on ecstasy: He mistook certain gestures of somebody he was in love with for real affection. While this is reminiscent of the women's accounts of the flawed judgment of people and of emotional connections, Chuck did not classify the person he was in love with as inauthentic, but instead referred to his symbolic misreading of somebody's gestures, similar to Costa. This is quite different from the notions of victimization that some of the women's narratives alluded to. Despite the disillusionment and the withdrawal from drugs, his clubbing- and drug-centred lifestyle overall was integrated into a narrative of transformation and self-realization. It had helped him reform his personality.

> It was very important to find the vehicle to be true to myself, all my life I've felt that, and you know at that time drugs and clubbing and, you know ,their relationship was a way of doing that for me, of finding truth about myself and things. (Chuck 2001: 30)

CONCLUSION

This chapter explored how the interviewees of this study framed the relationship between the reality of the club sphere and the everyday and how this affected their understandings of authenticity and identity. It illustrated the tendency to mark off the clubbing sphere as a separate order of reality, where everyday modes of being, everyday identities and modes of sociality were partly and temporarily suspended. Drug consumption is a central part of clubbing culture and in certain contexts signifies authenticity as a member. Drugs help fabricate a sense of transcendence and otherness, but also give rise to disjunctures between the reality of the nightclub and the reality of everyday life. Such disjunctures are resolved in various ways without, however, displacing the ethic of authenticity. The search for authentic involvement and relationships remained central. Drugs were used to deepen emotional involvement and attachment. At the same time this provoked scepticism and disillusionment about the authenticity and 'realness' of the affective bonds created in drug-induced states. In some cases this came to be assessed as inauthentic, whereas in other cases, insincerity, role-distance and simulation were anticipated and accepted as normal, partly also pleasurable elements of such spheres. The meanings attributed to this 'other-worldly' environment varied, and so did the evaluation of clubbing experiences and 'other selves'. They were either made concordant with identity in narratives of transformation, or they remained 'other' in narratives of disillusionment. The former represented clubbing experiences as a vehicle towards a more authentic 'self', while the latter ironicized these as expressions of a deluded or escapist 'self'. Some narratives obviously also combined both, images of transformation as well as images of delusion. The examples discussed in this chapter also demonstrated how participants attempted to come to terms with the blurring boundaries between reality and 'illusion', between simulated affects and authentic emotions, accounting for the ambiguity and impossibility of a clear-cut distinction.

The analysis was linked to the debate on the normalization of drug use in the context of clubbing. Clearly, the ways in which men and women freely narrated their drug experiences, expecting a normative context that was accepting and tolerant of drug use, reflects a certain degree of normality. Yet, excess and de-control not only signified a positive, transgressive otherness, but also marked a 'problematic' otherness in need of mastery. The ambivalent perspective on the pleasure and mastery of excess indicates that drug taking did not figure as a fully normalized practice. Both men as well as women described enabling and disabling effects of drugs. However, facets of a gendered discourse on drugs became manifest. In the two cases of the heterosexual/bisexual women discussed in more depth, drugs were assigned a cardinal function with respect to relationships, romance and sexuality. On the one hand, drug consumption was linked to sexual adventure and experimentation; on the other hand, it was also depicted as having undermined their (sexual) agency putting them at risk of victimization, illusion or self-estrangement. Whilst emphasizing their pleasures of constructing transgressive 'other selves' on drugs and the biographical changes brought on the way, they tended to ironicize and devalue this 'other reality' of their clubbing and drug taking. The male interviewees too reflected on the problematic side of (excessive) drug use, but they tended to integrate this potentially dangerous otherness into a narrative of overall personal, psychological transformation and self-realization, underscoring the consciousness-raising effects. With this emphasis on the enabling effect of drugs, their disabling effects (i.e. the loss of agency and control) also appeared less problematic and were embraced as either the risks and adventures of tragic–comic heroes or as a pre-stage to reorientation, mastery and transformation. The 'straight' females,[23] by contrast, expressed the disabling effects through images of dependency, victimization, distortion of perception and illusion. Nevertheless, they also designed stories of mastery and positive transformation mainly in terms of relationships and romance. Having highlighted these gendered aspects in these narratives on drugs, however, does not mean to suggest that these very same features also apply in other contexts of study or amount to general patterns beyond these cases. But they point, if rather tentatively, to the fact that the normalization or problematization of drug use does not apply to all social actors in the same way. General, sweeping arguments about the normalization of drug use are in need of being specified and qualified in relation to the social and discursive positionings of particular social groups.

Transformation and disillusionment were the key devices for dealing with the dialectic of self and other-than-self in these drug narratives. These devices are indicative of the justificatory structure of 'tamed hedonism': the engagement in hedonistic pleasures and lifestyles is rendered legitimate either when these pleasures are aligned to the wider aim of self-realization or when they remain insignificant to the deep structure of the self (Sassatelli 2001: 98). Narratives of mastery, transformation and self-experimentation serve to present protagonists who indulge in hedonistic pleasures but stay in control of their passions and desires (ibid. 99). As Sassatelli pointed out, 'in contemporary culture even intoxication, so long as it does not last too long, so long as it is confined to certain spaces such as the rave party, or to certain phases of life such as youth, may be accepted' (ibid. 98–99). To this extent drug consumption may have become culturally normalized.

6   Identity Projects and Spectacular Selves

I always felt like I was made for clubbing and I was stuck in Norfolk. I feel like I still haven't done the clubbing that I need to do . . . I still feel like I haven't got where I wanted to be. (Giselle 2000: 5, 16)

I suppose I was in the place at the right time, when a scene was beginning and part of the things that I did, helped to establish it. (Chuck 2001: 10)

When you're clubbing, it makes you feel privileged to be young; you feel like you're living the youth culture where you're participating and giving to the youth culture, and that's quite powerful, because there is an awareness of how much of the future lies in our hands. (Clare 2000: 22)

These quotes of clubbing participants portray clubbing as a highly meaningful biographical experience. As the last chapter demonstrated, not all interviewees of this study linked the biographical significance of their clubbing to such notions of self-realization and achievement. Interviewee Yong envisaged his clubbing and drug experiences as a step towards becoming an artist. Sally, another interviewee, mainly evoked meanings of luck and coincidence rather than achievement in accounting for changes in her life through clubbing and drug taking. It is one thing to evaluate certain events and experiences in terms of their relevance for biographical changes; it is another thing to measure them against the ideals and dreams of achievement, or to view them as part of an active accomplishment of what appears to have been a goal all along. By emphasizing self-realization, clubbing experiences came to be framed as what I shall call 'projects' of the self. Taking as its starting point four in-depth case studies drawn from the interview data generated in the context of this study (see the introductory chapter), this chapter compares several such examples of how clubbing experiences were narrated as 'identity projects'. It delves into the question of the significance of such projects, in particular, whether these can be seen along the lines of an investment orientation or learning mode to life indicative of the social positioning of certain middle class strata in the UK.

IDENTITY PROJECTS

As outlined in Chapter 4, a certain strand of research focused on the collective nature and the modes of sociality created in clubbing cultures, stressing the 'de-individualizing' force of dancing crowds. This view, as I argued, somewhat tends to overlook how individuality and collectivity are entangled and how the search for individual recognition ('getting noticed') is counterbalanced and regulated by group ethos. In contrast to mere collective identification and unshackling of individuality, the identity projects discussed in this chapter put a pronounced weight on individuality whilst also stressing the community and group ethos. The term 'project' has gained prominence through Boltanski and Chiapello's notion of the project-based polis (Boltanski and Chiapello 2005), which describes a new ethos of capitalism characterized by a certain mode of social organization around networks and a highly flexible and adaptable personality type absorbed in constant activity and oriented towards expanding social capital. In the project-based polis anything, regardless of work or leisure, can take on the form of a project; life fragments into a series of temporally limited engagements. The project form demarcates a particular activity from others and frames it as a goal-oriented learning process. However, the notion of identity project in this context does not mean to suggest that clubbing was framed as a project and linked to certain aims of achievement in the sense of an 'in-order-to' motive (i.e. participants getting involved in clubbing, in order to pursue certain objectives that had been on their mind beforehand).[1] In contrast to this notion of project, what is proposed here is that autobiographical narratives about clubbing evaluated these experiences in terms of different aims of achievement (more in the sense of 'because' motives, see Schütz 1967: 86–95). 'Identity project' refers to a *retrospective* justification of clubbing, in which events and experiences are weaved together as part of the realization of an apparently pre-existing *telos*.[2] The way in which clubbing is retrospectively designed as a project may have some similarities to the project-polis of Boltanski and Chiapello (e.g. in the emphasis on learning); yet, the term 'identity project' does not intend to follow the arguments of these authors. The focus of this analysis is on a particular mode of ethical justification through images of self-realization, mastery and individual agency, which at the same time points to the fact that these interviewees did not necessarily assume that the ethical value of clubbing was or could be taken for granted in social contexts outside club culture. However, such identity projects were not only narrated from the point of view of successful accomplishment, but the theme of achievement could also be thematized from the point of view of (potential) failure or difficulties. In some cases clubbing was narrated and problematized as the cause and pre-cursor for the (re-)orientation towards other identity projects. In this sense, the project encompassed the coming to terms with problematic aspects of, and possible negative transformations through, clubbing. Crucially, identity projects presented the involvement in clubbing culture as a learning experi-ence mobilizing these experiences as a *resource* for a future-oriented project of becoming.

The notion of identity project was also discussed in the debates around the new middle classes, especially within culturalist re-formulations of class theory (Bourdieu 1984, Eder 1993). Klaus Eder argued that the avail-ability of resources and capacities to construct individualized identities has become a key momentum of social stratification (Eder 1993: 174–175). The 'new petit bourgeoisie' as Bourdieu had termed this stratum—though much debate ensued as to whether such a class grouping could indeed be identified (e.g. Longhurst and Savage 1996)—were located within the lower service industries, involved with the production of symbolic goods and services. A particular fraction of the new middle classes was seen to constitute the 'new cultural intermediaries' sensitized to postmodern culture. The typical trajectory of the cultural stratum of the new middle classes was considered to be status-inconsistency and a downward mobil-ity compared to their social origin, either because of their non-certified cultural capital; because of a level of educational qualification lower than that expected of their background; or because of the lack of chance to convert cultural into economic capital. As a rehabilitation strategy, it was argued, the new cultural intermediaries try to utilize their non-certified cultural capital within the new economy of culture and adopt an invest-ment orientation or autodidact learning mode to life (Bourdieu 1984; Lash and Urry 1987: 295–296; Featherstone 1991: 90–92). Likewise, the concern with consumption, body-culture and self-presentation was seen to compensate for the uneasiness with their insecure social position. According to Eder, the new middle classes were engulfed with individual-ized identity projects, concentrating on the search for happiness in the life-world, embracing a new romanticism of nature, direct experience, and, as Featherstone added, expressive lifestyles (Eder 1993: 145–148, Featherstone 1991). Alluding to Bourdieu's point that the 'morality of duty' has mutated into a 'morality of pleasure as a duty' (1984: 367), Featherstone also suggested that these new middle classes turned lifestyle into a life project for displaying individuality. Being prepared to experi-ment and to calculate risks, they would pursue their pleasure in the form of a 'calculating hedonism' (ibid. 86), for which Sassatelli (2001) identi-fied particular legitimatory styles. For example, self-experimentation is one such discursive tool that enables subjects 'to produce a strong self-narrative' but 'provides them with a measure of distance from both desires and pleasures' at the same time (ibid. 99). One may find acceptance for indulging in pleasures as long as not really giving in to them.

This points to another theoretical angle from which identity projects may be examined. They can be seen as an expression of the 'ethicalization of existence', which requires individuals to take responsibility for their well-being and to work upon themselves in the 'name of freedom', autonomy and personal authenticity (Rose 1999a). Elaborating on the freedom discourses that shaped notions of modern government and subjectivity, Rose highlighted three main threads: freedom as *discipline*, freedom as *solidarity* and freedom as *autonomy* (1999b: 65). Freedom as discipline and mastery works through technologies of responsibilization implemented to domesticate passions and vice that could get out of hand. The second thread highlights webs of social solidarities and interdependencies as realms of freedom, and the third centres on the notion of individual autonomy and choice, projected, for example, onto the domain of consumption (ibid. 66–87). The clubbing narratives that will be discussed in the following tend to emphasize the strands of autonomy, solidarity and community. Needless to say, however, tensions and contradictions may arise between these conceptions of freedom. As the discussion of the plot structure of drug experiences in the previous chapter demonstrated, the choice to consume illegal drugs may be liberating at first, but may eventually be experienced as a loss of control and increasing dependency in need of being counteracted with self-discipline. In stressing that these problematic elements have been overcome, the narratives then evoked the freedom of mastery. As this overview meant to suggest, identity projects can be analyzed from various theoretical perspectives: as illustrations of a project-based polis; in terms of the constitution of subjectivity through freedom discourses; or, as I shall consider them in the following, as a mode of social positioning in the context of class dynamics.

NARRATIVE AS A FORM OF SOCIAL POSITIONING

The method of in-depth narrative interviewing and analysis provides a tool to study leisure practices such as clubbing in the broader life-context. This highlights the varying modes of affiliation to club and dance culture, which often change throughout one's biographical phases. It also allows for comparing the significance attributed to clubbing with other areas of life. Before outlining how narrative may be understood as a form of social positioning, I shall note some general points about the demographic characteristics of clubbing audiences in the UK.

Going out clubbing is not confined to people in their twenties, although market research in the UK shows that regular, intensive clubbing takes place mainly between 18 and 25. Over the age of 25 and with marriage or cohabiting, regular visiting of nightclubs drops off and bars become more popular (Mintel 2000a: 42, 2004: 5, 29).[3] Despite its stronghold among the young population, a far wider age-range of people is attracted to clubbing,

which has been associated with the extension of youth and the prolongation of youthful lifestyles into later life-stages.[4] While clubbing is simply
a regular leisure activity for some participants typically accompanying
teenage years and late adolescence, it may be connected to special periods
and biographical transitions in other cases such as (educational) migration
to (foreign) cities, time-out periods of travelling, sexual coming-outs and
other transitions in the youth and adolescent life course.

Participation in club culture in general is neither confined to certain
socio-economic groups, nor is there a direct correlation with income level
except that the lowest-income groups also have the lowest share of regular clubbers and of those who never visited. The share of frequent visitors
is highest in the middle- and high-income groups (Mintel 2004: 32, 61).
Yet, as has been argued, the segmentation of nightclubbing scenes catering
to particular strata of cash-rich or cash-poor consumers points to socio-
economic divides (Chatterton and Hollands 2003), which partly overlap or
crisscross with other divides based on sexual identification, ethnicity/'race'
and age. Even in those clubs that attract a socially mixed audience, processes of segmentation occur. Socio-economic position, involving symbolic
economies of class, also provides scripts for different ways of participation
and modes of storying (Wynne 1998, Longhurst and Savage 1996, Carrington and Wilson 2004).

In investigating narratives as forms of social positioning, the following analysis draws on constructivist and sociology of knowledge perspectives on social stratification. These explicitly thematized—instead of
an objectivist mapping of class groupings in social space—the symbolic
(or analytic) processes of classification itself (Devine, Savage, Scott, and
Crompton 2005). Bev Skeggs, for example, investigated class formation
at the symbolic level, exploring how historical processes, technologies and
knowledge practices got inscribed onto bodies through particular regimes
of value and classification (Skeggs 2004). The autobiographical genre too
has been moulded by class-specific ways of representing life-history, i.e.
enforced confession for the working classes in the context of institutions
of social control and individualized self-presentation in the bourgeois context (ibid.). Autobiographical narratives articulate a symbolic positioning
in the social cosmos. They are stories about (dis-)identification and location
as social actors place themselves within hierarchized social categories as
well as dissociate themselves from certain ascriptions (Anthias 2005: 41,
Skeggs 1997). Such narratives are inscribed in collective stories, discourses,
representations and normative systems, in stories told within families and
by significant others; and they are shaped by certain expectations of what
the audiences addressed deem appropriate (Anthias 2005: 42). According
to Floya Anthias, who conceptualized 'narratives of location' as a means
to reframe the study of social stratification, attention should be drawn
to the interplay between social position and positioning.[5] Social *position*
involves not only the allocation of economic but also cultural resources.

It is circumscribed by unequal chances of access to certain resources and to the participation in social, political and public spheres. This includes the answering characteristics of social institutions that define rules of eligibility and functional requirements for participation in these institutions (Gershuny 2000: 45). Social *positioning* refers to the ways in which people understand and experience, articulate and interact, with these ascribed positions, which are, to a significant extent, structured by denial and disidentification (Anthias 2005: 43).

As mentioned at the outset of this chapter, the analysis presented here builds on a comparative case analysis of interviewee narratives about clubbing. The four cases singled out were each analysed in depth[6] before being drawn together for comparison of the identity projects they designed. The initial case studies explored how the interviewees related their involvement in club cultures to other aspects of life outside clubbing. These narratives were not typical for the way in which interviewees of this study generally represented their experiences of clubbing. Of course, narrative interviewing incites self-reflection on biographical progress, but not all the narratives shared this emphasis on achievement, progress and individual development that was characteristic for the cases discussed here. They were selected because they stood out precisely for this emphasis and therefore constituted a distinctive type of representing clubbing experiences. The aim of the analysis was to outline the features of this mode of representation, to highlight the commonalities and variations between these cases, to contrast them with other cases[7] and to explore how middle classness, gender and sexuality textured these 'narratives of location'. Although several other narratives displayed similar features, not all the interviewees who could structurally be located within the (new) middle classes framed their experiences in such highly meaningful ways. The analysis thus shall not be misconstrued as claiming that members of such social strata generally present their clubbing experiences as 'identity projects'. It does not delve into the questions as to who would typically design such types of narrative and why.

As outlined above, this comparative analysis seeks to describe a particular type of narrating clubbing experiences, in which they were framed as identity projects. This involved various identity *themes* and accentuated individual development, agency, achievement, learning and mastery. In the cases discussed here, this included the (autodidactic) acquisition of artistic and creative skills or other competences; processes of professionalization of these skills and the change of career perspectives; the aestheticization of the body through masquerade, dance or sexual experimentation; love and romance; psychological self-realization and authenticity (as in coming-out stories); the achievement of insider or 'stardom' status on the clubbing scene; or the productive transformation of aspects considered as problematic such as intensive drug consumption. Before delving into more detailed analysis, the four cases shall briefly be introduced first, in terms of their social and family backgrounds and their trajectory in social space as delineated in their narratives; second, in terms of the biographical contexts of the involvement in clubbing; and last, in terms of the general configuration of continuity and change and the identity project(s) they designed.

Chuck: Transformation and Reformation

At the time of the interview Chuck was in his late thirties. He had been brought up in a fairly affluent middle-class Catholic family in a wealthy area outside London. But, due to the divorce of his parents during his teens he experienced, as he depicted it, a sudden decline in wealth. Another side-effect of this family crisis was that he 'went a bit off the rails' (Chuck 2001: 15), and eventually dropped out of school shortly before his A-levels. Yet, he managed to find work in profitable businesses of the time where he earned good money. However, whilst working as a self-employed sales manager for a company selling computers, he ran into large debts. After having paid them off, he decided to drop out of his 'yuppie lifestyle' and went travelling to Australia, where he eventually settled down for a few years and got involved in dance culture and other cultural and social activities. After returning to England he started an art foundation course. However, within a year he found out that he 'was not going to make it as an artist' (ibid. 45) and subsequently changed to design education. During his stay in Australia Chuck began to explore his sexuality and labelled himself bisexual. His narrative delineated far-reaching transformations and took many unexpected turns, not only in terms of his sexual identity, but also with respect to his overall personal change from a late-1980s yuppie towards a post-materialistic attitude. Except for the initiation into rave and ecstasy culture that had taken place in England, the involvement in club culture was marked off as a sort of time-out experience during his stay in Australia. This period was related to several projects; first, a 'hedonist' phase of sex, drugs and clubbing; second, this led to work involvement in the dance-culture scene and other cultural and social initiatives. These work roles and the acquisition of artistic skills were central components of his narrative of self-realization. This was grounded in the responsibilities he had taken on within the dance-culture scene and other communities, but also acquired a more individualized meaning. The successful conversion of his artistic skills into institutionalized educational capital was part of his identity project which overall served to illustrate his personal 'reformation'.

Giselle: Alienation and Vocation

Giselle, who was in her mid-twenties at the time, had been raised in a less affluent, but culturally hybrid and geographically mobile middle-class family of continental European descent. Her parents were self-employed in the service sector in the East Anglian countryside. Giselle stressed how the misjudgement of her family as economically privileged incomers by Norfolk locals, contributed to her marginalization and distance from the rural working-class community. In her view, this social division also shaped her education in a local all-girls convent school and sixth-form college, both of which were mainly attended by middle-class kids. One or two years after her A-levels and a break in which she travelled and worked in agricultural production and social care, she started studying mathematics, but eventually switched to study dance at an academic institution in London. However, Giselle quit her studies before obtaining her degree and went back to East Anglia, where she took up social and factory work. When she was studying, Giselle came out as a lesbian. Giselle outlined two significant 'psychological' changes. These were first, her sexual coming-out, which led her to reinterpret and refashion her feminine identity; and second, a period of depression, in the course of which she gave up her dance studies. Overall, Giselle's narrative oscillated between continuity and change. Clinging on to romantic discourses of the vocation to become a dancer, she also stressed her desire to constantly 'reinvent' herself, to start new things and move to new places. While she was studying, Giselle got involved in clubbing. When she quit her dance studies and moved out of London, she also withdrew from clubbing. Her 'project' of clubbing was linked to sexuality on the one hand and to her aim of becoming a dancer on the other hand. Notably, her initial narrative was composed of a series of chronologically arranged experiences of going out dancing and clubbing. The nights out were processed and evaluated extensively, whereby clubbing appeared as a test ground for the self. Giselle evaluated her performance and enjoyment of particular nights and reworked these experiences into anticipations of future enactments in clubs. This indicated a high degree of reflexivity about the development of particular skills, roles, body looks and practices illustrating a 'learning mode to life' (Featherstone 1991: 90–92). Her withdrawal from clubbing and dance entailed a revaluation and questioning of (herself in) these action contexts and was followed by a new identity project.

Clare: Self-experimentation and Missionary Role

Clare, who was also in her mid-twenties when interviewed, traced an affluent middle-class origin, in her words, 'a privileged family background' (Clare 2000b: 32). Growing up in a quiet suburban area in South London, she attended an all-girls local school before going on to a prestigious boarding school outside London. Straight after school she went on to university to study English; however, not at a high-status university her secondary education would have prepared her for. Clare did not present the transition to university as a significant matter of personal deliberation. Her future career aspirations of becoming an environmental campaigner might not guarantee her a similar socioeconomic level as her parental background. Clare identified as heterosexual and was engaged at the time. Her narrative emphasized continuity throughout various transformations. In contrast to the two cases outlined above, she did not address changes at the psychological level. Instead, the changes she described merely appeared to accomplish what a certain model of heterofemininity requires, in that case marriage. The most significant change she described was the engagement with her boyfriend. Clare was involved in clubbing during the time of her secondary education and her university studies. Her 'real' clubbing, which she assigned to the past, was followed by her work involvement. This was portrayed as the fulfilment of her dream to become a dancer. She sketched her clubbing and dance work as a secret, unconventional dimension of her life that allowed for the occasional 'coming-out' of an alter ego running alongside her everyday life of education. This 'parallel' life did not lead to a reorientation as in Chuck's case; yet, clubbing too appeared as an all-encompassing lifestyle joining together work and leisure, friends and relationships. Informed by notions of stardom, Clare's identity project centred on her work as a dancer and on her playful experimentation with sexual roles. Her self-understanding as a dancer and how she positioned herself in relation to 'the crowd' were crucial elements in this regard. But clubbing was also linked to another life project—that of love and marriage. Her withdrawal from clubbing and from dance work, depicted as a slow fade-out, did not lead her to question her experiences or modes of participation as in Giselle's retrospect view, not least, because her boyfriend and fiancée was also part of her clubbing life.

Alex: Managing Excess and Control

At the time of the interview Alex was in his early forties and was cohabiting with his partner. Originally from a North London working-class background, he was working as a primary school teacher. This upwardly mobile trajectory differed from the other three cases. Alex did not focus on his life history in much detail, but he mentioned that he had identified as a punk, played in a punk band and had worked, amongst other jobs, as a cat-walker, strip dancer and actor before arriving at the 'respectable' career of a teacher. He had always lived in London and finished his university degree in his thirties. Alex identified as gay and had lived in several relationships before, some of them long-term. Similar to Giselle and Chuck he expressed change in his life strongly in terms of psychological progress. His relationship at the time was relatively new and initiated a re-interpretation of, and demarcation from, his 'previous self' and the relationships it had experienced. The crisis caused by a nervous breakdown was also evaluated as progress because of the therapeutic change it instigated. However, Alex did not unfold a story of biographical development from past to present, but mainly concentrated on his present life and only briefly cast spots into the past. This synchronic mode of self-introspection centred on ethical and moral questions with respect to clubbing. Clubbing was not narrated as a past activity rather than as a regular weekend routine of relaxation together with his boyfriend. This evoked the image of conspicuous, excessive consumption, but at the same time the problematization of clubbing was more pronounced than in the other narratives. Although Alex certainly experienced clubbing as biographically meaningful—he met his partner on the Millennium night—he did not present it as having achieved or completed a project. The narrative of romantic love, his contemplation about relationships and psychological development, as well as his attempts to make ethical aims and moral norms compatible and to harmonize the different spheres and activities of life came closest to such a project.

IDENTITY PROJECTS IN THE CONTEXT OF CLUBBING

In the following parts I shall discuss and compare these cases in more detail focusing on the particular themes that were addressed in these identity projects: first, work roles in clubbing; second, dance and sexuality; third, romantic love and relationships; finally, I shall highlight an example of an identity project that arose from the problematization of, and the withdrawal from, clubbing. The various themes are closely related and overlap, yet, each of the sections will feature certain cases so as to be able to discuss the identity projects in the context of the respective case.

Skills, Competences, Professionalization

As has been argued, over the past two decades micro-economies of culture including popular and club cultures have become increasingly important as alternative labour markets that offer opportunities to eke out a living (McRobbie 1999a, 1999b). Work in the clubbing, music and party sector is frequently construed as a harmonization of work and enjoyable leisure, underpinned by discourses of self-enhancement and creativity (du Gay 1996, McRobbie 1999 #896: 148). The following examples demonstrate that work involvement in dance culture indeed serves as a basis for narratives of artistic or creative self-realization. In actual practice, however, work in a bar or a club is slightly less romantic. Given the variety of work roles within such contexts, not all involve (only) creativity, but are often as dull and monotonous as other jobs in the service industry. A closer look at the working conditions in the night-time economy (in more detail see Chapter 3) indicates a high degree of casual, informal, part-time work or self-employment with payments often below the minimum wage adding up to a supplementary income at best. The possibility of creative activity sometimes comes at the cost of long hours and exploitation. Although employment in these economies traverses the boundaries of class, ethnicity and gender, social position still defines different opportunities in the dance and music industry (e.g. music production and DJing is still a male domain). Gender (and possibly class) also provides scripts for the meanings derived from such work.

In contrast to these rather mundane aspects of work in clubs, the work experiences narrated in the interviews discussed here evoked notions of self-realization and creativity. Work roles were framed either as a responsible position within a collective; or as artistic practices; or as a mission; or as personal development and fulfilment. Crucially, they are everything else but a job.

Chuck's narrative offers some illustration of these points. Beginning with the story of his first clubbing experience, his narrative was structured by the theme of loss and gain. In the late 1970s, at the time of the crisis around the divorce of his parents, Chuck attended soul parties of the African-Caribbean community in his town. In an acrobatic frenzy of human pyramid building, people were trying to get as high as possible, before it collapsed and passed into nothing. This sense of taking part in a community context contrasted with the enterprising self that he sketched in relation to his first work experiences in computer business several years later.[8] As he pointed out, in his early twenties he was an

> archetypal yuppie in as much that my only goal was my career and making lots of money, and I really didn't give a shit about anybody else apart from my family. (Chuck 2001: 12)

Yet, the culture of the company he worked for and the lifestyle of his colleagues hardly corresponded with the ideal of Thatcherite enterprise-culture at the time. Instead of a morality of responsibility and hard work that was to curtail the utilitarian individualism, these 'enterprising' selves engaged in conspicuous consumption, excessive alcohol drinking and, as for Chuck, ran up debts. The freedom of consumption was also conjured up in his stories about the hedonistic lifestyle of sex, drugs and clubbing in Australia at the beginning of the 1990s, in which the sovereign consumer had nearly disburdened himself of the duty to be productive. This lifestyle, set 'outside of' his world (ibid. 7), turned the routine of a 'normal' working life upside down. Indulging in a paradisiac permanent holiday, he was going out seven nights a week, getting up late, going for coffee at lunchtime, spending the afternoon on the beach and going out clubbing at night.

> We were having sit-ins and love-ins and some of these events were, for me personally were, they were great fun; they were great exploratory experiences, I mean, sexually and also, in the club world and in drugs . . . I was bisexual at that time and had ah, I had a girlfriend and two or three boyfriends and I was also working as a male prostitute, so I was having a lot of sex (laughs). (Chuck 2001: 7)

Yet, the earthly paradise did not come free. The exploratory experiences of sexuality and drug taking eventually opened up the opportunity to economic capitalization, enabling him, as a non-legalized immigrant in Australia, short of a work permit, to earn a living. To some extent, the enterprising-self awakened once again. He started to supply drugs to friends and others, without however, as he was at pains to point out, intending to accrue big profits. Prostitution likewise was portrayed less as work rather than as part of his lifestyle and his search for maximum sexual pleasure and fun. The third work involvement in the realm of clubbing though marks a transition from an enterprising self to an active citizen committed to the service of the dance community. Two Australians in their late thirties had accumulated a 'warehouse full of furniture, carpets and tables' (Chuck 2001: 8) to set up chill-out areas at parties and raves. As they withdrew from the dance scene, they handed over the equipment to Chuck with the mission to make good use of it for the community, 'to keep it going' (ibid. 9). Moreover, with this gift the responsibility of a heir was placed on Chuck. He was to preserve the equipment for the son of the friends who had given it to him. Through this new work involvement he experienced the 'spirit of collectivism' that gave him a lot of hope and further motivated him to engage in artistic practices. It was coupled with a notion of mastery as it helped him cut down on his drug consumption. Yet, Chuck also delineated his disillusion about the dance community. In the course of his involvement he came to realize that some party producers subordinated the collective purpose to their private business interests.[9] For some time he put up with the 'menace', the 'violence' and the 'ugly commercial side' (ibid. 11) of some promoters who withheld his pay, until his equipment got destroyed at a party. In this story the protagonist appeared as a failing enterprising-self, who had miscalculated the risks of this venture because of having been tempted to participate in the production of a large-scale party. In the further course of events, by acting responsibly for the community, he interfered with the promoter's private financial inter-est. This led to a big argument. Chuck's story accentuated how his care and engagement for collective interests also undermined his own interests and, moreover, were punished rather than rewarded. In addition, the breakdown of his individual business thwarted the mission assigned to him and disrupted the hereditary relationship. The story, therefore, sketched the failure to fulfil his responsibility on three counts: for himself as enterprising individual, for friends and family and for the dance community.

Despite his disillusionment about the lack of solidarity in the party business Chuck did not withdraw from it, but found new opportunities in other community-related contexts. After working for the Sydney Mardi Gras, he took up social work embarking on safety and information cam-paigns aimed at young people. At the same time he started to take part in clubbing as a consumer again. This phase—connected to a newly opened S&M club and marked once more as sexual exploration—designated a further transition. His (artistic) participation within the collective con-text of the dance scene assumed a new, more individualistic meaning: not at the service of a community, but aimed at making the people stare at *him* as a spectacular body and star. He described how he made 'really elaborate costumes' (ibid. 12) in order to be noticed and given a VIP pass and how he achieved public recognition in the magazines.

Similar to his introduction to clubbing, Chuck's decision to return home and to withdraw from the clubbing lifestyle was related to a family affair. In particular, it was initiated by his father's intervention.[10] After returning to the UK, Chuck reduced his clubbing to occasional visits, framing it from a similar, individualistic, if not therapeutic viewpoint. Clubbing, as he said, enabled him to balance his emotions, allowing for a certain outlook on the world. Overall, he evaluated clubbing for the impact it had on his psychological transformation: it had helped him open up to people, become less judgemental, build trust, and forgive and forget about problematic experiences of his life. Simon Reynolds pointed out that ecstasy and rave culture marked an end of the Thatcher-inculcated work ethic (1998: 47). But he also noted the continuity to Thatcherite politics in the 'rampant hedonism' of youth and dance culture, arguing that 'acid house's pleasure-principled euphoria was very much a product of the eighties: a kind of *spiritual materialism*, a greed for intense experiences' (ibid.). Chuck's narrative of the time-out period of clubbing, his exploration of drugs and sexuality and his eventual turn towards inward-oriented self-development very well illustrates this shift from materialism to the consumption of experiences.

Aestheticization of the Body

Both Giselle as well as Clare designed dancing (in clubs) as identity projects, albeit in different ways. The focus on dance as a central area of achievement and self-realization reflects a gendered discourse on the body and dance. Unlike studies which emphasized how clubbing participants drew from the energy of collective dancing in a crowd (Malbon 1999); these narratives accentuated an individualized notion of dance as an art form alluding to romantic tales of becoming a dancer. These unite images of luck as well as achievement, talent as well as hard work (McRobbie 1984, 1997a). Giselle, for example, constructed her passion for dancing as a feature of her character and a 'natural' predisposition. She marked significant beginnings of her dancing and history of going out at the ages of 6 and 9. In her narrative, dance was seen to express personality traits such as individuality, confidence, creativity and erotic power. It also appeared as a means of gaining recognition. As Giselle described her practices, dancing in a club wedded together dance as art form with the pursuit of sexual interests. Both the sexually charged, flirtatious aspect as well as the artistic, experimental aspect were evaluated in terms of the attention and recognition she gained. In contrast to Clare's project of sexual experimentation, for Giselle dancing in a club was part of her sexual identity project of successful (lesbian) cruising, in this case, of securing as many flirts as possible. Her self-image as a sort of femme fatale who optimized her choice and managed multiple contacts was textured by the freedom of consumption. However, in taking

into account the possible offence caused by her playful attitude and in setting moral limits to her flirting, she appeared self-critical and responsible.
The accentuation of agency in Giselle's account of sexual cruising in clubbing contrasted with the emphasis on the constraint of freedom, agency
and the opportunity of achievement. Constraint was a central theme in
her identity project of becoming a professional (art) dancer. She sketched
the ambivalence of, and the struggle between, the successful liberation and
expression of an 'authentic' self on the one hand and its repression and
constraint due to mechanisms of social closure in the dance institution
on the other hand. Giselle ascribed the lack of opportunity to realize her
vocation of dance to the body ideals and rigid norms in the dance world.
As, according to her, these body types are regarded as apparently natural,
unchangeable dispositions, not having a 'dancer's body' deprived her of
the chance of achievement. Her critical distance from the institutional culture of 'egocentrism', 'self-indulgence' and 'competition' was another reason that Giselle named for the inadequate achievement. Instead, because of
showing consideration for other people in the dance class, Giselle felt that
she had to constrain her movements in the class. As a result, her potential
for developing 'crazy', 'special', extravagant movements remained unreal-
ized and unacknowledged. Exclusion and marginalization, typical of new
cultural intermediaries (Lash and Urry 1987: 296; see also Rose 1999a:
268) were emphasized throughout Giselle's narrative and intricately linked
to her body and femininity. Her vocation to dance contrasted with her self-
perceived failure to pass as feminine. From her childhood onwards, Giselle
felt that her body was not seen as 'naturally' feminine, but as a body to
be worked at in order to become more feminine. Body height and weight,
ways of walking and sitting, were targets of her mother's regime of correc-
tion and monitoring. Referring to her partly French background, Giselle
described how she was taught 'feminine' comportment by her mother. Since
her childhood Giselle's body was marked as 'clumsy', 'messy' and 'tall', but
all the same she was encouraged to develop her performance skills and was
sent to dance training.

Against the marked deficiencies of femininity, Giselle posed her preco-
cious accomplishments of femininity. She related this image-consciousness
and insecurity to her parents' concern with look and their view of children
as 'products'. As Beverley Skeggs noted, 'the appearance of women, via
their lack of/or associations with femininity, is often the means by which
class becomes read as embodied' (2000: 133). In Giselle's narrative femininity was doubly coded; it appeared as the source of exclusion and difference
on the one hand and as a vehicle of distinction to lay claim to middle-class
identity on the other hand.[11] The problematization of femininity illustrated
the experience of incompatible spheres with contradictory values. Both the
lack of, as well as the association with, femininity were constructed as a
cause for social marginalization, either in the dance class or within lesbian
scenes (see also Chapter 8).

While this conflictive reading of femininity constrained Giselle's identity projects, Clare's identity projects built on and affirmed heterosexual femininity. Clare's story of how she became a dancer similarly alluded to a romantic discourse, combining notions of talent and natural predisposition with notions of work and achievement. Although the naturalization of dance as an element of feminine disposition undermines the acknowledgement of it as skill and work, Clare affirmed agency and achievement in her identity project despite appearing as a rather passive agent in some of her stories. Having fulfilled her desire to become a dancer, Clare conceived of the clubbing sphere as a utopian egalitarian world (McRobbie 1984: 135), which bestowed recognition of talent even though she did not have an 'ideal' dancer's body. Her role as a dancer in clubs oscillated between the notion of work on the one hand and artistic expression and sexual experimentation on the other hand.[12] Clare was involved in different types of dance work including fetish clubs, table-dancing clubs and podium dancing in clubbing and at festivals. Clare presented her dancing as part of a secret, naughty and adventurous dimension of herself and also defended her dance work, especially the table dancing, against preconceptions of immorality and lack of respectability. In addition, she accounted for her dance work (on the clubbing scene) as socially valuable. This understanding of her role as a dancer may be traced back to her secondary education. The boarding school she had attended had combined the academic education of a 'social elite' with a 'life-world' education of socially responsible citizens. It conveyed values of confidence, hard work, self-discipline and leadership along with values of art, creativity, self-development and consideration for less-privileged people. Apart from the academic subjects the syllabus also comprised of art and theatre work, environmental and service work for the community.

Clare had not intended to become a dancer in fetish clubs, but when meeting the agent of the Fetish Band through a friend, she was 'found and selected' on the spot.[13] The agent had asked her in a kind of set-up test situation to try on a fetish outfit and proved her apt to perform. This was when her interest in fetish was awakened. She endorsed the view that fetish dancing fulfilled her personal interest in wearing fetish outfits, but she drew the line at practicing it sexually. Similar to Chuck, the fetish dance-work oscillated between a profession and a lifestyle. It was connected to socializing with other members of the Fetish Band and went along with an exploratory attitude towards sexuality and drugs. The performances meant to express this lifestyle and attitude:

> . . . the dancing is very important, but it's also the image that we project. (Clare 2000a: 3)

Taking on a work role in clubbing appeared as a process of maturation, growing up and achievement of celebrity status on the clubbing scene. Discourses of stardom, as Richard Dyer (1979: 43) noted, construct the star as ordinary and special character, as one of the crowd, yet different. Accordingly, Clare set herself apart from the crowd. As somebody who added atmosphere to a club night, she thought she should be allowed free entrance to clubs even if not working. Instead of dancing with the crowd, she felt the stage was the right space for her extravagant freestyle dancing.

> When I'm dancing on the dance floor I feel as though I'm out of context, because I don't dance like normal people dance, normal people just repeat their movements . . . I'm doing all this crazy stuff and I require, I demand quite a lot of space. (Clare 2000a: 24)

Clare mediated leadership and egalitarianism also by speaking on behalf of the ordinary customer and sketching out her policies as the would-be mayor of clubbing, proposing that everyone should be allowed in free to clubs. She justified her prominent position and attention-seeking as part of her professional role, which would require being outstandingly crazy and creative. The narcissistic gain of being watched and noticed was vindicated by pointing to the reciprocity of her dancing. She viewed herself as part of the youth-cultural elite and as a role model who was embarking on the mission to encourage and inspire female clubbers. She also wished to open up people's minds, for example, by staging bisexuality in her dancing. The leadership image, however, involved the commitment to professionalism and excellence in return for the privilege to perform on stage. On the one hand this articulated work ethic and emotional labour; on the other hand, the work aspect was overlaid by a notion of voluntary care for the audiences.

> I have done my job, if I am being noticed by people to take pictures, then I am doing my job properly . . . I somehow find it quite egotistical when I describe it . . . but I don't do it so that people will think I am great, I do it to make them happy. (Clare 2000b: 50)

Similarly, Clare likened her work as a table dancer with the role of a psychiatrist, who listened to the problems of clients. By contrast, Yong, who also understood himself as a transmitter of messages and moods and framed his role through notions of leadership and stardom, conjured up images of masculinity and sexual potency (see Chapter 5). Clare repeatedly emphasized her dance role, especially in the fetish clubs, as personal fulfilment. The downsides of it as a 'job' were mentioned less explicitly and related to podium dancing. This type of dancing involved choreographed sets and therefore was a fairly routinized job compared to the freestyle dancing and partying lifestyle in the fetish clubs. It involved more emotional labour than fun, also because she worked in clubs that did not match her personal taste. Clare called them 'meat market' clubs and associated them with aggressive and abusive behaviour of the audience (Claire 2000a: 6).

As for the identity projects of Yong and Clare, another difference is to be noted. For Yong DJing was the first step of his professional ambitions in cultural and creative production. He intended to acquire other artistic skills and to eventually become a film director. Clare's club dancing, by contrast, did not pave the way for further professionalization of her artistic or creative skills. Instead she kept it separate from her official career path and planned on partly replacing her dance work with a day job after graduation. She only considered taking up a managerial role in the entrepreneurial activities of her fiancé, a gym trainer, whom she envisaged setting up a business as a dance agent for clubs. Nevertheless, dance work was a core element of Clare's narrative of achievement. It supported a general optimistic outlook on her ability to realize other aspirations alike.

> As things have been turning out so far, a few years ago I wished to be a dancer and now I am; when I started my degree, I wished to get a two-one and now I have one, so. Hopefully, I will get into . . . [= environmental NGO, S.R.]. (Clare 2000b: 52)

While working as a dancer in a club was everything *but* a job for Clare, Sally, who worked for the same agencies and did the same types of dance work, framed it as a simple job. A mother in her early twenties living in South London, she had started dance work after having worked as a dental assistant for one year. She first started table dancing before getting involved in dance clubs. Her dance work was a more or less enjoyable job that helped her earn an additional income.

> It wasn't very interesting at all, it was just a way of getting money every week to go out and get mashed up at the weekend. (Sally 2000: 14)

Sally mentioned her dance work in her narrative, but unlike Clare did not make it a central theme. As she said, 'there is not really much to tell about that' (Sally 2000: 16). According to her, it was merely by chance and luck that she was 'at the right place at the right time' and got involved in dance work (ibid. 16). For her the Fetish Band was neither a lifestyle nor connected to personal fulfilment, transformation or achievement. Although she enjoyed performing on stage and the attention from the crowd, and even though she stressed the biographical relevance of her involvement in the clubbing scene—it had incited the relationship with the father of her child (see Chapter 5)—she did not present this as self-realization.

> For me the Fetish Band is a big act, a big act to go on stage with a bit; it's not something that I take home with me. It's something purely for the stage . . . it's all pretend for me, all fiction, not really true. (Sally 2000: 17–18)

Even though Sally and Clare both did the same jobs for the same agencies, their understanding of their role as a club dancer differed markedly. Clare's narrative contained certain moments of dis-identification and dissociation: on the one hand, against conventional, middle-class ways of life and heterofemininity; on the other hand, against sexualized, commercial 'meat market' clubs. She aimed for an innovative framing of gender identity through the aestheticized experimentation with a sexualized clubbing lifestyle, trying to overcome conventional models without, however, becoming associated with disreputable images of femininity.

Love and Romance

Research studies suggested that rave and ecstasy culture had made manifest a shift in gender relations and, in particular, signalled a transformation of predatory male behaviour in clubs (e.g. Pini 2001; see also Chapter 7). It was argued that for women taking part in rave culture, dancing and socializing gained priority over romantic or sexual encounters (for example Measham et al. 2001: 31). Nevertheless clubs still are perceived as contexts where potential (sexual) partners can be met (Mintel 1996: 29), and discourses of romance continue to shape the scripting of clubbing experience. In fact, several interviewees related a romantic relationship that was sparked off in this context. In the following, Clare's narrative of romantic love shall be compared with a similar narrative provided by Alex. Clare's account of the relationship and engagement with her partner was intricately linked to her identity project as a dancer. Not only was her boyfriend a club dancer himself, but he also brought her in touch with other dance agencies. The relationship therefore extended to the work sphere. They started to dance together; they made their costumes together and performed as a couple. Moreover, her boyfriend was cast as a 'rescuer', as the relationship instigated her withdrawal from drug taking and table dancing. In this respect, the narrative of love was interwoven with the narrative of mastery. The relationship not only constituted the kernel of her overall story of success, but it also justified the sexually experimental fetish dance-work. The classic heterofeminine romance narrative culminating in engagement and the prospect of marriage was thereby spiced up with a spark of unconventionality. The story of the engagement ritual conjured up Hollywood fairytales. It took place on the Millennium night when both Clare and her boyfriend were performing in a club. Her boyfriend surprised her with his proposal on stage at the climax of the night. This story articulated a very mixed capacity to act (agency). On the one hand, Clare appeared as a rather passive agent. The action context that was created by others almost forced her into a certain role.[14] On the other hand, she appeared as a star; she was not only a centre of attention, but also the integral part of the Millennium event. Despite this 'actively passive' role and the moments of luck that Clare sketched in her narrative, it also expressed a strong sense of achievement (for example, in her successful seduction of her would-be boyfriend; see Chapter 5).

As this example demonstrates, narratives of romantic love often bring coincidental elements, events, times, objects and people into meaningful, symbolic relationships with each other. Such stories also conjure up notions of authenticity and self-realization. Alex' narrative, similar to Clare, evoked the symbolic connection of a particular with something general. The turn of the Millennium night coincided with a significant change in his life marked by the beginning of a romantic relationship. Alex was waiting for something special to happen on the Millennium night. However, he did not actively search for it; but instead, a possible object of desire appeared by chance.

> I walked in and I saw him, and that was it (claps his hands). I was like, 'I want to be with him.' (Alex 2000: 3)

At this point Alex started to actively pursue his object of desire by inviting his future boyfriend to join him to another club night. In the following course of events the protagonist, as a consequence of heavy drug-taking, lost control and passed out. Similar to Clare, his to-be boyfriend looked after him and became his 'rescuer', which initiated the romance. Alex' narratives about his experiences with relationships came close to an identity project as defined at the beginning. His reflections on previous relationships and his psychological progress connoted a sense of learning and achievement. But the allusion to achievement was offset by luck and coincidence and the constraint of agency. Alex sketched a rather provisional picture of his transformation worrying about 'slipping back' into his 'old self' (ibid. 15) and that he was trapped in self-perpetuating structures of behaviour. His narrative conveyed the 'coming to terms' with, and control of, his emotional burdens rather than achievement. Although he talked about self-development, Alex did not measure or relate this development against desired goals of becoming. In contrast to the identity projects discussed above, he did not integrate his clubbing experiences into a narrative of progress. Instead, the main thematic concern of his talk was how to integrate partly conflicting values and principles of night life and day life. Despite also conveying a sense of achievement the following quote demonstrates this emphasis on integration and harmonization.

> I've got my job, I've got my love and I've got my life. (Alex 2000: 24)

Yet, in harmonizing different roles and areas of life Alex was also anxious about possible incongruities. Indulgence in pleasure and hedonism was to be balanced by social responsibility and a commitment to duty. Alex' consumption of club culture did not involve the use of time in order to accumulate (sub-)cultural capital by developing artistic abilities and professions, but rather appeared as a ritual of excess and expenditure of time (Lash and Urry 1994: 58). However, this expenditure of time in weekend rows of clubbing and drug taking was to be managed and controlled. On the one hand, clubbing figured as a practice of relaxation providing for a temporary distantiation from daily routines; on the other hand, the disruption of time routines caused unease. Unlike Chuck, who glorified the liberation from daily routines of work during his stay in Australia, Alex disapproved of the reversal of day and night time-structures. His narrative sketched a struggle between the night-life consumer, who tended to forget the duty of work, and the working and day-time self, who was to set limits to night-time enjoyment. Overall, his involvement in dance culture appeared as a source of moral concern in as much as it was inscribed with pleasure.

THE PROBLEMATIZATION OF CLUBBING AND NEW IDENTITY PROJECTS

Both this as well as the previous chapter highlighted the ethical ambivalence manifest in the interviewees' accounts of clubbing experience. For example, while Clare depicted the Fetish Band as an action context of personal fulfilment, she also described it as overwhelming and absorbing. Talking about her worthy identity projects of work and relationship balanced what she perceived as problematic aspects of her drug consumption. Despite stressing the pleasant sides, Chuck, Alex and Clare, as well as other interviewees, also critically reflected on excessive consumption, mainly in relation to drugs and time. Narrative identity projects emphasized the ethical merit of clubbing in the light of its problematic sides. They constituted a justificatory structure proving that clubbing, instead of being a meaningless, superficial or escapist activity, as critical views of mass and popular culture would imply, has ethical value. Some identity projects, however, also emerged as a result of withdrawing from clubbing. Giselle's turn to a new project, for example, was based on a self-critique of her dancing, clubbing and flirting 'obsessively'. Giselle associated these practices with an other-directed decoration of herself with mere images, similar to the construction of femininity through the creation of looks. These practices, once signifying authentic self-realization, were ironicized as inauthentic in retrospect. She re-directed the ethical aim of authenticity to her 'inner self'. She said that she needed to work 'from the inside out' rather than from the outsice in (Giselle 2001: 80).[15] After quitting her studies in the final year due to severe health problems, Giselle moved back to East Anglia, started to work in agricultural production, began to write prose and poetry and to explore other creative skills. Similar to her accounts of clubbing, the move to East Anglia was narrated as an identity project linked to certain goals. She conjured up the image of a writer in the countryside, living at a distance from the local people, 'who are really much in their own culture' (ibid. 73). Giselle's writer self, similar to Clare's dancer self, was designed as a missionary role of instilling progressive ideas and worldviews into rural culture. Correspondingly, her farming work appeared not to be driven by economic necessity, but was idealized as a learning practice and immersion in the local community and culture, much like an experiential and existential mode of tourism (Hetherington 1998: 117). She took a semi-permanent exile from her culture and consciously exposed herself to a context in which she had always felt alien. This new identity project was linked to a therapeutic reworking of past place identities and class identity. In a way, the romance of nature and the aestheticization of the countryside replaced the romance of dance (Urry 1990: 100).[16] Although Giselle's narrative did not evoke the discourse of stardom, this post-materialist, ascetic form of justification, symbolized in the image of a 'rebel' type of 'independent woman' and bohemian déclassé, clang on to such discourses (Dyer 1979: 52, 54).

In summarizing the discussion of these case studies, which narrated clubbing as identity projects, Clare's narrative demonstrated individualistic optimism. Her involvement in the clubbing sphere enabled her, amongst other things, to extend her role repertoire. The change that she sketched was brought on the way through the mastery of problematic aspects and appeared as the unconventional fulfilment of a heterofeminine script of romance and marriage. Chuck's time-out experience in the Australian clubbing and dance scene led to a permanent transformation, stressing the discontinuity of identity. It recalled Christian plot structures of reformation and salvation. Giselle similarly stressed transformation and reformation. However, her story outlined the failure of her identity projects connected to dancing and clubbing. The dis-authentication of her 'clubbing self' and the reorientation to new projects embodied what could be called an ethical asceticism. Alex' account merged an ethics of pleasure with moral concerns. Clubbing was portrayed as pleasurable and problematic at the same time and was carefully balanced by a morality of duty and responsibility in relation to work and family. All the four narratives were embedded in discourses of freedom, and predominantly alluded to freedom as autonomy and choice, especially with regards to sexuality or drugs, followed by notions of mastery, in relation to the withdrawal from drug taking. Giselle, Chuck and Alex' accounts were partly framed by a coming-out narrative. It became clear that each narrative raised ethical and moral issues in relation to the involvement in clubbing culture. In Alex' case this problematization was most pronounced and explicit in the ambivalence of pleasure and concern. While similar anxieties were also articulated in the other narratives, their mode of ethical justification was to present them as having been mastered, emphasizing agency, transformation and achievement.

CONCLUSION

In Chapter 4 I argued that aestheticization could be conceived of as a construction of play-realities. This realm of play implied a disruption of sameness identity (Ricoeur 1991) through identificatory practices of acting 'as-if', e.g. as in playful roles and masks that involve the idealization of the desired other, the staging as other (dissimulation), or the miming of other (simulation). As this chapter demonstrated, the desirable transformations and identifications provided for the possibility of being designed as identity projects. These retrospectively framed the involvement in club culture as an achievement of (apparently pre-existing goals of) self-realization and self-transformation. However, participation in clubbing could also entail transformations that were perceived to tip over to the problematic side and therefore needed to be held in check and justified. Chapter 5 pointed to the gendered modes of ethical justification indicated by the varying tendencies to either 'ironicize' (see Chapter 4, Pollner 1987) experiences of clubbing or to accentuate their transformative outcomes. The analysis of this chapter indicates that aestheticization in contexts of clubbing might also be textured by class. In particular, it suggested that the narration of clubbing experiences as an identity project revealed traits of the habitus of the new middle classes. For example, their identification with a border zone of legitimate culture was mobilized as a resource, and problematic elements were re-interpreted as learning experiences and forms of mastery. To some extent this implied a perception of clubbing as a devalued realm of popular culture along the lines of the high–low culture hierarchy, connoting, for example, passivity, escapism and hedonism, loss of control, dependency and lack of meaning. While some moulded their experiences into worthy identity projects, others distanced themselves from their clubbing past or present by belittling their experiences. The symbolic dissociation from, and the ambivalent relation to, amusement echoed not only images of mass culture, but also the gendered, classed (and raced) character of this discourse, threatening certain social groups, more so than others, with immoralization.

7   Between Style and Desire
Sexual Scenarios in Clubbing Magazines

Club and night life, as well as youth music cultures, play a crucial role in the wider social processes in which gender and sexual identities are reproduced, modified or transformed. This is rarely taken into account in the mainstream of gender studies research, but regularly emphasized by scholars focusing on the study of youth culture (e.g. Frith 1978), frequently interested in charting images, meanings and modes of conduct that depart from dominant values and moralities. Rave, club and night-life cultures in Britain too were seen to manifest, or even contribute to, the reconfiguration of heterosexuality and heteronormativity. Researchers stressed the emergence of new sexual codifications, the weakening of the divide between straight and gay scenes and the liberating ambience that opened up the possibility of enjoying 'erotic pleasures beyond sexual boundaries' (Pini 2001: 164–165, McRobbie 1994, A. Bennett 2001: 134, Measham et al. 2001: 56). It was argued that in rave culture gender relations assumed a more equal character shifting away from the 'sex market' ambience and predatory male behaviour of earlier discotheques, bars and clubs. This was seen as liberating and empowering particularly for women (e.g. Pini 2001, A. Bennett 2001). Other works on British clubbing scenes pointed to the sexualization of urban night life in the last years with a rising number of fetish, S&M, naked nights and sex clubs emerging on the night-life scene. The diverse aspects of sexual experience—the search for sex, the public expression of sexuality, the play with sexual characters and roles, the participation in sexual communities and the exploration of new forms of eroticism and desire in sexually charged environments—were all invoked as central elements of clubbing (P. Jackson 2004: 35).

This can be seen in the context of a wider 'sexualization of culture' (Attwood 2006), i.e. the preoccupation with sexual values, practices and identities; a more permissive attitude and the disintegration of moral consensus about sexuality; a proliferation of sexual texts, discourses and imagery in the mass media and the public fascination with sex scandals and moral panics; the destabilization of clearly marked sexual categories and identities and, overall, the intensification of mediation and virtualization, which blurs the boundary between the real and the representational, the act and the image (Plummer 1995: 137, Attwood 2006: 81). Gay and queer night-life cultures too are claimed to have had a considerable impact in the sexualization of clubbing (Chatterton and Hollands 2003: 118, Buckland 2002, P. Jackson 2004). However, scepticism prevails among cultural analysts reflecting on the mainstreaming of gay villages, who argue that this reinforces heteronormative and homonormative constructions of gender and sexuality. These analyses all seem to concur in the view that the growing appeal of gay lifestyle marks the fetishization of only particular segments of gay culture enforcing a 'new homonormativity' (Duggan 2002) whilst other segments become more marginalized. Gay space was also seen to become '(re-)heterosexualized' (Bell and Binnie 2004; Skeggs, Moran, Tyrer, and Binnie 2004b; Casey 2004: 453). Although sexualized night-life landscapes are generally more accepting of a plurality of life-forms and sexual practices (Chatterton and Hollands 2003), these analyses stressed that heteronormative structures continue to exist.

The 'mainstreaming' of gay and queer sexualities was not only explored at spatial levels. Much debate in recent years concentrated on the political significance of the increasing representation of previously marginalized sexualities in the media and in popular visual culture. As mentioned above, the sexualization of culture is intricately linked to the sexualization of the mass media, advertising, the Internet and popular culture. A whole new way of understanding and practicing sexuality has been opened up by the internet challenging 'the essentializing of the self and of sexuality' (Ross 2005: 342, Slater 1998). The representation of sex and sexuality generally is a core element in the marketing of lifestyle magazines, popular music videos and CDs, films, celebrities and branded products (Reichert 2003) as well as in the marketing of clubbing. Sexuality appears in various television formats (e.g. advertising, drama, documentary) and in a range of discursive and visual forms. Magazines too, especially lifestyle magazines addressing men or women, make extensive use of discourses and imagery related to sexuality. This includes the representation of same-sex eroticism, homo- or bisexuality as new and eye-catching content. Popular drama on Western television quite frequently includes peripheral gay characters, but recent years saw the launch of TV series such as *The L Word* or *Queer as Folk* featuring mainly gay protagonists and their night-life spaces (Manchester's gay village, respectively Pittsburgh in the US version of *Queer as Folk* and the lesbian scene L.A. in *The L Word*). However, same-sex desire is not always approved of in the mass media. Women's magazines such as *New Woman* and *Essence*, for example, cast homosexual inclinations of women as a normal element of heterosexuality, but problematize male bisexuality as a threat to the heterosexual couple (Gadsden 2002). Male homosexuality also figures as the abject other in men's magazines that promote a 'New Lad' iconography of heterosexual promiscuity and drinking (Edwards 2003). Even when constructed as normal and tolerable, the visibility of gay or queer sexualities is ambivalent as it risks fetishization and a colonialist appropriation of the other (Phelan 1993).

The analyses of this and the following chapter take a closer look at the (re-)configuration of gender and sexuality in club cultures. Unlike other studies which tend to exclusively focus on certain sexual sub-scenes (Buckland 2002, Whittle 1994, Lewis and Ross 1995, Pini 1997), attention shall be put on the relational nature of sexual boundaries and identities on the clubbing and night-life scenes in London. This chapter concentrates on the role of sexuality in the marketing and mediation of clubbing. Just as a considerable amount of pop music, clubbing too is sold via the spectacularization of sexuality, which helps signify it as a site of transgression, playful experimentation and self-transformation. Club cultures are sustained by a range of media providing promotion, information and communication platforms, a large part of which is internet-based, but complemented by printed magazines, posters and flyers. Magazines, in particular, figure as mediums for the distribution of free music samples; they pick up and help codify clubbing slang, and they shape classifiers for music genres, dance styles or modes of behaviour. The subsequent discussion centres on the visual representation of sexuality in printed clubbing magazines. However, rather than a comprehensive content analysis, it offers a close reading of a certain subset of visual scenarios.[1] The selection of these scenarios was guided by the analytical question in what ways the representation of sexuality challenged or reconfigured the implicit heteronormativity of these magazines.

The analysis is based on two mainstream clubbing magazines in the period between 1999 and 2001. Unlike other clubbing-related magazines at the time, these magazines, *Mixmag* and *Ministry*, included reviews and photographic coverage of a range of UK clubbing spaces. The strong presence of a sexually charged imagery places them in the sexual-political economy of mass media and magazines described above. Yet, they also differed from other media representations. Although they presented forms of sexual and erotic expression previously marginalized or stigmatized as deviant, they did not prominently feature gay, lesbian, bisexual and transgender/transsexual night-life and clubbing scenes themselves. For example, they challenged the ideal of monogamous heterosexual coupledom by presenting images of female hypersexuality, promiscuity and same-sex eroticism. In addition, scenarios of drag seemed to suggest a playful confrontation of the notion of natural gender differences. The question arises as to whether or not the representation of these constructions of gender and sexuality unfolds similar dynamics as in other media contexts and in what relation these are placed to heterosexuality. As said above, the analysis does not chart a general picture of the role of sexuality in the visual representation of clubbing, but focuses on specific scenarios that appeared repeatedly and regularly in two magazines over a certain period of time. *Ministry* no longer exists, and *Mixmag* has somewhat changed its design and editorial tone since (see below). Yet, in their recurring mode, these scenarios stand for typified forms of representation that are, to some extent, also to be found in other media contexts of the past and present and thus warrant closer investigation, even though they may not (or no longer) amount to a typical or general feature neither of these nor of other clubbing magazines.

At the time, *Mixmag* and *Ministry* were two of several clubbing magazines on the British market. Based in London and reporting mainly from the British clubbing scene, these magazines were also available internationally. They combined photographic and textual coverage of past events, information and listing of future events, reviews of music and fashion and features with celebrity and upcoming DJs. Other magazines such as *Muzik* (1995–2003) and *DJ* (1991–) by contrast, catered for a predominantly male audience with special interests in music, technology and DJing. According to an audience poll of December 2007, *DJ*, also London-based, is mainly read by men, many of them single and working, for instance, as DJs or promoters in the music industry. *Mixmag* magazine was launched in 1982 as a black-and-white dance music magazine and was acquired by independent publishers Development Hell Ltd in December 2005. *Ministry*, its closest competitor, was also a monthly music magazine that belonged to the Ministry of Sound Group (see also Chapter 3) and ran from January 1998 through to December 2002. In the late 1990s the contents of these magazines were aligned to an audience primarily based in the UK, drawn from 18- to 25-year-olds who attended branded, well-renowned clubbing events and large-capacity clubs throughout the country. These audiences possibly had a greater share of female readers than the aforementioned magazines. *Mixmag* was relaunched in 2006 as a more upmarket style magazine with a stronger emphasis on fashion, aiming to address a wider and slightly older readership rather than the young, committed, hard-core clubber. According to its website, its certified circulation in the past few years has been in the range of 40,000 and its estimated readership is at 276,000. Apart from *M8* magazine (1988–), which lies in the range of 30,000 sales and also offers global coverage of club and dance culture, *Mixmag* is still the most well-known mainstream magazine in the UK[2] complemented by smaller magazines catering for different market niches (e.g. *Upfront*, *Knowledge Magazine*, *Sleeve*). In addition, there is an uncountable number of e-zines, websites and forums, supported by directories and content suppliers; however, an increasing amount of web contents or newsletters is reserved to the exclusive use of subscribers. In varying degrees, clubbing-related websites function as formats designed for advertising and online shopping (see also Chapter 3). More content-based websites as well as magazines usually centre on reviews, club and music features, and event listings. Photo galleries are a typical feature of magazines, e-zines as well as club websites. They differ in style and emphasis, ranging from portraits of individual participants (by the majority females), groups of friends, outrageous costumes, DJs and the crowd. By including images of 'ordinary' members of the clubbing scenes, the magazines bestow public recognition and symbolic capital. While homosocial bonding and physical closeness amongst males and females are a regular element of photographic representations, the imagery of the clubbing magazines (e.g. *Mixmag*) is less sexually charged than in the previous years. The representation of female same-sex eroticism, too, has been toned down. Such imagery, however, continues to be found on the websites of clubs that provide sexualized environments, for example, fetish clubs.

Heteronormativity regulates sexuality and gender through the institutionalization of heterosexuality as the privileged norm via the exclusion of abject others. This norm however, can be expressed in various ways allowing, to a certain extent, for desires and practices that cross its boundaries (J. Butler 1993). Heteronormativity is constituted and remade at a number of levels: the structural, the level of meaning, through everyday practices and routines, and through individuals' conceptions of heterosexual identity (S. Jackson 2006: 108). The following analysis considers two of these levels: first, the level of meaning by reflecting on the visual scenarios of the magazines, and second, the level of subjective understanding of sexuality and identity. A link shall be made between the analysis of visual representation and the reading of actual spaces and practices by social actors. The visual scenarios open up particular interpretive repertoires and modes of (self-)recognition. More specifically, they disrupt, institute or maintain norms of intelligibility for conceiving of the relations between sex, gender, sexual practice and desire (J. Butler 1990: 17). They make available certain codes that orient the practical reading of spaces (Skeggs et al. 2004b: 1840–1841); for example, they specify requirements and practices of roles, and 'provide the understandings that make role entry, performance, and/ or exit plausible for both self and others' (Simon 1996: 40).[3] Such visual scenarios also imply certain regimes of symbolic value in selecting who and what should be made visible or not; they help establish notions of who and what is considered to be 'in' or 'out' of place. Hence, they are central for 'the processes through which people learn of their entitlement to different physical and social spaces' (Skeggs 1999: 214). In order to illustrate the affinity between the semiotic structures of the media scenarios and subjective self-understandings, the analysis is also supported with examples drawn from the interview data generated between 1998 and 2001 with participants of the London club scene (see introductory chapter). However, this by no means amounts to a systematic exploration as to how the media scenarios are transposed into people's forms of classification, let alone suggests a neat transfer between them. As Buckland quite rightly remarked, 'the sexual politics of representation are contested in clubs themselves' (Buckland 2002: 112). The iconography of the media is ambiguous and allows for different ways of decoding and re-interpretation. At the same time the interpretive repertoires of social actors are 'over-determined' in the sense that neither the particular scenarios nor the media in general can be seen as the only causal mechanisms at work.

Instead of merely supplying semiotic structures that, to some extent, orient participants' modes of symbolic classification and that codify certain roles and modes of conduct, the wider significance of these visual representations in the clubbing magazines lies in the emphasis on the performative. They shape performative understandings of identity and sexuality. As Polhemus noted, clubbing is a cruising through style-worlds, which turns practices into performative resources (1996). For example, fetish, once closely associated with certain forms of erotic desire of a minority of S&M-practicing people, was re-signified into a style that signifies glamour, outrageousness and campiness (ibid. 111). Similarly, other forms of sexual expression, as this analysis shall show, are affected by the re-signification of sexuality as a practice of aestheticization and self-fashioning through dress, masquerade and body performance. Sexuality is thereby thematized as a form of stylization oscillating between the expression of sexuality and its representation, between style and desire (Buckland 2002: 113–114). This bears similarities to the transfiguration of sexuality through the internet, in particular, the disassociation between doing and being that it affords by creating a space between fantasy and action. One can experiment with several sexual personae 'without actually being' (Ross 2005: 343). Investigating how the aestheticization of sexuality affects common-sense notions of the categories of gender and sexuality, I shall argue that, whilst evoking a notion of the fluid and plastic nature of sexuality, this does not automatically destabilize heteronormativity. In the particular context discussed here, non-heteronormative articulations of sexuality were designed as virtual scenarios to be claimed and disclaimed by a heterosexual audience. This created new forms of (playful, temporary) identification, but at the same time reinforced symbolic markers of heteronormative constructions of gender. Notably, the blurring of sexual identity boundaries was tied in with the naturalization of gender difference.

CLUBBING AS A SEXUALIZED SPECTACLE

As Hobbs et al. pointed out (Hobbs, Lister, Hadfield, Winlow, and Hall 2000: 712), contemporary British night-time economies rest on a 'structured provision for liminality'. They promise liminality by invoking a 'repertoire of liminal symbols' (ibid.) such as overt sexuality or inebriation. The representation of clubbing as a sexualized spectacle was at the heart of the media scenarios in the two magazines *Mixmag* and *Ministry*. Not only overt sexuality figured as a liminal symbol, but also the aestheticization of roles and practices once considered strange, exotic, weird, déclassé or perverse. Still coated by a whiff of otherness, they were presented as normal and acceptable at the same time (Simon 1996: 46). The imagery combined two discursive strands: on the one hand, a notion of the liberation of desire, and on the other hand, a liberal notion of choice and lifestyle. These refer respectively to a freedom of expression and the promised sovereignty of consumption (Rose 1999b). The liberatory strand evokes bohemian adventure, spontaneity and passion, resting on the belief that the truth of oneself resides in one's sexual being, in particular the transgressiveness of sexuality (Wilson 1999: 21). It is linked to the ethic of authenticity and a therapeutic narrative of freeing one's true desire, which appears as destiny. By contrast, the liberal strand highlights sexuality not as an ability to open up to one's repressed or quieted true potential, but presents it as a matter of choice, invention, stylization and performative self-construction.[4] Both these discursive threads emphasized the transformability of sexuality and sexual identity.

Inevitably, by thematizing sexuality, these scenarios also framed gender. In playing with and revaluing once-stigmatized articulations of femininity and masculinity, they reframed gender at the level of sexual or erotic enactment and stylization whilst reinforcing traditional markers of 'feminine' or 'masculine' look. They called for 'coming out' and acting out intimacies that used to be neither respectable nor desirable. Public performance or enactment in the nightclub appeared as the means to liberate one's most intimate desires. At the same time, this enactment was visualized as ambiguous and playful, if not mere ironic stylization. However, while sexual desire was cast as varied, fluid, ambiguous and playful, gender remained fixed as heteronormative, binary difference. The scenarios therefore evoked an ambiguous process of disrupting and re-fixing heteronormativity, through which non-heteronormative elements were incorporated into heterosexuality. Heterosexuality was assigned a hypertext of possible identifications with sexualities that were once constituted as its others. In this way, same-sex desire and other non-heteronormative elements could be aligned to the heteronorm by oscillating between 'real' and 'play'. It is precisely this ambiguity between authenticity and performative stylization which was codified in this imagery as a mode of recognition. Conversely, these scenarios allow for the recognition that conformity to the heteronorm (or the 'homonorm') in terms of looks does not necessarily commit the agents to those norms. Quite paradoxically, this disrupts yet also calls upon a body symbolism whereby sexuality and gender are read off from visual bodily markers.[5]

The 'Naughty Girls' Scenario

One way in which these clubbing magazines created a notion of clubbing as a sexualized spectacle was through presenting women as visual spectacles. The 'naughty girls' scenario ironicized longstanding discourses about stigmatized forms of femininity (Bailey 1990 Nead 1988: 179, Walkowitz 1992: 69, Frank 2003: 89–90, 107); discourses in which the respectable body was white, de-sexualized, heterofeminine and middle class (Skeggs 1997: 82) and marked off from the public expression of sexuality, which was considered deviant and close to prostitution. This scenario plays on such images of stigmatized femininity, re-signifying them as signs of an anti-bourgeois and unconventional attitude. In this respect, nightclubs were represented as places where the performance of sexuality can generate symbolic value and, if carefully coded and mantled in an image of glamour, can be brought into line with respectability and femininity. As Beverley Skeggs pointed out, 'glamour is the mechanism by which the marks of middle-class respectability are transposed onto the sexual body' (Skeggs 1997: 110). Glamour emphasizes attitude, appearance, desirability and stardom. The 'naughty girls' scenario is quite typical of media representations of young women's sexualities in 1990s Britain (McRobbie 1997b), which depicted women as active, lustful, pleasure-seeking and confident, up for 'shagging, snogging and having a good time' (ibid. 195–196). This social typing included irony, naughty humour and sex scandal (ibid. 197–198). It can be seen in the wider context of the re-evaluation of sexual promiscuity (of women) and the playful re-appropriation of derogatory slang expressions by female authors, music groups, alternative online media and high-street fashion (e.g. such as the term 'slut'; see Attwood 2007).

In July 2000 the opening pages of *Mixmag* magazine portrayed a number of clubbers who had supposedly revealed a 'personal secret' in response to the question 'What rumour would you start about yourself?'[6] Among these were several females who were attributed transgressive sexual roles or practices, evoking images of the feisty 'bad girl' or 'sex radical': 'We secretly have threesomes together'; 'That I am the doctor of love'; 'I have been medically diagnosed as a nymphomaniac, and I haven't taken my tablets tonight'; 'That I'm a top lass'; 'I used to be an Amsterdam porn star'. The photographic portraits staged spectacular, expressive bodies. First name, age, city or town and profession of these persons were cited below the images. These portraits codified self-confidence, creativity and irony and highlighted naughtiness as identity, ability and practice. They touched on notions of otherness by embracing, for example, excessive sexual lust and prostitution. The young females were presented as experienced and knowledgeable in sexual matters. The disclosure of a personal rumour alluded to the liberatory discourse, whereas the visual appearance itself already signified a liberated and open mind. The liberatory coming-out discourse was wedded to a liberal notion of picking funny and naughty play-roles. The identity claims attributed to these clubbers were unhinged from a clear-cut referent. The images played on being decoded as fun roles, disguise and masquerade. The *act* of dressing up and self-stylization was more important than the actual role. The images suggest a liberal 'anything goes' atmosphere; however, this may also shape a normative expectation that females in clubs are sexually 'up for it', that they are 'off their head' and that things can be pressured on to them (see Hutton 2004: 233, whose study demonstrates that females, especially in mainstream clubs, still face risks of sexual harassment).

This type of aestheticization of female sexuality can be compared with pop star Madonna's public staging of sexuality, which emphasized the plurality of inauthentic sexual profiles instead of expressing a sexual identity (Andermahr 1994: 30).[7] The 'naughty girls' scenario alluded to a mode of self-construction, in which authenticity gives way to the spectacle of masking and passing in ephemeral sexual characters, suggesting highly flexible entries into, and exits out of, these roles. It presented female sexuality as a game of indeterminacy and performative stylization. However, this imagery of the moderate and nice 'bad girls' and 'sex radicals' did not challenge binary gender codes. Instead, it presented quite clear-cut profiles of sexual transgression embedded in respectable everyday personhood and in an unambiguously feminine gender.

Scenarios of 'Hot Lesbo Action'

> . . . while their kiss cannot undo the historicity of the ways in which men produce their space as the site of the production of gender (Woman) for another (men), the fact that a woman materialises another woman as the object of her desire does go some way in rearticulating that space. The enactment of desire here can begin to skewer the lines of force that seek to constitute women as Woman, as object of the masculine gaze . . . making out in straight space can be a turn-on, one articulation of desire that bends and queers a masculine place allowing for a momentarily sexed lesbian space. (Probyn 1995: 81)

In the above quote, Elspeth Probyn argues that the enactment of female same-sex desire can reconfigure a heteronormative context and articulate a temporary lesbian space. However, as Probyn acknowledged, this is delicate and ambiguous rather than straightforward. The enactment of same-sex desire may undermine the constitution of women as objects of masculine desire, but just as easily it may be drawn into heteromasculine constructions of space, vision and gender. Moreover, both dynamics may be at work at the same time. Same-sex sensuality or desire between women (as well as men) in the context of rave or club culture was frequently put down to the effects of drugs such as ecstasy. Other authors noted that heterosexual women used 'lesbian masquerade' in straight dance-scenes as a strategy to create a safe, hassle-free space (Skeggs 1997: 135). While gay male culture became sign-values of hip and chic, lesbian scenes and lifestyles have been less exposed to fetishization (except perhaps for the most recent TV soap *The L Word*). As space for lesbian night life is much more limited than unmarked or gay codified space, the bars and clubs that cater for women-who-desire-women tend to be more protective of their space. Most of them maintain door policies that invite heterosexuals only as guests of their main clientele, not least because these spaces precisely seek to disrupt the long-established and powerful visual regime that constitutes women as objects of the masculine gaze and desire. The pornographic genre has been quite central for the masculine fetishization of female same-sex eroticism. In this context, the playful allusion to lesbian sex is used as a resource for affirming heterofemininity and desirability. Such visual regimes are also at work in heterosexually codified (i.e. unmarked) dance scenes. Similarly, the visual representations of female same-sex enactments in the clubbing magazines were inscribed into codes of heterosexual desirability. This was based on, amongst others, quite explicit pornographic poses and on captions and commentaries (e.g. '*Mixmag* photographers fall for this every time', or the journalists asking two women, 'fancy engaging in hot lesbo action for us then?'). Female-to-female eroticism may have articulated a lesbian space, but the (pornographic) fetishization by the journalistic gaze re-fixed and re-framed it as an affirmation of heterosexual desirability rather than as a queering of heterosexual space.

In contrast to the invention of the homosexual as an identity in the late nineteenth century (Foucault 1979), homosexuality here was reinvented as a series of *acts* ambiguously coded as normal ('who cares?') on the one hand and as transgressive or spectacular ('look at this!') on the other hand. These same-sex acts were clearly demarcated from *lesbian identities*. While the photographic coverage of the gay and lesbian Mardi Gras night represented lesbian identity through butch style,[8] the other imagery depicted same-sex desire in the context of femininity. It could be supposed that thereby this scenario undermined the stereotypical representation of lesbian sexuality through images of butch. However, butch style was evoked as the representation of 'real' lesbianism, whereas the other images alluded to the symbolism of the femme, whose sexual identity is clouded by ambiguity and confusion.[9] The pornographic frame too reinforced the recognition of desirable (hetero-)femininity. Lipstick lesbian discourse, as Beverley Skeggs noted, 'enables straight women who are invested in glamour to "pass" as lesbian' (1997: 135). This particular scenario vice versa enabled females posing in same-sex intimacies to pass as straight, providing for same-sex action to be recognized as an element of heterofemininity rather than (simply) as an expression of sexual desire between women.

Another example, which thematizes self-stylization through metaphors of otherness, demonstrates how lesbian sexuality was re-signified through butch style.[10] It shall be sketched briefly in the following: The image featured a comic-style photographic narrative of a young man being dressed up in drag and glamour by two women. The irony of the story, titled 'Substance girlies! Suits you sir or madam?', resulted from the rather clumsy attempt of the man to go drag. After the protagonist failed to pass as either female or as a man in drag, he resorted to a different masquerade, exemplified by a T-shirt saying, 'Nobody knows I'm a lesbian'. On the one hand, the secreted lesbian identity that he claimed was supported by his quasi 'butch', masculine appearance. On the other hand, the final punch line lay in the inauthentic embodiment of female *gender*, the bad imitation of woman-ness, which would nevertheless be required for passing as a lesbian. In this respect, the visual appearance undermined the identity claim as a lesbian. Although the latter is associated with masculine look or butch style, masculinity remains its other and apparently could not be made to disappear in this narrative. While the sequence alluded to the plastic nature of gender and sexuality, it reinforced the fixity of 'natural gender' through a masquerade that failed. The inadequate performance disclaimed the performativity of gender, which drag aesthetic in a sense suggests. The image staged the playful transgression of masculinity, but the failure to convincingly perform and imitate femininity implied that masculinity, respectively gender in general, is anchored and fixed in the body.

A similar script characterized the female homoerotic scenario. It claimed certain aspects of otherness and at the same time provided codes that either made possible to disclaim it as a game (of acting 'as-if') and to realign it with the heteronorm. This scenario prepared the grounds for a mode of recognition that disentangled female-to-female intimacies from the identity category 'lesbian'. By situating such enactments in the framework of femininity, this scenario opened up the symbolic boundaries of heterofemininity to include practices that were traditionally marked as other to the heteronorm. It allowed for assuming such a position and still be recognized as part of the norm. Homosexuality thus did not figure as an imaginary threat, but rather as an inherent possibility of heterofemininity itself. At the same time, it reconstituted the 'masculinized woman' as the abject other of the heteronorm and thereby affirmed heteronormative constructions of gender. Although it was argued that androgyny finds increasing acceptance in nightclubs (Hennessy 2000: 107, Hemmings 1997: 17), the clubbing magazines did not highlight such constructions of gender. Quite the opposite, in both visual scenarios discussed here, the freedom of sexual stylization and homoerotic enactment by females rested on an otherwise respectable body that was (mostly) white and (hetero-)feminine. In allowing for the possibility of identifying with non-heteronormative sexual roles, these representations opened up heteronormativity. Yet, this came at the price of conforming to heteronormative constructions of gender. Actual club settings may be less liberal than this imagery suggests. As Hutton pointed out, women expressing same-sex affection, especially in mainstream clubs, frequently fear censure and aggression (2006: 110).

The discussion so far suggested that clubbing magazines incorporated and revalued non-heteronormative articulations of sexuality as forms of aestheticization. In particular, the expression of female sexuality was scripted as a liberal form of stylization and self-invention through notions of otherness epitomized, for instance, in images of excessive hypersexuality, the display of glamorous sexual characters, and female same-sex intimacy. These media scenarios provided ways of understanding particular non-heteronormative sexual roles or desires as part of, rather than in opposition to, heteronormativity. They prepared the grounds for combining non-heteronormative enactments with traditional articulations of gender and sexuality. This allowed for experimental, playful and non-committal identifications with, for example, female same-sex enactment, bisexuality and drag. Male homosexuality by contrast, was not, or only rarely, part of the magazines' imagery. The sexual discourse generated in these magazines rested on irony, excess and camp as well as on pornographic iconography, emphasizing a 'New Lad' male hedonism and 'tongue-in-cheek' sexism (Williamson 2003) combined with post-feminist visions of an active, self-determined and liberated female sexuality.[11]

PLAYING/DOING/BEING: EXPERIMENTATION
BETWEEN RECUPERATION AND ABJECTION

What subject positions do these cultural scripts create, what effects do they have on the formation of subjectivity, and what modes of (self-)recognition do they open up? Chatterton and Hollands argued that much of the supposed boisterous sexual behaviour and predatory sexual attitude of women in nightclubs is of a symbolic nature (2003: 76, 156). Such self-stylization is often wedded to traditional, heteronormative concepts of romance and gender. Interviewees' accounts of clubbing were in many instances scripted through practices construed as unconventional or even deviant (e.g. drug consumption, dressing-up in characters, excessive partying). Especially the female interviewees frequently referred to some kind of sexual experimentation. Same-sex desire was only one way in which this was expressed. This may reflect a contradiction that heterosexual women face in managing their sexual projects. In trying to avoid being sexualized within the heteronormative visual regime yet keeping intact their (hetero-)sexual projects, they draw on new scripts of sexual autonomy, competence and experimentation, which allow for ambiguity and misrecognition (Skeggs 1999). The reference to self-experimentation can also be read as a particular configuration of desire and control in which contemporary consumers are placed (Rose 1999a: 263–264, 1999b: 66–87). Individuals are encouraged to promote their desires and pleasures, but at the same time they have to keep mastery over them (Sassatelli 2001: 94, Featherstone 1991: 24). The rhetoric of self-experimentation serves as a particular legitimatory style for the temporary or contained discharge of desire, as it enables subjects to 'produce a strong self-narrative', which at the same time 'provides them with a measure of distance' (Sassatelli 2001: 99).

In contrast to experimentation through acts of stylization, the following example accentuates the fun and excitement gained from misrecognition, respectively passing in non-heteronormative roles. The indeterminacy given off by the body performance created scope for playful identification. Emine, a media student in her mid-twenties, originally from Turkey, related some incidents in which her gender and heterosexual identity were apparently misinterpreted by other clubbing participants. When visiting a gay and mixed club in Paris with her boyfriend, she was approached by a woman, who mistook her as a lesbian or bisexual. She emphasized that such incidents happened frequently. Despite persistently negating this attribution by, for example, repeatedly referring to her boyfriend as a 'proof' of her sexual orientation, she effectively passed as a gay female.

> Once I went with my boyfriend, and it was funny because there was this girl, she came to talk to me, thinking I was totally a lesbian and he came, she came with a gay friend of hers and he was thinking my boyfriend was gay as well, so they were both like trying to, you know, open up a conversation, and she was totally convinced I was. And at the end she asked me "Are you gay or" you know, "bisexual?" And I said, "I'm afraid I'm not", and so "Come on, don't wind me up", "Seriously, I'm not, I mean, it's even my boyfriend." And she totally didn't believe he was, "He looks very skinny, and he is more like feminine than he is masculine." She didn't believe. (Emine 2000: 2)

While Emine provided an explanation why her boyfriend was perceived as gay (or 'effeminate'), she did not mention in what way her own body appearance could have given reason for her being mistaken as a lesbian. However, she referred to lesbians as 'demanding' or 'pushy', which conjured up the image of the butch lesbian and might suggest that she found herself positioned on the boundary between femininity and masculinity. Emine provided another story that unfolded how her gender was called into question. In a club she was asked by transsexuals whether she was a 'real' woman with 'real' breasts or a transsexual who had had a surgery. Apparently, she was asked to disclose her biological body. She may also have been read as 'naturally' female but teased and ridiculed in a sort of fun interaction.

> The funniest is with transsexuals, because in that club we used to go in Paris, there was a lot of transsexuals as well, and it was so funny because, I have a friend and she is really pretty, but sometimes you can think she looks like a transvestite or—sometimes not—believe I'm a woman, but then, you see your breasts [sic], they see your breasts and they are like totally, "Are these real" kind of thing, and they are always making these comments, you know, "Did you have a surgery? Are you a man, are you a woman?" to my friend as well. She has curly, long hair and they're like, "Is this a wig, is this real? Are you a woman, are you a man?" You know, it's just their relationship towards women is the funniest. (Emine 2000: 2)

These mis-readings were not framed as stories of offence, but as fun-stories that did not involve serious face-threats. These stories emphasized how her body attracted attention and caused puzzlement. She described it as an aesthetic, indeterminate body that resisted stereotypical categorization by others. This aesthetic body seemed to enable her to pass in several non-heteronormative roles (lesbian, bisexual, transsexual). It thus appeared as a (passively) transgressive body that did not require any *act* of transgression.[12] Emine's response to the misrecognition as a lesbian and her allusion to the image of the masculine lesbian could be interpreted as a form of repudiation (J. Butler 1993). Yet, hers is not an abject identification that 'does not show' (ibid. 112). Instead, these notions of 'otherness' were integrated into her narrative of heterosexual identity as virtual roles and possible modes of (mis-)recognition by others.

The second example illustrates how same-sex enactment may be integrated as a possible bisexual dimension into the narrative construction of heterofemininity. Clare, a club dancer in the UK, notably framed her performative acts as a fetish dancer, who was 'messing around' with other girls on stage, not in the context of homosexual or lesbian desire, but in terms of bisexuality (Clare 2000a: 12). In this respect, she differentiated between 'wearing' (fetish outfits) and 'doing' (fetish sexuality). Performing in fetish costumes was considered by her as an element of her personality rather than sexual desire.

> With the freestyle dancing that I do for the . . . [name of the dance crew, S.R.], it's really, it's quite sexual, it's quite suggestive with the girls and the guys and I really enjoy that, because I think everyone has an element of bisexuality in their personality; and although I don't sort of actively go out and have sex with girls, to be able to sort of simulate that on stage, is, it makes me feel brilliant because it's non-committal, and it's ah, it's not me actually saying "I am bisexual", it's just the suggestion of being bisexual, which I really enjoy. I like girls, but I wouldn't want to have a relationship with a girl or actually have sex with a girl necessarily, but just to be able to play with a girl and make the crowd think that I'm, you know and vice versa, even though we not actually do anything, we're just making it look like we are doing, it's a very powerful feeling. Especially the guys you know, they are standing, like they are really amazed because two girls are messing around on stage. (Clare 2000: 12)

In this extract the homoerotic scenario is presented as a form of stylization and is detached from (homo-)sexual desire. Clare's depiction of bisexual simulation seems similar to the pornographic framework of 'hot lesbo action' discussed above. It appears to have been enacted in order to stimulate the crowd's desire and to enhance Clare's desirability. As noted before, Clare integrated bisexuality into her personality as a playful element and put-on. It was clearly demarcated from bisexuality as a sexual practice or identity. This account reminds of the way in which female homoerotic enactments were framed in the magazines. Although Clare evoked the liberatory discourse of opening up to one's transgressive desires, she did not accentuate the expression of a formerly repressed real sexual desire. Instead she emphasized the ability and confidence to simulate erotic roles and to act as a sexualized persona. Clare presented herself as a 'naughty sex-radical', yet also counted on it being read as a temporary masquerade. However, whether the bisexual dimension was anchored in real desire or was just an erotic role on stage was something that Clare was 'not a one hundred percent comfortable with yet', as she disclosed in the course of the interview (Clare 2000b: 40). In this respect, the narrative construction of her sexual identity remained ambiguous and indeterminate. She disclaimed homosexual desire by describing it as a mere stage act, or she acknowledged her sexual experiences with other women but mitigated them at the same time.

> I mean I've had a couple of experiences with girls before, but not really, always when I've been on drugs or when I've been drunk, never ah, never really straight . . . I like kissing girls, but I don't really like sleeping with girls. (Clare 2000b: 39)

> I just see it as taking a friendship one stage further, ah, especially if it's just kissing. And kissing a girl is completely different from kissing a guy. It's fun and it's silly and it's like little secret, naughty thing. . . . I mean I've slept with probably ah twenty guys and one girl really, two girls, so it's not an even balance and I think bisexuality is balanced, isn't it, and like I said, you can see yourself in a relationship with somebody of the same sex, which I can't. You know, I want to be with a man, but occasionally I see a girl and think "mhm, she is really nice." (Clare 2000b: 41)

Here homosexual desire is disclaimed by relegating the homoerotic experiences to states of restricted consciousness or intoxication.[13] Same-sex eroticism is limited to specific acts such as kissing or, is linked to a state of passivity. Homosexuality is viewed as naughty and silly secret in the framework of friendship rather than relationship. The reference to the substantially larger number of heterosexual encounters serves as another element in renouncing bisexuality. Nevertheless, this 'other' sexuality is integrated into the narrative construction of heterosexual identity. It articulates an unconventional, ambiguous and transgressive overflow, which allows for expressing a bisexual element without the (self-)recognition as bisexual. Despite the denial of homosexual desire, the heterosexual subject position here is not just constituted through a disavowed identification with abject homosexuality, but is defined in relation to a virtual scenario of homo- respectively bisexuality. In this example heterosexual femininity was neither completely subverted nor simply reproduced; it was scripted and narrated as having other sexualities as *possibilities*, sometimes actual, sometimes virtual, attached to it.

CONCLUSION

This ambiguity between claiming and disclaiming non-heteronormative positions calls to mind Judith Butler's argument about the logic of repudiation (Butler 1993). According to Butler, heteronormativity is constituted through a threatening outside of abject, unthinkable bodies and desires, which themselves may become eroticized as transgressive sites (ibid. 96–97). These identifications are activated and disavowed at the same time, they 'never show' (ibid. 112). From Butler's viewpoint, the sexual enactments represented in these magazines seem to displace heternormativity, but may follow the logic of repudiation and actually reinforce heteronormativity by providing ritualistic releases. In the scenarios discussed here, however, other sexualities were not just constructed as abjected regions, but were designed as virtual becomings or play-roles to be temporarily claimed for heterofemininity or -masculinity. Nevertheless, this highlighted a boundary between those elements of otherness that were incorporated into these virtual scenarios and those elements that remained excluded. In the examples discussed here, to identify with bisexuality meant to accept it as a stage simulation but to reject it as a life-form. To pass as a lesbian or transsexual made anxious about being pathologized as a masculine woman. 'Lesbo action' was assimilated into heterofemininity but disarticulated from lesbian sexuality or identity, which was resymbolized through the butch body. Female same-sex enactments were normalized when framed by the symbolic recognition of feminine desirability, suggesting that it is tolerable if (also) performed for the male gaze. This partial claiming and disclaiming of sexual otherness is more like a form of repossession, through which marginalized positions are reconstituted as *objects* of consumption (Žižek 1997b, Skeggs and Binnie 2004a, Skeggs 2005). Such acts of appropriation assimilate certain elements of otherness and convert these qualities into symbolic capital. At the same time they redraw the boundaries to those others who are not considered to be assimilable and who continue to serve as the repudiated, constitutive limits of the (hetero-)normative positions (Skeggs and Binnie 2004a).

The dynamics of recuperation and abjection, fetishization and exclusion that are prompted by these representations are never transposed into the spatial contexts that smoothly (Butler 1993, Hennessy 2000, Skeggs and Binnie 2004a). As the debates on the commodification and aestheticization of difference in urban culture show, these may also facilitate and intensify politicization and contestation (Jacobs 1998) and therefore leave scope for unpredictable shifts and reconfigurations of heteronormativity. Yet, such recuperation not only creates new lines of exclusion but may also have disempowering effects for the agents of recuperation themselves. (Playful) identification with non-normative sexual roles and desires may challenge heteromasculine and -normative visual regimes but may come at the price of positioning women as empowered only if objects of male desire. 'Fluid' sexualities, the multiplication of sexual scripts and the aestheticization of self through sexual stylization may call into question the fixity of sexual identity. But this may also become the new fix for heteronormativity, which renews its scripts of love, desire and romance through transgressive releases

that are anchored in, and reinforce, binary gender norms. Sexual stylization in public may serve well for gaining symbolic recognition and status or
for empowering one's sense of identity, but it may also become a vehicle of
power and subjectification, whereby particular groups are recognized and
normalized through their sexuality.

How are other kinds of intimacies affected by these configurations of
heteronormativity? How do these processes alter the positioning of gays,
lesbians, bisexuals and transgenders in social space? As has been argued,
the development of these sexual communities has been based on the principles of visibility, recognizability and territorialization (Castells 1983, Bell
and Valentine 1995). However, in the past decade the boundaries between
straight and gay scenes have become more blurred; first, because of its
appeal to straight audiences; second, because of the perceived risks of self-
ghettoization and homogenization on the gay scene. Interestingly, this was
not reflected in these clubbing magazines. Although these visual representations did not construct bi-, trans- or homosexualities as intolerable or
outside the norm, they were not embraced as part of the norm either. Queer
cultures remained largely invisible, which confirmed rather than challenged
the implicit heteronormativity of unmarked clubbing space. In case these
sexualities were made visible, they were either exoticized or recuperated as
noted above. It can be assumed that the visual scenario of female same-sex
intimacy intervenes into the structures of recognition for lesbian sexualities, as it renders the symbolic markers through which lesbian and female
same-sex desire are read more unstable. On the one hand, the detachment
of female same-sex desire from lesbian identity opens up positions for the
expression of a variety of forms and styles. On the other hand, these processes of recuperation also provoke defensive closures of lesbian identity
through the intensification of boundary work. This becomes manifest in
struggles over authentic embodiments of lesbian identity and in contests
over entitlements to space (see for example, Casey 2004, Eves 2004: 486–
487, Skeggs 1999: 225–227). Such types of visual representation of female
same-sex desire as discussed here circulate in the media at a larger scale and
contribute to a revaluation of femininity also in lesbian club cultures with
the consequence that butch or androgynous styles are curtailed and marginalized in gay-mixed contexts. If these recuperated elements of lesbian
sexuality also constitute the basis of a 'new homonormativity' within the
women's scenes, warrants further investigation.

8 Allegorical Anarchy, Symbolic Hierarchy
Sexual Boundaries in Two London Dance Clubs

Academic representations of contemporary youth club cultures since the late 1990s can broadly be divided into two strands. On the one hand, club and dance cultures are deeply infused with images of transgression and liminality. Some authors interpreted dance cultures as a manifestation of a post-subcultural era, in which the demarcation of subcultural boundaries has given way to a postmodern style eclecticism (Muggleton 1997, 2000: 47; Polhemus 1996) and to more flexible and transient neo-tribal formations (A. Bennett 1999, 2000).[1] Other accounts conjured up images of the social inclusiveness of dance cultures beyond boundaries of class, sexuality or ethnicity or even beyond 'the scene of identity politics' (Melechi 1993: 38). Especially the drug ecstasy was seen to weaken clear-cut sexual identifications (see also the discussion in Measham, Parker, and Aldridge 2001: 48–51 and Hutton 2006). On the other hand, academic studies emphasized the continuing centrality of boundary work within clubbing scenes and dance cultures and the segmentation of dance spaces into 'mainstream', 'residual' or 'alternative' spaces attracting particular strata of cash-rich or cash-poor youth (Chatterton and Hollands 2003: 3–6). Dance cultures were described as 'taste cultures' characterized by constant disputes over the legitimate taste and the struggle for symbolic capital via 'subcultural ideologies' modelled on Bourdieu's concept of distinction (Thornton 1995: 3). Such practices of classification not only demarcate boundaries between music genres and scenes, but also between subjects and types of practices (e.g. 'E-heads' vs. 'Beer Monsters'; see Moore 2003b). It has been claimed that music policy and drug consumption patterns are key factors for the segmentation of clubbing scenes (Measham 2004: 341). Moreover, they articulate and remake social boundaries of class, ethnicity, gender and sexuality. These stratifiers circumscribe varying notions of belonging and entitlements to certain spaces opening up different types of participation. Clubs provide arenas for the construction and mutual (mis-)recognition of identities through the meanings negotiated in social practices. Instead of merely expressing existing social boundaries, the clubbing scene can be seen as a medium for the institutionalization or de-institutionalization of symbolic and social differences.[2] Such lines of differentiation, though nebulous and shifting, remain significant despite the broad popularity of dance culture across the youth population (Measham et al. 2001: 50–54, 65).

This chapter takes a closer look at boundary work in the context of clubbing and how it is tied in with the remaking or reconfiguration of social boundaries. As explained in Chapter 4, symbolic boundaries include all sorts of conceptual distinctions by which commonalities and differences between people are established and typified (Lamont and Molnár 2002). From this perspective, the symbolic boundaries at work are more complex and manifold than the three main lines of subcultural distinction exposed by Thornton (1995, see Chapter 1, p. 10). Boundary work means to draw lines of demarcation against rival others in order to stake out claims to authority, resources and status (Gieryn 1983). Staking out claims naturally goes along with negotiation, acceptance or refusal, whereby social actors 'support and challenge' existing classifiers, identity categories and categorization processes (Gerson and Peiss 1985: 318). Classification of 'others' is at the basis of boundary work. However, as suggested in Chapter 4, boundary work does not only involve binary oppositions; spaces that encourage simulation and play also evoke more fuzzy boundaries articulated against a horizon of possibility and virtuality.

Following on from the analysis of media representations of sexualities in clubbing (Chapter 7), the subsequent discussion concentrates on gender and sexual boundary work in dance cultural settings, in particular, in gay(-mixed) and lesbian venues. Gender boundaries, in particular, were defined as divisions of women and men into certain spheres of action (e.g. the public and the private; Gerson and Peiss 1985: 318). Although not gender-divided in this sense, except for men- or women-only scenes, gendered positionings in relation to night life shape modes of participation in, and ethical justifications of, clubbing (see Chapters 5 and 6). The term sexual boundary refers to symbolic or social–spatial groupings and separations of people on the basis of either categorizing their sexual identifications or attributing certain qualities relating to sexual identity. In the particular context of the club, such boundary work may be geared towards staking out (and also denying) claims to inclusion, belonging and recognition. Focusing on sexual boundary work does not mean to suggest that interaction in clubs is generally characterized by this or any other kind of boundary work. Rather, the intention is to explore in what ways such boundary work and negotiation of sexual boundaries occurs in these contexts. In particular, the question arises as to what extent sexual boundaries disappear or are remade in club contexts that wish to reach a sexually mixed crowd.

As the previous chapter demonstrated, heteronormativity in club contexts is to some extent reconfigured through sexual play-realities and sexualized stylization. Gay villages and night-life clusters have been popularized among certain segments of heterosexual, especially female audiences. New labels and codes have evolved on the club scenes to create more inclusive spaces regardless of sexual identification. These processes have disrupted the structures of visibility, recognizability and territorialization and the identity markers that once underpinned sexual, e.g. gay or lesbian communities (Castells 1983, Bell and Valentine 1995).[3] A largely critical discourse has unfolded about the implications of these transformations for notions of gay or lesbian identity. The fetishization of gay culture was seen to bring about a 'new homonormativity' (Duggan 2002). On the basis of two case studies, a gay (respectively gay-mixed) and a lesbian club in Central London, the following analysis investigates as to what extent and for whom identity boundaries and sexual divides on the clubbing scene are weakened or reinforced. It delineates the ways in which aesthetic stylization and performative understandings of sexuality may contribute to both the queering as well as the normative closure of identity categories. The case studies rest upon data that were generated through ethnographic fieldwork and narrative interviews with clubbing participants. As set out in the introductory chapter, ethnographic fieldwork was carried out in a cross-section of about twenty straight, gay, gay-mixed, 'polysexual' lesbian dance clubs in London. The interviews took place outside the club contexts with people of mixed backgrounds (gender, class, age, nationality, sexual orientation) and related to varied clubbing contexts in London and elsewhere. They did not specifically focus on the two clubs discussed here unless they were covered by the interviewees themselves. More detailed ethnographic research took place in the two clubs under study and included promotional material (e.g. the venues' websites), media articles as well as interviews with the manager/owner of the women's venue and the promoter of the gay-mixed club of the time.[4]

A tentative argument shall be sketched out in the following chapter suggesting that these two clubs tended to feature different types of boundaries and boundary work, and hence different structures of experience and identity. Whereas the women's club encouraged highly symbolically marked in-group/out-group distinctions, the gay-mixed club provoked more hybrid and allegorical boundaries of membership and identity. The first section of the chapter addresses some of the mechanisms and frames for the (re-) production of sexual boundaries in dance culture by focusing on clubbing scenes as cultural economies and by looking at the history and position of gay and lesbian scenes in these markets. Following on from this, the second part provides some background to the clubs under study and describes their promotion and image work. This highlights the entanglement of sexual and aesthetic codifications, which are either used to further limit or to open up sexual boundaries. The third part elaborates on, and briefly illustrates, the types of boundary work activated in the clubs' door policies and admission practices and in the social interactions inside the clubs. It should be clear that this neither covers all aspects of boundary work nor claims to be representative of all such encounters. This chapter reflects upon the structuration of social relations and experiences in these clubs and the negotiation of sexual boundaries in the context of institutional modes of operation and the wider cultural discourses which frame these particular clubbing scenes.

MECHANISMS AND FRAMES FOR THE REPRODUCTION OF SEXUAL BOUNDARIES IN THE CLUBBING MARKET

Economic sociologists such as Michel Callon and his collaborators (Callon, Méadel, and Rabeharisoa 2004) elaborated on market making in service economies as a process of qualification and re-qualification, in which qualities of goods are defined, redefined and transformed (see also Slater 2002a, 2002b). The creation of goods and sign-values itself can be described as a form of boundary work. Goods are qualified in relation to other goods, within a space of goods. Qualification is twofold: goods are singularized (individualized, made distinguishable from) and normalized (made comparable to) other goods, a controversial and political process that depends 'on the joint work of a host of actors' (Callon et al. 2004: 65) and transforms the product throughout production and consumption. In the case of dance clubs, the qualification of goods is mediated by the club's self-promotion, the media representations and word of mouth. Qualification is split between contexts of co-presence and mediated images of particular scenes. Needless to say, not all the agents involved in the 'profiling' of a good receive equal recognition. As the qualities are stabilized to some degree through the credibility of the consumers, these agents in reverse have to 'qualify' for inclusion. This means goods and agents are inserted in a web of mutual legitimization and qualification, a point that anthropologists of consumption have so convincingly demonstrated at the intricate linkage between the system of goods and the social distinctions (Douglas and Isherwood 1979). As was elaborated in more detail in Chapter 3, cultural economies, i.e. economies occupied with producing cultural, symbolic or immaterial goods and qualities, depend on a careful balancing of symbolic and economic capital (Entwistle 2002). This often leads to ambivalent processes of opening to increase profit and of social closure to sustain credibility. Scarce space naturally intensifies the credibility contests for consumers, whereas highly saturated markets create unstable and unpredictable consumer attachments. The profiling of the good and audience is a constant process as parts of the audience withdraw or new groups wish to be accepted. Demand and supply are highly temporalized and accordingly, how permeable the boundaries are around spaces varies considerably. The ambivalence between opening and closure can be considered a general mechanism for the reproduction of boundaries within cultural economies such as dance clubs. In order to gain a clearer understanding of the dynamics that shape the boundary work of gay and lesbian clubs in particular, attention shall be drawn briefly to the market contexts and the cultural discourses which affect these scenes.

Gay and lesbian club scenes veer between two different frames regarding their functions, the organization of social relations and institutional processes. These frames are entangled with each other, and the contradictions and tensions they generate reflect wider social changes. Night-life spaces serving the gay and lesbian communities in Britain (and elsewhere) grew a more visible presence in the wake of the identity politics of the 1970s. In a largely hostile societal context, these spaces intended to provide safe environments and meeting places for people seeking their commonality in a shared sexual identification and aiming to create symbolic expressions of this shared identity (see also note 3). These types of spaces were constructed as (bordered) territories of identity and underpinned by according institutional processes. As these 'sexual community' spaces became permeated by a growing interest in, or pressure for, profit making, they developed into more full-blown service spaces, situating themselves in a market context and specializing in the provision of certain services to gay 'consumers'. With the increasing emphasis on style codes, design and aesthetic elements, the institutional boundary work became less concerned with preserving a strict sexual codification, allowing more openness while preserving the gay sign-value. Although today such clubs are mainly accentuated as service and consumption spaces, the community discourse continues to inform the framing of these spaces. As Bell and Binnie put it quite aptly, gay spaces 'are caught between imperatives of commodification and ideas of authenticity' (Bell and Binnie 2004: 1807).

In the UK and elsewhere, the past decades, especially the 1990s, have seen an increasing, yet uneven and ambivalent, acceptance of sexual minorities. Particular segments of gay, lesbian or queer culture, such as the Gay Pride festival, became 'marker[s] of cosmopolitanism' (Chatterton and Hollands 2003: 163) and have been mobilized for cultural consumption by a wider, non-gay audience. Several UK city councils recognized the potential for regenerating run-down urban areas through the promotion and support of gay consumption and businesses (see Chapter 2, Chatterton and Hollands 2003: 167, for the US see Castells 1983). This resulted in visible changes in the urban geography of gay and lesbian night life since the 1980s and especially the 1990s. Once relegated to the margins and fringes of the city, gay cafés, bars, clubs and gay villages evolved in the very centre of mainstream, heterosexually dominated night life. However, cultural critics bemoaned that the greater visibility of non-normative sexualities is a market-driven, capitalist 'appropriation of gay styles for mainstream audiences' (Hennessy 1995: 143), resulting in the fetishization of particular segments of gay (male) culture—dubbed the 'beautiful people syndrome' (Whittle 1994: 39)—and the continuing marginalization of either the less well-off, the older generations or those 'queer' scenes that cannot be assimilated into the fetishized image. Venues for gays, lesbians, bisexuals and transgenders continue to exist on the fringes of cities, in remote or unsafe areas.[5] Structural gender divides have been reproduced with gay male spaces by far outnumbering spaces for females in most cities (see also Valentine 1993).

Despite these ambivalent developments gay clubbing culture has heavily influenced youth dance cultures in terms of music, fashion and an orientation towards pleasure seeking. Especially heterosexual female and student populations have become attracted to gay or gay-mixed spaces (Chatterton and Hollands 2003: 163, Casey 2004, Eves 2004). Straight women, in particular, visit these venues because they perceive them as women-friendly and safe, and because these venues enable them to enjoy a sexually charged atmosphere without having to fear harassment or worry about consequences. Gay clubs are also frequented because they are seen as fabulous and spectacular, as glamorous and stylish, fostering an atmosphere in which imaginative possibilities of self-fashioning through dress, interactions and dance can be realized (Buckland 2002: 36).

Due to these developments, gay male and women-only dance scenes have redefined their boundaries. They have been struggling with the question as to what extent they should stay 'bordered territories of identity', preserving a safe space[6] for sexual minorities that are still targets of homophobic violence in public space, or should open up to include people regardless of their sexuality. In actual practice, boundary work becomes particularly pertinent in relation to the labelling of the clubs and the club nights, and in relation to admission policies. The ongoing dominance of heteronormativity and the risk of stigmatization and violence in unmarked (i.e. straight) scenes and spaces are often named as reasons for holding on to sexual codifications. However, this is also increasingly perceived as self-ghettoization and as negative segregation; exclusion on the basis of sexual identity would not be acceptable in straight scenes either. Mixed spaces are believed to reduce the emphasis on sexual cruising and competition. Yet, the opening up of the identity borders also provokes unease that these venues loose their gay character and become usurped by heterosexual consumers (Chatterton and Hollands 2003: 174, Casey 2004, Eves 2004). In some respects, the opening and 'mainstreaming' of gay spaces may produce reverse effects. As for the gay village in Manchester for example, Hobbs et al. argued that Canal Street became 'a victim of its own success' as it had turned into a late-night entertainment village with the highest concentration of violence in the central area prompting some gay entrepreneurs to develop a 'New Gay Quarter' for a 'strictly' gay clientele (Hobbs, Hadfield, Lister, Winlow, and Waddington 2003: 101–102).

The clubbing scene in London consists of a predominantly unmarked segment of clubs with no explicit sexual boundary work, but more or less implicit heteronormativity; and a segment of clubs catering explicitly for gay, lesbian, bisexual, transgender or queer folks, many of them accepting straight visitors as 'guests' of their core customers, but not admitting groups of solely straight people. Some established gay clubs responded to the demand of straight audiences by explicitly promoting sexually mixed club nights.[7] On the one hand, the label 'gay-mixed' suggests a sexually mixed audience, yet in practice the majority of the audience often is gay male. On the other hand, some club nights have replaced the principal codification as 'gay' by other labels. For example, 'polysexual' suggests a pluralistic, inclusive policy that explicitly highlights that a variety of sexual identifications is welcomed. However, even this does not necessarily sidestep the gay codification as it is sometimes based on an implicit gay majority policy in order to avoid alienating the original gay core market. As the promoter of such a night pointed out in the interview (Freeman 2000: 2), the label polysexual mainly was used to highlight a non-discriminating atmosphere, in which sexual labels could be rendered irrelevant. Yet, in practice it would mean 70 to 75 per cent gay clubbers. He further stated that in order to make sure that gay customers feel secure, 'we would always keep a balance in the favour of gay' (ibid.; see also Mintel 2000b: 64). In addition, sexual labels such as 'gay', 'gay-mixed' or 'polysexual' are also invoked as aesthetic sign-values believed to appeal to a fashion-centred, cutting-edge consumer segment regardless of their sexual identity. For instance, the same promoter also noted that he primarily aimed for an audience with taste and an understanding of music and fashion.

As stated before, it can be suggested that such scenes have become caught up between two different and partly contradictory objectives, driven by imperatives of commodification and ideas of authenticity. This produces highly complex, overlapping and disjunctive borderscapes around such spaces. On the one hand, they position themselves as spaces serving particular sexual communities and as territories of identity. On the other hand, they are lifestyle and consumption spaces mobilizing aesthetic sign-values that appeal to certain consumer segments. Thereby, the codes 'gay', 'queer' or 'polysexual' partly came to stand in for aesthetic codifications. As the recognition of gay or lesbian sexualities is grounded in certain body markers and styles, the latter have become the main vehicles for claiming (or denying) recognition and membership in a sexually codified space. But sexual and aesthetic codifications may become entangled in different ways; aesthetic sign-valuing may be deployed in order to target a particular aesthetic or lifestyle niche within the sexual community or, it may open up the sexual codification in order to address a wider, mixed audience and to create an ambience where sexual boundaries can submerge (see Figure 8.1). However, even the marketing of such gay-mixed or polysexual spaces tends to require essentialized notions of gay, lesbian or queer sexualities for the realization of its sign-value. These aesthetic–sexual borderscapes provoke complex contests over spatial and social inclusion stirring up, but also disrupting disciplinary and normalizing power in the authentication of bodies. In this process, symbolic systems of sexual identity are called up and reconfigured.

AESTHETIC AND SEXUAL CODIFICATIONS
IN CANDY BAR AND HEAVEN

Back in 2000, a survey of the gay entertainment market[8] suggested that gay male consumers, having high disposable incomes, were frequent users

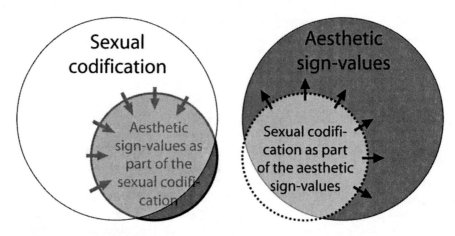

Figure 8.1 Aesthetic–sexual borderscapes

of bars, pubs, clubs and restaurants (Mintel 2000b: 1). The market survey further indicated that gay people keep visiting nightclubs until much later life stages than heterosexual club consumers (ibid. 11). However, it also pointed to the gender difference among gay consumers in terms of income and night-life consumption (ibid. 30–33). Women were found to be in majority infrequent or less frequent visitors of nightclubs. Another finding of the survey was that the gay scene did not cater well enough for the diversity of the gay consumer segment (ibid. 64). Both genders equally—66 per cent of all the respondents—articulated the desire for a better variety of gay venues (Mintel 2000b: 12). However, this constraint of choice and variety has different meanings for male and female audiences (transsexual or intersexual audiences were not included in this survey). The gay male clubbing scene in London is a fairly saturated market. While club nights come and go, there is generally a range of nights on offer each night of the week. Despite a great number of events, the gay male scene is sometimes perceived as too homogeneous (see also Chatterton and Hollands 2003: 173), which is also linked to the perception that gay customers themselves are homogeneous, with the same groups and tribes moving from club to club in their weekend rows or even weekly cycles of clubbing. By contrast, a weekly cycle of clubbing in lesbian codified spaces would be fairly difficult as most events take place at weekends, and only few women's dance nights are on offer mid-week. The main issues regarding the constraint of choice in the lesbian clubbing scene are therefore the shortage of events on offer and the scarcity of clubbing space. This goes along with a high fluctuation of events (see also Wolfe 1992: 151). Due to lower income levels and drink sales, women's nights are less profitable, often a point of contention for venue owners, which is why it is difficult to find attractive and affordable venues for women's nights and to sustain events more long-term (see also Chapters 3 and 4). Cheaper venues are often located in dodgy areas with poor transport facilities and are not particularly attractive to female audiences. Many women's nights take place in small venues with tiny dance floors, which involve a dynamic visual interaction in contrast to clubbing spaces with large dance floors, which make it possible to 'disappear' in the crowd.[9] Clubbing events tailored to a female gay or bisexual audience are often set up as either fortnightly or monthly (more rarely, as weekly) events in spaces that are otherwise used to cater to either a gay male or a dominantly straight audience. Only a few venues in Central London (i.e. transport zone 1) are owned and managed by lesbians and run for a mainly lesbian or female audience. Door policies are often more restrictive at women's events than at gay male venues due to the scarcity of clubbing spaces, their smaller sizes and also in order to avoid sexual objectification.

Both venues this analysis focuses on had a somewhat unique status within the gay and lesbian night-life scenes. At the time of this study, the first venue, Candy Bar, was one of two seven-day, permanent women's bars in London and the only one in Soho.[10] A number of other women's club-nights and bars have started up in Central London since, but Candy Bar tried to create distinctive events, for example, by acquiring a license to stage strip nights. Candy Bar is a small, independent company, owned by Kim Lucas. The idea to open a women's bar took shape in the first half of the 1990s, when many gay men's bars opened in Soho, particularly Old Compton Street. One of the main problems in setting up the company was, as the owner pointed out, finding a venue, which she eventually rented from promoters of a big gay club-night. 'I felt the only way I was going to get any sort of backing was to put my ideas into gay men's heads' (Lucas quoted in Garett 2000: 13). In 1996 Candy Bar opened in a quiet backstreet of Soho, and after a temporary relocation to another Soho venue between 2000 and 2002 reopened again in the first venue. Due to its small capacity of 150 persons and a weekend license until 2 a.m., Candy Bar is a hybrid bar-club and mainly a late-night drinking venue with a small dance floor. The second venue, Heaven, operates in a more saturated market. It is also located in central London, but not in Soho. When the club opened up in 1979 with a weekly Saturday men-only night, it had moved into a venue that was owned by British Rail, which secured a relatively cheap rent over the years.[11] Heaven has a reputation for having shaped the new character of the 1980s and 1990s London dance scene, not only because it was one of the first of a new generation of large-scale, technically well-equipped dance spaces, but also because it was one of the first places in London to promote house music by hosting Ibiza-influenced dance nights at the end of the 1980s. This is one reason why the club became well known among a straight audience. In 1991 Heaven was bought by Richard Branson and belonged to the Virgin Group—a fact that has been kept rather secret—until it was sold off in 2002/03 and is now (2008) owned by three shareholders. In the 1990s the club underwent refurbishment and was remade by a labyrinthine structure connecting three dance floors, eight bars, two performance areas and a members-only lounge, with an overall capacity of 1,695 persons. Until the mid-1990s Heaven had the largest capacity for a gay club (Mintel 2000b: 21). In 2002, between 8,000 and 10,000 customers passed through its doors each week on five different nights.

Unlike more alternative night-life spaces, both clubs pursue active branding strategies. Candy Bar sought to establish a lesbian brand for franchising at a national and international level. Another branch was opened under the same name in Brighton in 2000 and a Sydney branch is under consideration. Heaven was never marketed through the Virgin brand, but tried to create an individual brand out of its name, planning to branch out to Ibiza in 2009/2010. Both clubs used sexual labels in their promotion and admission policies. In 2002 Heaven was still advertised as 'the most famous gay nightclub',[12] but in the years before, it had continuously toned down the sexual codification of its traditional Saturday flagship night from 'strictly gay' to 'for a mainly gay male crowd'. Its website highlighted neither a gay codification of the club as such nor of the Saturday night.[13] In the same period, Candy Bar maintained a clear codification and partly reaffirmed its codification as a lesbian space: 'a 7 nights-a-week lesbian bar . . . Men welcome as guests' (*Time Out* November 1999), 'London's leading venue for lesbians, bisexual women and their gay male guests' (*Time Out* December 2001), 'the premier meeting place for Lesbians, where ever we are',[14] 'the world's most famous lesbian brand'[15]. Candy Bar aimed to address a particular aesthetic-ethic niche within the lesbian and bisexual communities by latching onto the place-image of Soho and by endorsing a lifestyle along the lines of images of the gay male lifestyle: fashion consciousness, clubbing and sexual cruising. As only a hybrid between a bar and a club, it amplifies an ambience of clubbing by running club nights at other club venues or festivals. The social composition of the bar staff was an essential part of the sign-valuing of the venue. The 'Candy Bar girls' usually wore T-shirts with the brand logo and were designed as role models of the bar. To some extent, this resulted in them being perceived by visitors as exclusive in-crowd. Knowing or even befriending them was believed to create insider status in the bar. By contrast, according to the promoter Angela Reed (2002), Heaven intended to be an open, accessible mainstream club for everyone and a gay club at the same time. This ambiguity also caused some tension in the club's admission policies. On the one hand, the promoter implied that the club aimed to provide a safe space for a gay and lesbian audience, particularly for people who had just had their coming-out and wished to get involved in the gay scene. On the other hand, she expressed the view that sexuality had become secondary to taste and aesthetics and suggested that sexual identification was no longer the primary focus of clubbers when selecting a club night. She regarded Heaven as a particular aesthetic and ethic environment that cut across sexual boundaries.

> Nowadays it's not so much of a gay thing or a straight thing, it's a club thing . . . Entry into Heaven isn't about your sexuality, isn't about

whether you're a boy or a girl, it's about your attitude and if you fit in. (Reed 2002: 1–2)

The primacy of aesthetics and attitude over sexuality was also reflected in the way in which the club incorporated a 'drag' element. It not only encouraged members of the crowd to dress up in drag but also employed a team of drag queens in order to foster a party atmosphere. Drag was less seen as an element of queer culture rather than a visual spectacle and marker of glam and flamboyancy:

> Drag in its very nature has changed over the years as well. It used to be a very big part of gay culture of years ago. Now it's a different sort of drag, it's all about glam, it's all about the dressing up, and that's why we incorporate the drag into, not because 'oh, look there is a bloke in a dress' . . . it's sort of added value . . . drag is a focal point, it's very visual, it's very exciting, it's very escapist. . . . It's an entertainment. (Reed 2002: 3)

ALLEGORICAL AND SYMBOLIC BOUNDARIES: DOOR POLICIES AND SOCIAL INTERACTION

It is of particular interest if and how the clubs' image work and codification, as well as the wider cultural context of gay and lesbian clubbing, framed people's classification practices and the negotiation of identity in the clubs. The following analysis describes and illustrates different types of boundary work that were accentuated in these spaces, which ultimately impacted on understandings of membership and belonging. As Chapter 4 unfolded, dance clubs are spheres for the aestheticization of the body through stylization and sensation, spaces where aesthetic, embodied reflexivity is a central element in self-presentation, dance and interaction. Identity and boundary work through self-presentation and the reading and classification of others not only involves conceptual distinctions, but also aesthetic classifiers and modes of reflexivity (i.e. concrete particulars such as sounds, mimetic gestures, movement, objects). Lash and Urry distinguished between allegory and symbol as two different modes of aesthetic reflexivity in contemporary life (Lash and Urry 1994: 51–58). The symbol rests on a unity of signifier and signified, whereas allegory disrupts this unity. For example, a symbolic reading of body appearance renders the body as an expression of qualities or essences of self/identity. In allegorical readings, such assumptions about the coherence between appearance and essence are destabilized; allegory refuses closure and leaves a space of indeterminacy. Stylization, for example, can work in both ways, either by using the body as a surface for displaying symbolic codes and signs in order to construct particular notions of authenticity (e.g. as in modelling a certain type of lesbian identity), or as an allegorical play with body symbols that challenges fixed typifications and a surface–depth model of identity (e.g. as in creating masks).[16]

The following part sketches examples of these two types of boundary work. One highlights 'either/or' modes of classification through binary categories. The other emphasizes a 'both/and' logic of classification, in which distinctions and categories become blurred and categorization as either one or the other impossible. The latter suggests a weaker form of boundary work where othering processes are contested or made more difficult by ambiguous and indeterminate enactments. These modes of reflexivity and classification were present in both night-life spaces. Yet, Candy Bar showed a stronger tendency than Heaven towards more rigid in-group/out-group distinctions and a concern with purity, while the second type of boundary work was more prevalent at Heaven. This assumption, of course, is built on a limited range of interview and ethnographic data, and is therefore insufficient to assess the general validity for the encounters in these or other spaces. However, the question arises as to how these tendencies towards certain types of boundary work might be connected to particular institutional modes of ordering in these club spaces and to the wider cultural shifts in the regime of heteronormativity spurred by processes of recuperation and fetishization (see Chapter 7).

These points shall be illustrated by four telling examples of boundary work at a) the entrance to these spaces and b) in the social interaction inside the clubs. Narrative accounts of experiences in the women's bar were strongly framed by the category of belonging or non-belonging, of feeling part of its culture and of being able to relate to the crowd. This partly reflected the degree to which visitors gained recognition of complying with the sign-values of the space. The ambitious efforts of the management to shape and typify a particular lesbian lifestyle created a space with a strong, appealing sign-value. However, to some extent, this space tended to be read as a closed and standardized, if not normative aesthetic environment. It was seen to feature a certain body look and a 'cruisy' attitude that marginalized feminine style as other. Sexual identification was no longer perceived as sufficient to claim access, or belong to the space. Narrations included many tales about in-group and out-group distinctions entwined with the hierarchization of styles. The gay-mixed club illustrated a more general trend towards casting off its sexual codification and was more willing to accept external others; in that sense it was more like other sexually unmarked public spaces. In contrast to Candy Bar, experiences of the gay club, as represented in the interview data, were not so much framed by the issue of belonging. Instead, the club tended to be decoded as a 'space-to-move-through'. This not only applied to the night out, but was also indicated by individuals' long-term clubbing pathways. Punters new to the gay club scene regarded Heaven as a good place to start, but eventually moved on to explore other clubs. The non-place aspect is contrasted by claims to territory. The image work of the club as a 'gay club' and also a 'club for everyone' resulted in ambivalent processes of openness and closure and partly caused concerns among gay audiences about a 'straight colonization' of 'their' space.

However, as the examples shall demonstrate, despite the tendencies towards certain types of boundary work, Candy Bar was not simply a space of internal differentiation and hierarchization; and Heaven was not merely a space of heterogeneity and complexity, where stereotypes of gender and sexuality were disrupted. Even in this mixed, partly queer space sexual boundary work did not disappear, not simply because heteronormativity became renormalized through the visibility of heterosexual bodies, as some authors argued (Casey 2004), but because (gay and lesbian) visitors themselves deployed heteronormative discourses in the reading of (hetero-)sexuality (see also Eves 2004: 481, 487).

Membership, Boundary Work and Door Management

A significant element in the institutional ordering of dance and night-life spaces is the regulation of people's access to clubs through admission and door policies. This involves a visual classification of bodies and a simultaneous evaluation of whether or not these bodies fit in with the desired club clientele. In the case of sexually codified spaces, this visual practice invokes symbols (or stereotypes) of gender and sexuality. However, as the previous section highlighted, aesthetic codes may overlay or even supplant sexual identity categories. The door policies and interaction practices at the door of both clubs revealed the complex entanglement of sexual and aesthetic markers. Aesthetic criteria were frequently seen by visitors to constitute tacit, vague and flexible rules underneath the official policy.[17]

As for the women's bar, aesthetics were understood to create additional boundaries further confining the sexual identity boundaries when negotiating access and cultural membership. The aforementioned notion of the in-crowd pointed to processes of hierarchization and social closure. For legal reasons, Candy Bar, when it opened up in 1996, started off with members' licenses. All visitors, upon entering the bar, had to sign up their name and address and were issued a membership card.

> I went to the Candy Bar not so long ago . . . I've sort of signed the book months ago, never got a card . . . but then you know, because I've got longish kind of hair, I mean the door-women were just insisting that I wasn't going in, and it was just, there you go, put my name in the book, I'm a member of here, but I haven't got a card . . . I just stood there saying 'My name is in the book, my name is in the book, give me the book and I bloody show you my name!' And in the end she was like, 'Oh, okay, okay, you'll have to sign a new card, and you have to fill your details in again' . . . I couldn't figure it out. (Kay 1999: 17)

In this situation access to the bar was described as a negotiation about formal criteria of membership. The issue at stake was whether or not the rules and procedures were followed. These, however, failed to appear consistent and systematic to Kay. The inconsistencies made her suspect that the official admission procedure was just invoked to conceal the (aesthetic) judgement of her bodily appearance. Thereby, the bar was perceived as a normative style environment favouring expensive, short haircuts, a certain body size and a toned, sporty body (Kay 1999: 18). This called upon and reinforced Kay's awareness of symbolic codes of lesbian identity and incited her self-classification as an outsider to the bar crowd. In referring to her 'longish hair', which alluded to femme style, non-belonging oscillated between failing to pass as a member of the sexual community and failing to pass as a member of the aesthetic community.

By contrast, the gay-mixed club Heaven was interpreted as an open and accessible space. A young woman, Lisa, who identified as heterosexual, recounted how she and her female friend both dressed up in nurses' outfits and queued up for a Saturday 'gay' night at Heaven, but were turned away. At the top of the queue, a man in front of them was having an argument with the door staff.

> He said, 'Look, why can't I get in, I mean, you're gonna let those two in, aren't you?' pointing at us, and I was pretty sure that if he had not opened his trap, she would have let us in. And she then turned to us and said, 'You do know this is a gay club, don't you?' 'Yes, we do', and she said, 'Well, are you gay?', and we both went, 'Yeah' [high voice, S.R.]. And she then sort of said, 'Well, you're very welcome to come back on a Wednesday or Friday night or Monday, but I can't let you in tonight'. And I just stood there and said, 'Do you really think, if I was straight, I'd be wearing an outfit like this?' And she went, 'I don't know, do I?' (Lisa 2000: 7)

Despite not proving successful in this instance, aesthetic performance was seen to get one through the door even on the Saturday gay night. The fact that Lisa and her friend chose this night suggests that they either counted on passing as lesbians, or that they expected the door policy to be rather flexible, assuming they could get in even without passing as lesbians, just by wearing a spectacular outfit. Being turned away was construed as an unexpected situational outcome resulting from the security's attempt to appear rule-consistent. Officially, the door supervisor justified the refusal of access on the basis of sexual categorization rather than aesthetic evaluation. Lisa implied that they were turned away not for aesthetic reasons, but for failing to pass as members of the sexual community: 'apparently we looked too straight' (Lisa 2000: 6). This phrase indicates that the negotiation and categorization of sexual identity was strongly grounded in body looks and performative enactments. According to Lisa, the door supervisor rendered visual signs such as the costumes and the body performance more reliable than verbal questioning. In rejecting their identity claim she called upon symbolic markers of lesbian identity. However, in explicitly negating the possibility of identifying the young women's sexual orientation through the costume, these symbolic codes were also destabilized.

Social Interactions

As the example in the previous section indicated, a short haircut was considered part of the style norms in the women's bar. Longer hair, as a sign of femininity, was seen to be a marginalized style. Indeed, several other interviewees' accounts were aware of this and other aesthetic norms. Feminine appearance, body size and the lack of the right fashion labels were also understood to differentiate out-groups from in-groups, causing feelings of non-belonging. Giselle, a lesbian-identified woman in her mid-twenties, alluded to different readings of hairstyle. Having visited the bar with long hair she felt herself being perceived (or 'blanked') as 'special', 'novelty' and 'probably not even gay' (Giselle 2000: 34). By contrast, when she frequented the bar with a shaved head, she felt 'more accepted' and part 'of the gang' (ibid. 26-27). Nevertheless, in the following extract Giselle related an incident in which the status achieved through hairstyle was threatened yet again. Similar to Kay quoted above, being denied recognition and cultural membership called up and reinforced certain classification systems.

> I went in there [= Candy Bar, S.R.] recently, and I had short hair and I was wearing jeans, but had a tight top on, and so I was classified as girlie by this woman . . . She was like, 'Oh, yeah, you've cut your hair, but you're still a bit of girlie, aren't you?' (Giselle 2000: 34–35)

The classification as a 'girlie' further entailed an assignment and hierarchization of sexual motives and attitudes. This converged on the opposition of a 'cruisy', casual sex attitude on the one hand and a 'relationship approach' on the other hand.

> She was like, 'I am really into one-night stands. I bet you girls [referring to Giselle and her friend, S.R.] are nice girls, aren't you, I bet you girls are', you know, 'just want a relationship.' She was implying that sort of thing; and yeah, it's just so weird that suddenly she just feels she has to say this kind of attitude, this kind of analysing us and saying what we have been like, just because we look a bit less, we're not hiding our bodies. (Giselle 2000: 34–35)

Giselle construed this interaction as an unwanted assessment of her body and an attack against her membership status. She rebutted it by establishing a different

scheme of classification hinting at the 'butch' body and its 'lack' of femininity. Nevertheless, the dis-identification with the assigned category (a 'nice
girl looking for a relationship') and the very fact of being classified created
feelings of non-belonging.

As mentioned before, Heaven was understood by heterosexual visitors
as open and accessible despite its 'strictly gay' door 'policy' on a Saturday
night. A more diverse and bigger audience and the spatial setting make
visual observation and the classification of people more difficult. Internal
boundary work (within the categories gay or lesbian) seemed to be less
prevalent than the demarcation of boundaries against the external, straight
other. The acceptance of straight visitors into the club caused mixed views
among the gay clientele. Positive feelings were contrasted by concerns about
the segregation of gay and straight people who would converge on different
dance floors. Gay visitors, such as Bruce, felt ill at ease about 'straight men'
who performed their sexuality ostentatiously. He framed the gay club as a
territory for gay people in the first place and wished straight clubbers were
more aware of their 'guest' role:

> You're in my space, you are here and I mean it is not your right to be
> here, you are privileged and the privilege is probably granted by the
> fact that you know a gay person who brought you here tonight. (Bruce
> 2000: 8)

Lesbians likewise were anxious about the 'invasion of their territory' in gay-
mixed nights as it reinforced their minority position even in a gay space (see
also Skeggs 2000: 140). Hailey, who identified as heterosexual, described
how she got into an argument with a group of lesbians when kissing her
boyfriend in Heaven.

> I was with my boyfriend and we were having a kiss in the corner or
> whatever, and all these lesbians got really angry with us, started throw-
> ing lemons at us and things because we were having a snog, and they
> were like, 'Get to your own place blah blah blah'. And I can understand
> that to a degree, but it's really rude. So then my boyfriend turns around
> and starts and snogs my friend Ted and then snogs this friend, I mean,
> it was just, we were just being really silly. (Hailey 2000a: 16)

The lesbians appeared to have framed this situation as a 'straight colonization' of 'their' space. Their reaction comes to the fore as a result of
their feelings of marginalization in heterosexual space (Hailey quoted
them as saying, 'we could never do that in a straight club', 2000a: 17).
Hailey's friends subordinated themselves to the club's sexual codification
by mimetically integrating homosexuality as a performative, 'silly' act that
criss-crossed a clear-cut reading of their (hetero-)sexuality. This allegorical
boundary not only disturbed the classification by strangers:

He [i.e. her boyfriend, S.R.] feels comfortable in his sexuality. My boy-friend knows, I think he knows that he is not gay, maybe he is, maybe that's the problem, could be actually, ahm no but no, but he feels very comfortable, he likes being with women and you know, he is—is not gay, which is why he can have a laugh with my friends and have a snog, which has happened a couple of times. (Hailey 2000a: 16)

As this example shows, in claiming membership status, clubbers identifying as heterosexual, carved out a space for playful experimentation by inte-grating homosexuality as aesthetic performance and a subjunctive mode of acting 'as-if' that oscillates between imaginary and symbolic identification (see Chapter 4 and Žižek 1997a: 141–143).

CONCLUSION

This case study started out with the question as to what implications the changes in the urban night-life geography of some UK cities—in particular, the trend towards the opening up of gay clubbing scenes to heterosexual audiences and the emergence of new sexual codifications—have for the for-mation and negotiation of sexual identities. The mobilization of non-nor-mative sexualities for cultural consumption is a debated issue. In contrast to research on club and dance cultures that puts great emphasis on emerg-ing transgressive sexualities and on the opening up of sexual identity cate-gories (e.g. Pini 2001), the exemplary analysis in this paper revealed a more complex and ambiguous entanglement of the weakening and strengthening of identity boundaries.

Both dance clubs were decoded by visitors as aesthetic environments as much as being recognized as sexually defined spaces. However, in the wom-en's bar, aesthetics and style were seen to further constrain the boundary established by the sexual codification and were seen to confine cultural membership, in line with the branding, to a particular segment *within* the lesbian consumer group. In the gay club, aesthetic stylization was used by ('heterosexual') visitors as a way to open the gates and to (re-)establish membership status in the face of exclusion.

The constitution of, as well as the exclusion from, membership in sex-ually codified night-life spaces is thus strongly grounded in practices of aestheticization and aesthetic classification. Aesthetics allow for the desta-bilization, and for the re-symbolization of sexual identity at the same time. This particular case study shows that the aestheticization of sexuality does not necessarily prompt a symmetrical, general weakening of identity boundaries and sexual divides, but prompts an uneven redefinition of sex-ual boundaries. In the above examples, flexible, playful appropriation and experimentation by heterosexual visitors was contrasted by the protective and normative closure of identities, especially by gay and lesbian visitors.

In this respect, the internal differentiation processes and the stronger symbolic boundaries around lesbian identity may be related to the reframing of heterofemininity in the context of club culture more generally (see Chapter 7 and Pini 2001). However, ethnographic research as well as repeated visits to the bar in the subsequent years suggested that femininity was not quite such a marginalized 'other' as implied in the interviewee accounts discussed here; quite the contrary, it seemed to grow a visible presence and perhaps also greater acceptance and appreciation in the women's scene. Perhaps this can even be seen as an effect of the 'new homonormativity' propagated in media representations. Even if the above results are preliminary, the question that warrants further study is: Who can deploy aesthetics as a resource of play and appropriation, and on whom do aesthetics work as disciplinary, normalizing power?

In contrast to celebratory readings of contemporary dance cultures, this chapter has shown that dance spaces, despite offering the possibility of abandon and new forms of collective identification, are also deeply contested territories. This contestation provokes operations of disciplinary and normalizing power manifested in the examination and judgement of bodies in relation to symbolic hierarchies (Foucault 1977). Thereby bodies are 'invested with certain properties and inserted into regimes of truth' (McNay 1992: 28). Thus, clubbing scenes are technologies of subjectification and normalization producing docile bodies and differentiated individuals as much as they constitute spheres for transgressive or 'limit' experiences.

Notably, normalization is not only effected through a repertoire of authenticity (symbolic modes of recognition), but also performativity (allegorical reflexivity). Both draw on and redraw hetero- and homonormative discourses. The awareness that performative enactments create only a visual illusion of authenticity is linked to a simultaneous belief in this very illusion. Performative enactments are questioned and at the same time called upon as symbols of identity and authenticity. The attempt to resist categorization by means of allegorical enactments can itself be seen as a form of normalization in its fixation on the body as an arena of control (Bordo 1995: 272–275, 296). However, bodies are always ambiguous and can neither be authenticated by oneself nor another. But this ambiguity, as Susan Bordo noted, is 'unsettling and challenging' (Bordo 1995: 293). Therefore, whilst aware of the shortcomings of a body symbolism, everyday/night actors hold on to their attempts to construct intelligible, unambiguous bodies despite the incoherences and puzzles they may face in the reading of the other.

9 Conclusion

AESTHETICIZATION AND MARKETIZATION: BETWEEN TRANSGRESSION AND NORMALIZATION

Compared to other books on the subject, this book might be perceived as taking a rather prosaic and unsentimental perspective on clubbing cultures, failing to pay tribute to the special nature of the elevating and uplifting experiences that one can have in such contexts. Indeed, it aimed to break away from the romantic and celebratory appraisal of youth- and popular-cultural practices that forms an underlying thread in so many studies in these fields, no matter whether they are vested in subcultural, post- and after-subcultural or any other fashion. The focus on spectacular and extraordinary practices often carries with it an implicit assumption that these are more resistant, oppositional and creative than other, less-spectacular activities. This is because these spectacular cultural practices under study tend to become surfaces onto which identifications, hopes (and worries) of the researchers are projected. But Simon Frith (2004: 176) asks quite rightly, why would a person who is ostentatiously pierced all over the body be necessarily more 'resistant' to dominant culture than a person who joins a choir? Studying the spectacular components of youth lifestyles may deflect attention away from more mundane aspects and processes that structure the lives of (young) people. It may also contribute to popular images that suggest that such spectacular practices are widespread or that problematize such lifestyles and people engaging in them as either being 'in trouble' or 'causing trouble' (Cieslik 2003: 5). It is all the more important to bear in mind that clubbing participants are also ordinary people with ordinary lives and problems to think about. Likewise, the spectacular aspects of clubbing need to be viewed against the backdrop of its ordinary and routine features and the humdrum experiences in day and night life. It was one of the aims of this book to consider clubbing experiences in the context of the prolongation of youth and of biographical transitions such as from education to work; family and relationships; travel and migration; and the formation of sexual codes and identities. It was another aim to bring into focus, and to contextualize, clubbing experiences within the broader framework of (urban) governance and the regulation of night-time entertainment; the leisure market, the development of the night-time economy, the business strategies and market-making of nightclub companies as well as the institutional processes of ordering crowds.

The study of clubbing cultures can be taken into new analytical directions that are not driven by the hopes, dreams or fears frequently projected onto these spheres. This particular book situated clubbing cultures in the debates on aestheticization and prosthetic embodiment, suggesting that these perspectives help conceptualize the kinds of practices and body experiences as well as the play-forms of sociality typical for clubbing spaces. Putting it more acutely, we might say that aestheticization provides a key structure for the framing of experience in these contexts. It fosters specific experiential, cognitive styles or perhaps even a certain *Menschentyp* who is versatile in performative practices, subjunctive modes of acting 'as-if' and a 'fuzzy-minded' ordering of reality as both real and virtual. Welsch (1997: 15) called this ideal-typical figure the *homo aestheticus*. Of course, such experiential styles are not confined to clubbing or similar ludic environments of night life, but particularly pronounced in such contexts. While playful and aesthetic practices always have a potential for critique and for carving out alternative ways of being, the *homo aestheticus* is not per se an oppositional, transgressive or critical actor, but can be understood as a form of subjectification. As such it involves a mode of relating to one's 'self' as a malleable and flexible entity, by way of focusing on the capacity of transformation and self-invention. From this perspective, attention is directed to aesthetic and prosthetic transformation as normative elements or ethical repertoires (in contrast to Foucault's aesthetics of existence as a buffer against normalizing pressure). To some extent, this weakens the ethic of authenticity even though deep involvement and 'real' connections with others remain a central part of what is required and aimed for in clubbing contexts. Aesthetic and prosthetic forms of embodiment can be vehicles for achieving such 'authentic', deep involvement, but they also disrupt the logic of authenticity, i.e. the surface–depth model of self.

Clubbing cultures provide experiential commodities; more precisely, they supply stimuli that enable the consumers to fabricate certain sensuous/emotional states such as spontaneity, expressivity and excitement. Similar to other economies of experience, they rest on the commodification of authenticity—an inherently paradoxical and contradictory process (Boltanski and Chiapello 2005). Marketization is based on the codification of special qualities and differences, which makes possible the transfer and reproduction of these features. However, as soon as something is codified, its multiple and indeterminate character, which is part of its appeal as unique and authentic, tends to give way to schematic and planned scripts, which makes the good appear as less interesting and 'authentic' (ibid. 480–481). This inherent tension plus the fact that experiential commodities are time- rather than substance-based trigger a cycle of permanent renewal. Images of 'sell out to the mass market' illustrate the suspicion of the 'loss of authenticity' and the demands for new, more authentic spaces. Boltanski and Chiapello's reflections on the role of critique, in particular, the critique of inauthenticity, for the renovation of capitalism provide another perspective on the ongoing problematization of authenticity in clubbing and popular (music) cultures. The symbolic opposition between the mainstream and the underground, a variation on the 'mass culture' and 'high art' dichotomy (Huyssen 1986: 53), apart from informing distinction processes and the competition over 'subcultural capital' (Thornton 1995), reflects this very paradox of the marketization of authenticity.

This can be illustrated at the example of drugs in clubbing culture. On the one hand, drugs serve as prosthetic means of deepening the authentic emotional involvement; on the other hand, they provoke scepticism and partly disillusionment about the authenticity of the emotions and affectual bonds created in drug-induced states. Narratives of disillusion conjured up the inauthentic escapism of mass and consumer culture, but they also alluded to a different semantic thread in the critique of inauthenticity—one that centres on insincerity and artificiality rather than on standardization or de-individualization. The suspicion of inauthenticity registered in images of the club as a 'general illusion' and even extended to the perception of self and others in these spaces, for example, in the retrospective mistrust in the friendship ties forged in drug-induced states. Similar to the project-based polis (Boltanski and Chiapello 2005), we might say that clubbing contexts sway between an authenticity norm and a flexibility norm; a deep expressivism on the one hand and a depthless virtualism on the other hand. They adhere to, and reactivate, the reference to authenticity at the same time as they admit to the impossibility or irrelevance of distinguishing between the authentic and the inauthentic.

The ambivalent evaluation of clubbing experiences that was highlighted in this book can be seen in the wider context of critiques of inauthenticity and of the tensions inherent in the marketization of authenticity. Clubbing was associated with the liberation of desire, self-abandonment and positive notions of transgression and excess; but it also provoked fears of losing control and of being carried away, of de-realization and of the possible 'pathological' or immoral facets of the 'excessive' consumption of substances or time. As an object of ethical reflection it was embedded in the justificatory structure of 'tamed hedonism': transgression and excess appeared legitimate when confined to certain spaces and times and when held in check by self-control. Self-experimentation served as another semantic field for producing a strong narrative with a certain degree of distance. This also became evident through the narrative representation of clubbing as an identity project. These projects emphasized agency; control and mastery; and individual progress and achievement. They turned identifications with night-life entertainment, often discredited as 'escapist', 'hedonistic' and 'superficial', into an ethically and morally justifiable project of authentic self-realization. This testifies a need of disarticulating clubbing experiences from possible connections with derogatory images of 'mass'/night-life culture. But it also reflects processes of recuperation, whereby border zones of legitimate culture are turned into resources for working on identity. Such recuperation was more prevalent in the context of masculinity and middle classness. By contrast, speaking from social positions that are more closely associated with 'problematic otherness' entailed a mode of self-distancing by affirming critical notions of the superficial or insincere character of mass culture. By adopting such images, the value of one's clubbing practices and experiences was partly called into question.

The participation in clubbing cultures opened up possibilities for exploring alternative ways of being and for playful identifications beyond heteronormative models, but at the same time upheld such models. For example, in the context of femininity the exploration of, and experimentation with, sexuality was combined with romantic tales of love and marriage. The imagery of clubbing magazines promoted and codified the entry into non-heteronormative sexual roles, but fashioned such scenarios within the limits of heteronormative, binary constructions of gender. Thereby, certain play-roles of otherness were integrated into heteronormativity, whilst the boundary to non-assimilable elements, serving as the constitutive other of (hetero-)normative positioning, was redrawn. Aestheticization prepared the ground for identifications which blurred identity categories and destabilized the symbolic markers supporting these. But this also provoked intensified boundary work between authentic and inauthentic embodiments and reinforced regimes of normativity. There is, therefore, no straightforward, one-dimensional change of gender relations and sexual boundaries in club cultural spaces towards more equality and acceptance of diversity. Instead, the complex entanglement of dynamics of recuperation and repudiation produces ambivalent effects and varied consequences for different groups of participants, challenging as well as reproducing heteronormative scripts. The frame of play and simulative acting opens up opportunities for non-committal experimentation with virtual roles, but at the same time provides a basis for passing off less-acceptable forms of behaviour such as machismo, (hetero-)sexism, racism or else in the mantle of irony. Acting 'as-if' can be taken in all sorts of directions and oriented towards different ends. As hinted at above, aestheticization may be a resource of playful appropriation and experimentation, but it may also be a vehicle of normalizing power by supplying a repertoire of aesthetic symbols of authenticity, i.e. style codes. The question to be addressed is: Who can deploy aesthetics as resource of play and on whom do they work as disciplinary, normalizing power?

Furthermore, whilst aestheticization allows for new identifications and helps create experiences of the extraordinary and the 'elsewhere', it is set against the backdrop of the ordinary. The semantics of transgression and their translation into situated practices are informed, amongst others, by everyday identities and social locations as the gendered narratives indicated. Despite taking issue with the problematic side of 'excessive' drug consumption, men more easily accentuated the 'freedom of excess' in their narratives of adventure, risk and a total loss of control, featuring a grotesque body-out-of-balance or out-of-place. In women's accounts, the complete loss of control, notwithstanding positive notions of pleasure and excess, tended to be associated with the risk of victimization, immorality or self-estrangement. Clubbing expresses identities that are anchored outside the club sphere. Social positions to some extent circumscribe what particular modes of participation in clubbing contexts are deemed legitimate and appropriate; and they also influence the ways in which experiences of clubbing are or are not linked to projects of identity and authenticity. Even though education-to-work and family transitions are key dimensions in the reproduction of class, gender and ethnic inequalities, youth cultural and clubbing sites too mediate the institutionalization and (re-)production of symbolic and social boundaries. At the same time they allow for new identifications through which such boundaries may be challenged. Clubbing is not only a site for temporary, leisure-based weekend or night-time identities, as it may well be (Roberts 2003: 22), but— as biographical case studies show—it can also become a sphere (combined with other spheres) where identities, world views and attitudes are remoulded in more profound ways.

This, however, is not necessarily always experienced as empowerment (see also Hutton 2006), but can also signify possibly problematic transformations that initiate a reorientation as indicated in narratives of mastery. Sexual stylization and play with non-normative roles may be empowering in one sense, but may come at the price of risk or sexual objectification. As should have become clear, club cultures are not simply sceneries of transgression and liberation from repressive normalization and disciplinary power that structure, at least in part, everyday life and the social institutions that govern the lives of (young) people. Clubbing contexts too are partly structured by operations of disciplinary power and normalization, not only in terms of intensified surveillance by the authorities and club managements, but also in terms of the interaction and categorization practices of participants themselves.

The discussion of club cultural economies as well as of governance and regulation highlighted that night-life culture respectively its participants are not 'unruly' or transgressive per se, but that first, the invitation to transgression of the ordinary and the 'structured provision for liminality' (Hobbs, Lister, Hadfield, Winlow, and Hall 2000: 712, Turner 1974: 260) are central to contemporary urban leisure and entertainment economies; second, market dynamics such as growing pressures for profit exerted by property owners, landlords or shareholders of listed companies may contribute to and intensify problems such as binge drinking; and that third, the regulation of urban night-time entertainment through laws and administrative measures embedded in particular regulatory traditions is not external to, but is already implicated in, the cultures that become objects of regulation. Certain types of regulation may provoke and amplify precisely the transgressions that are sought to be contained in the first place.

NEW DIRECTIONS FOR CLUB CULTURAL RESEARCH

What is so interesting about the phenomenon of clubbing culture that it warrants future study and writing about it? Quite rightly, Phil Cohen (2003: 47) criticized that there often is a sense of déjà vu about youth culture studies, as they keep telling the same old research story and place themselves at the service of market research companies in need of information about the latest consumer trends. At least the former point contains a kernel of truth when considering the studies focusing on clubbing and contemporary dance cultures. Whilst there is no denying that this field has been flourishing over the past decade in terms of quantity, Cohen's critique points to the somewhat inflationary tendency such developments may have, especially if other important areas of research are neglected. The field of study, consisting of many single-site ethnographic studies, looks dispersed and not very well integrated. Comparison and synthesis are exacerbated by varied research foci, methodological approaches and theoretical perspectives that all contribute in their own interesting ways but lack orientation towards more general, overarching sets of questions. A debate is needed which synthesizes common themes and identifies different strands of research in order to map research agendas more systematically. Various such attempts have been made at theoretical level (A. Bennett and Harris 2004, Muggleton and Weinzierl 2003b). Clearly, new questions and themes such as the role of night-life entertainment in the post-industrial urban context (e.g. Chatterton and Hollands 2003) and the regulation and governance of night life (Hobbs, Hadfield, Lister, Winlow, and Waddington 2003, Talbot 2007) have shifted the field onto new terrains and have opened up the previous preoccupation with clubbers' experiences. Yet, a more thorough conceptual debate that reflects on the relevance of this field of study and particular strands within it in the wider context of socio-cultural analysis could prove beneficial. This would include a synopsis that first, develops overarching research questions that should be asked about club cultures in a broader analytical and explanatory framework and that second, discusses different theoretical paradigms within which such research can be situated. Sure enough this poses challenges, but also chances. For example, linking up the study of club (and youth) culture more closely to debates in other areas, from which it can productively draw from as much as contribute to, might alter its image as a specialist and rather insulated, 'island' type of research.

Firstly, what I conceive of the most important and promising route for future research is a more *systematic* comparative focus on different local cultures of clubbing, delving into the different meanings, practices and political/societal significances of 'clubbing' in various contexts at the intersection of the global and local. Comparison and synthesis of the scattered studies meets difficulties precisely because the similarities and differences between local clubbing cultures have hardly been made a topic of investigation. Systematic comparison would make possible a more nuanced understanding of the specificity of local cultures. As the formula of clubbing has become a widespread, nearly global signifier of 'going out dancing,' with many local traditions of dance, music and modes of sociality being articulated into it, the study (of local scenes) of clubbing is usefully advanced within wider debates on the globalization of culture, respectively, the interconnections of club cultural economies (see for example Schroeder 2006). Secondly, crucial to the analysis of clubbing practices and experiences is the grasp of clubbing as a cultural-economic field. This involves taking into account the key agents and forces and interfaces with other fields of practice. Significant agents are the venue owners and managers, promoters and DJs, the brewery and beverage industries, the music industry and record labels, event organization companies, radio stations and magazines, the security industry, sponsors and investors. What also requires careful analysis are corporate structures, diversification, subcontracting relations, the genre and star system, the role of advertising and branding as well as internationalization and franchising. Clubbing should be studied in connection with the practices it is interlinked with such as eating out; going to gigs, events or bars; holidaying and tourism. Notably, it is not always marketed as an end in itself, but is also used as a medium for advertising, social or business networking as well as for promotional purposes. These range from consumer products and retail outlets, fashion, design and music to art events, social movement initiatives and even campaigns of political parties, with the formats sometimes blurring and the ends blending into each other as in leisure-retail/night-life complexes. In view of this, club music and dance culture signifies more than a special night-time entertainment activity of young adolescents. It has become a general ingredient of popular and consumer culture, and, to a certain extent, it has even influenced political culture and campaigning. Its role is fuzzy and blurred, which makes it all the more interesting to trace its connections and manifold dimensions. Thirdly, it is indispensable to situate the study of local club scenes in the context of political, economic, social and demographic developments as well as of urban governance and planning, particularly the regulation of night-time entertainment. Exploring the pathways of development of night-time entertainment in two different cities (London and Istanbul) identified some common elements that may not be specific to only these places. This included de-industrialization, run-down city quarters where disused spaces became available for new uses; the transition to post-industrial urban finance, service, culture and experience economies; the expansion of higher education and the formation of new urban middle-class professionals. However, certainly not all urban contexts to which these elements apply saw the emergence of a club and night-life scene in their centres—therefore, this calls for more in-depth, systematic comparison.

Both in London as well as in Istanbul cultural strategies of development began to play a significant role within (urban) governance; however, local path-dependency led to different consequences for, and attitudes towards, night-time economies and clubbing cultures. In Britain, the transition from Thatcherism to Blairism went along with a shift from control and containment to a more explicit endorsement and promotion of the night-time economy. The conservative government had introduced a cultural-industries agenda since the 1980s and began a moderate promotion of the evening economy since the early 1990s. New Labour carried over and intensified cultural strategies of economic development in the visions of 'creative Britain' and 'cool Britannia', whereby youth and minority cultures' innovative potentials were to be resourced and 'converted into entrepreneurial forms of "creative industry"' (Cohen 2003: 50). In the wake of the 'creative city' and '24-hour city' concepts the evening and night-time economy too eventually came to be seen as important for the regeneration of city centres and found active support by some city councils.

In Istanbul, urban renewal of the centre mainly focused on its cultural history and architectural heritage for tourist promotion. Despite acknowledging and accepting the longstanding and ongoing tradition of night-time entertainment in the centre, the local authorities, Islamic or secular, tended to view the bar and club scenes more as a potential cause of decline and less as a vehicle of economic and social development. Nevertheless, the bar, club and festival scene experienced a substantial growth especially since the early and mid-1990s driven by the dynamics of economic liberalization and the import of Western consumer trends, music, lifestyles and media and an expanding culture and leisure sector geared towards the middle and upper classes.

Notwithstanding the different overall political perspectives on the night-time economies, London's West End and Soho bar and club area also parallels the development of Istanbul's central night-life cluster in that it was neither planned nor actively promoted by the local council. In this respect, wider economic and social processes such as the ones sketched out above seemed to have been more decisive than policy views on culture and the night-time economies. Even so, forms of night-life regulation and governance, especially licensing and planning, are important instruments that influence the scale and the qualitative and institutional features of night-time entertainment venues as well as the urban night-life geography at large. It became clear that both cities also face similar challenges in the governance of night-life entertainment. This includes conflicts arising from the regeneration and gentrification of city centres, from mixed-use developments, and the saturation of night-life areas. Again, these may be quite common problems in post-industrial urban settings regardless of the particular local circumstances.

In sum, contextualized, ethnographic studies of clubbing continue to be essential but should be approached from a more systematic, comparative perspective taking into account how particular local scenes are affected by the globalization of clubbing culture; the organization of club cultural economies; governance structures and the wider social, economic and political context. Experiences of club and night-life cultures can be explored for a range of issues, potentially open-ended. The brief outline of themes in no way meets the need of integration as set out above. However, I hope that this book overall has opened up new directions to be developed in the future.

Appendix

Interviews With Clubbing Participants

Age = at the time of the interview.
At the time of the interview all interviewees were resident in London. However, several had migrated there from other countries or were of mixed parentage (as indicated in the list below).
All the interviews were treated confidentially. Names are pseudonyms.

Aniela	30, Poland, law student and interpreter	02-02-2000(a)
		24-11-2000(b)
Alex	40, UK, primary school teacher	06-11-2000
Bruce	29, Canada, secondary school teacher	08-11-2000
Clare	early 20s, UK, graduate, club dancer	01-02-2000(a)
		05-07-2000(b)
Chuck	late 30s, UK, design education	24-01-2001
Emine	mid 20s, Turkey, media student, free-lance journalism	03-02-2000
Erik	late 20s, Germany, self-employed masseur	10-02-2000
Gary	late 20s, Canada, media student	13-10-2000
Costa	mid 20s, Greece, art student	04-07-1999
Gia	late 20s, UK, media graduate, cutter in film production	30-11-2000
Hailey	early 20s, Australia, media student, works in television	25-10-2000(a)
		06-12-2000(b)
Giselle	early 20s, UK-German-French parentage, dance student	18-04-2000
	factory work	26-02-2001
Kay	mid 20s, UK, art graduate, works in administration	17-11-1999
Lisa	18, UK, drama student	18-02-2000
Lennie	late 20s, UK, office professional	18-11-1999
Nike	early 40s, Greece, writer and artist	07-02-2000
Sven	late 20s, Sweden, translator	01-12-2000

Sheila	early 20s, UK, student in social work,	
	shop assistant	06-11-2000
Valerie	early 30s, UK, office professional	04-10-2000
Sally	early 20s, UK, club dancer	11-10-2000
Walter	early 20s, UK, student	09-02-2000
Steven	early 20s, UK, media student	11-11-1999
Yong	early 20s, Italy, Korean parentage,	
	media student	26-01-2001

Interviews With Club Promoters and Managers

London

Kim Lucas, Candy Bar	20-06-2002
Angela Reed, Heaven	18-10-2002
Lee Freeman, DTPM	08-11-2000
Tubbs West, Fabric	05-10-2000
Ingo, Club Wotever	20-02-2007
Lise, Club Hussy	20-02-2007

Istanbul

Arhan Kayar, Dream Design Factory	24-06-2007
Osman, Club Naya	25-06-2007
Koray, Studio Live	28-06-2007
Selma Sesbes, Sortie	02-07-2007

Interviews With Licensing Officers

London

John Smith, Lambeth Council	12-02-2007
Simon Gallacher, Islington Council	14-02-2007

Istanbul

Mr. Suayip, Beyoglu District Municipality	27-06-2007
Cemal Aksoy, Besiktas District Municipality	29-06-2007

Interviews With Journalists

Ben McArdle, Ministry magazine	05-10-2000

Notes

NOTES TO CHAPTER 1

1. Club Pacha opened in 1973.
2. Detailed accounts of the rise of dance culture in Britain can be found in Collin (1997), Garratt (1998) and Reynolds (1998).
3. See the Appendix for a full list of interviews that were conducted for this study.
4. Similar debates about post-traditional, individualized forms of association exist in the German-speaking context, where the concept of 'scene' received much attention in recent years. Hitzler, Bucher, and Niederbacher understand scenes as thematically focused cultural networks of people who share certain material or mental forms of stylization and interactively stabilize and develop their commonalities in specific settings (Hitzler, Bucher and Niederbacher 2005: 20).
5. A similar perspective was recently opened up by Gabriele Klein's analysis of pop and techno culture (Klein 2004a). She considered processes of aestheticization foremost in connection to mediatization at a more general level and described the techno scene as an aesthetic community.
6. Judith Butler (1993: 113), for example, summarized this position: a coherent identity position is produced through the production, exclusion and repudiation of abject spectres that threaten those very subject-positions.
7. Malbon for example, excluded gay clubs, because his aims were gaining 'real understandings' of club scenes relatively quickly and being able to empathize with people instead of becoming an ethnographic voyeur (1998: 51). A notable disregard of (lesbian) sexuality can be found in Pini's work (1997, 2001), which is even more striking in the light of her outspoken critique that females' clubbing experiences have been rendered invisible and her claim that women experienced sexually liberating aspects within rave scenes. Despite having also researched all-women events (2001: 89), lesbian sexuality was, if at all, mentioned as a moment of post-feminism or of 'new modes of femininity' (Pini 1997: 11, 42). Overall, lesbian sexuality or identity did not seem worth much reference in relation to the 'new feminine sexualities' and 'erotic pleasures beyond sexual boundaries' (Pini 2001: 164–165). In the early years of the new decade, studies on club cultures began to pay more attention to gay and lesbian clubbing scenes; for example, one of three clubs researched by Measham, Parker, and Aldridge (2001: 65) had a largely gay, lesbian and bisexual clientele. Other examples were Buckland's study of queer club cultures in New York (2002), and Chatterton and Hollands (2003), who considered the mainstreaming of gay clubs among heterosexual audiences. More

intensive debate has unfolded over the last years about the fetishization of gay villages (see more details in Chapters 7 and 8).

8. The particular method used in this study was originally devised by the German sociologist Fritz Schütze (1978) and further developed in contexts of biographical social science research (e.g. Rosenthal 1995, Sieder 1982; see also Chamberlayne, Bornat, and Wengraf 2000). It rests on the assumption that concentrated narrating may unfold a mimetic stream of remembering which resembles in its formal organization the course and motivational relevances of action (Schütze 1978). Interviewing comprises different stages and starts with an open and non-directive question giving interviewees room to talk with as little intervention as necessary by the interviewer. More direct questioning usually follows after the initial narrative generated by the interviewee.

9. While the large-scale research of Measham et al. (2001: 74–76, 90) as well as other studies such as Release (1997) demonstrated the feasibility of undertaking research in clubs, they also tell of the number of practical and ethical problems involved in doing in-situ research with (intoxicated) people in these high-noise settings.

10. Amongst other difficulties, the diversification of the club scenes renders this problematic (Measham et al. 2001: 63–65, Mintel 2000a, Release 1997). On local variations in relation to employment status of club visitors, see Forsyth (1998). Mintel market research (2000a: 7), which includes a very wide range of night-time venues, found that slightly more men and singles are among what the survey classified as the 'heavy visitors' (those going out once a fortnight or more).

11. The Appendix lists all interviewees by name (pseudonym), age, ethnic background and occupation.

12. Visual recording technologies would make possible other forms of documentation, but are outweighed by ethical, legal and practical problems. First, it is impossible to seek consent from all participants that could possibly be caught on camera. Second, due to the increasing prevalence of video surveillance in public space as well as in clubbing spaces filming is likely to be perceived as obtrusive. Third, the violation of privacy would raise data protection issues and finally, club managers and security usually do not allow recording inside the venues (except for their own security purposes or for media photographers and filmers) and therefore do not accept bringing cameras into clubs.

13. It shall be noted that this, of course, also remains short of covering *all* kinds of sexually codified dance clubs.

14. A similar empirical study focusing on notions of self-realization and self-stylization in youth cultural contexts in Germany, particularly rave and dance culture, was presented by Stauber (2004).

NOTES TO CHAPTER 2

1. The following sections are based on a range of different sources. Research literature served as the main source of information on Istanbul in addition to semi-structured interviews with two licensing officers from different district municipalities (Beyoglu, Besiktas) and with four club promoters and managers conducted in June 2007. Club promoters and managers were interviewed in English; the licensing officers were interviewed in Turkish with the help of a local translator. Interviews were transcribed and translated. In the case of London, the main research activities took place between 1998 and 2000 (see the introductory chapter), but additional

semi-structured interviews with licensing officers from different boroughs in London (Islington, Lambeth) and with club promoters were carried out in February 2007 (see the Appendix for a full list of interviews). Apart from interview data, the chapter is based on policy documents (e.g. licensing policies of various boroughs, urban development plans) and research and media reports on the night-time economy published since the early 2000s. Due to the increased political and economic interest invested in the cultural sector and the night-time economy and spurred by the legal changes affecting licensing and door security, there has been an enormous upsurge of academic, market and policy-oriented research on the night-time economy in the UK in the last few years.

2. For the period between 1991 and 2004 Mintel market research estimated a 10 per cent increase in the number of pubs, bars and nightclubs in the UK (Mintel 2004: 5, 10).

3. The former A3 class included a range of activities, between which premises could change without the need for planning consent (Tiesdell and Slater 2006: 145).

4. The Unitary Development Plan will be superseded partly by the Local Development Framework introduced under the Planning and Compensation Act 2004.

5. In 2004 the press took issue with the state of British town centres at night. In 2005 the *Daily Mail* mounted a campaign against 'binge drinking' (M. Roberts 2006: 334).

6. The London Plan, short for the Mayor's Spatial Development Strategy defines particular policy areas: a central activity zone (CAZ), largely identical with central London, five sub-regions (North, North East, North West, South East, South West) and a town-centre network. A network and hierarchy of centres is part of government Planning Policy Statement 6: 'Planning for Town Centres'. This policy also sets out the government objectives for town centres, which focus on enhancing consumer choice and on creating diverse retail, leisure, entertainment, culture and tourism functions.

7. In addition to the general policies set out in the London Plan, the mayor published a more detailed, non-statutory best practice guide on managing the night-time economy (GLA 2007) in order to develop a consistent policy approach. This also follows the government planning policy for town centres. Local authorities are to consider the cumulative impact of, and form partnerships to manage, the evening and night-time economy.

8. For example, the premises still open in Westminster after the underground stops running are capable of holding 156,000 people (Westminster 2008: 133).

9. For example, over a third of the residents of Islington Council in London are aged between 16 and 34.

10. Except on Friday nights between 1 and 6 a.m., when most reports related to incidents in nightclubs.

11. This also contrasts the former mayor's position that saturation policies would be more appropriate in mainly residential areas (GLA 2007: 42).

12. As the Licensing Policy Statement of a London borough put it, 'problem premises will be controlled, while those that seek to operate reasonably will not be subject to unreasonable restrictions' (Islington 2005: 10). Residual night-life spaces outside the mainstream commercial drinking culture are increasingly marked as 'other' or 'disorderly' (Chatterton 2002).

13. Upon entering fingerprints and a photo are taken from punters, which are then added to a database along with the date of birth and address taken from an ID. Fingerprint identification is used each time they visit the venue.

If visitors get banned from one premise, these 'offences' are recorded on the system, and the local Pubwatch scheme can ban them from one or all venues for a specified time.

14. Recep Tayyip Erdogan was Mayor of Greater Istanbul from 1994 to 1998 as a member of the Welfare Party (Refah Partisi). In 1997 the Welfare Party was banned for threatening the secular nature of the state and in 1998 Erdogan was imprisoned for promoting the banned Welfare Party. In 2001 Erdogan and a faction of moderate conservative reformists from the Welfare Party founded the Justice and Development Party (AK Parti).

15. *Pavyons* are best described as bars primarily visited by men to consume music, food and women. Although they are not officially considered to be brothels, they are practically on the cusp of prostitution. *Gazinos* are restaurants and music halls offering an on-stage live music programme; they are frequented by women and men.

16. Istanbul does not have a very strong historical tradition of urban planning or renewal. Historically, governance and planning was characterized by a high degree of informality, sometimes even referred to as 'anti-planning attitude' (Robins and Aksoy 1996: 8, Keyder 1999), which resulted in a patchwork of spontaneously evolving mix-use urban fabric. Urban planning was strongly shaped by a centralized top-down decision-making process, which consisted of formal statutory and legally binding master-plans and short-term informal infrastructure investment plans. But the formal land-use planning system was institutionally weak and overwhelmed by the explosive growth, which could only partly be regulated and was often dominated by retrospective legalization of illegal developments ('planning by amnesty'; see Kocabas 2005: 33). In the mid-1980s modernist functional zoning of urban space was introduced and districts were defined for working, shopping, culture and entertainment (Robins and Aksoy 1996: 9).

NOTES TO CHAPTER 3

1. Licensing records would obviously be a key source. However, as Valverde pointed out, licensing in Britain was a relatively low-tech, non-expert way of governance that until recently was never linked to the production of specialist statistical or expert knowledges (2003: 245–250). As a consequence, licensing records have neither been digitalized nor systematically collected in a central database. Despite recent efforts to step up and improve the knowledge base due to the changes in the governance of night life (see Chapter 2), licensing records to this day partly exist only on paper files stored by local licensing authorities.

2. This includes every business that makes tax returns (PAYE or VAT), but not self-employed individuals.

3. For this research the following databases have been consulted: Amadeus and Lexis Nexis for international company data and Fame, which includes all companies in Britain and Ireland.

4. Under SIC 2003 nightclubs were classified under Section H, Hotels and Restaurants, as part of Bars (55.4). Bars included four subclasses (55.40/1: Licensed clubs, 55.40/2: Independent public houses/bars, 55.40/3: Tenanted public houses/bars, 55.40/4: Managed public houses/bars). Within the new classification scheme (SIC 2007) effective in the UK from 1 January 2008, licensed clubs are categorized under 56.30/1, part of Section I/Beverage Service Activities. If the operation of dance floors excludes beverage serving, it is classified under Other Amusement and Recreation Activities (93.29).

5. Mintel defines nightclubs as 'establishments where the primary offer is that of dancing to music and where drink and food are offered as ancillary items. . . . In addition, an admission fee is normally, but not always, levied (2004: 1).' The venue possesses a Special Hours and a Public Entertainment License (License Act 2003). From 2004, Mintel began to include hybrid venues if they had a dedicated club or dance section, DJs and admission fees (ibid. 12).

6. Economic sociologists such as Michel Callon and his collaborators described market making in service economies as a process of qualification and re-qualification, in which qualities of goods are defined, redefined and transformed throughout production and consumption, a controversial and political process that depends 'on the joint work of a host of actors' (Callon et al. 2004: 65). Qualification involves boundary work, as goods are defined through relations of similarity to, or difference from, other goods within 'a hierarchy of exchangability' (Ryan 1992: 192–193).

7. See also Ryan (1992: 50–54) on the contradictions of the cultural commodity arising from the erosion of use-value (i.e. originality) through exchange value (the principle of equivalence).

8. A caveat relates to expenditures on eating and drinking out as well as DIY, parts of which are likely to be not leisure related.

9. According to Mintel, 78 per cent of the age group 18 to 24 and 61 per cent of 25- to 34-year-olds visit nightclubs (Mintel 2004: 27), and 42 per cent of the 15- to 19-year-olds identify as regular clubbers, going every week or at least once a month (Mintel 2006: 61).

10. Since April 2005 door security staff must be trained and licensed in England and Wales under the Private Security Industry Act 2001. Although the training period of about 28 days is quite short, due to high staff turnover and wage increases this entailed additional costs for operators (Mintel 2004: 6). The Alcohol Harm Reduction Strategy tried to clamp down on irresponsible promotions by the industry such as 'all you can drink' deals (ibid. 11). There are contradictory reports about the effects of the smoking ban, which was introduced in Scotland in March 2006. While the Scottish Licensed Trade Association noted a 10 per cent decrease in the sale of alcohol, Cancer Research UK reported that smoke-free premises managed to attract new consumer groups. A number of smoke-free clubs had their turnover up. Equally, it was supposed that those places that were able to provide outside areas for smoking would also become more popular. Yet, outside smoking raises issues for managing noise disturbances and crowds on the streets, as well as increases the risk of drink spiking because of drinks having to be left unattended inside (see Urban 2007: 17).

11. These figures must be treated with caution as nightclub operators tend to be fairly secretive about the amount of sponsorship as well as turnover.

NOTES TO CHAPTER 4

1. Victor Turner distinguished the liminal from the liminoid. He located liminality foremost in tribal societies and regarded the liminoid as a typical feature of contemporary societies, where contexts of play and experimentation develop apart from the central economic and political processes. While the liminoid resembles liminality, it produces no anti-structure to normative structure. According to Turner, leisure activities, but also art, science and political protest represent such liminoid domains (Turner 1982: 32–33, 52–55; see also Hetherington 1998: 110–113).

2. A similar theme was developed by Giddens (1991: 156), who spoke of the sequestration of experience. This refers to the (institutional) removal and concealment of certain life experiences and moral crises from the routines of everyday life, such as madness, criminality, sickness, death, sexuality and nature. In a sense, club and dance cultures themselves could be regarded as institutional arenas to which certain forms of emotional and bodily expression as well as transgressive behaviour are removed.

3. Hobbs et al. (2000) even suggests that intoxication too has become a normative requirement in such settings.

4. This also evokes the theory of subterranean values, which set apart youth cultures, leisure and hedonism from the sphere of production and formal work values. Subterranean values were seen to exist underneath the surface of official values of a society (Matza and Sykes 1961). See also Jock Young (1971: 126). More detailed discussions are offered by Hebdige (1979: 76–77) and A. Bennett (2000: 16).

5. See also Buckland's study of queer club cultures in New York: 'Some participants wanted to see the club as a space of escape from the outside world; others wanted to see these spaces as pre-political configurations of community that could blossom into political agency outside. Some saw their activity as an individual self-fashioning; others expressed that their decision to go to a club was born out of desire to be with others like themselves and still others found any realization of these desires compromised or unfulfilled in clubs'(2002: 86–87).

6. See also http://www.killingkittens.com/homepage.htm (accessed: 3 December 2008).

7. The turn involves a decision-rule (or rather a set of rules), which orders participants categorically or individually, or both ways (Goffman 1972: 35–38).

8. For example, the dress code advertised on the website of Plan B, a South London club, reads, 'We operate a casual dress code policy to ensure a relaxed and friendly atmosphere in the venue. Trainers are generally fine, but we don't allow baseball caps, hoodies or tracksuits and generally discourage scruffiness. . . . Management always reserves the right to refuse admission' (http://www.plan-brixton.co.uk [accessed: 25 August 2008]). However, not all clubs operate a dress code.

9. As the Mintel survey of 1996 (1996: 15) found, many operators strived for a gender ratio of 60:40 in favour of women, while in practice the crowds are usually equally split or lean towards a majority of men.

10. A number of studies on door work and 'bouncers' at British night-time entertainment venues appeared in recent years, which cannot be followed up here in much detail due to lack of space. This includes the studies by Hobbs et al. (2000 and Hobbs, Hadfield, Lister, Winlow, and Waddington 2003), who view private door and security work as a response to the intensification of violence and disorder in the post-industrial, liminal leisure economies that centre on alcohol consumption. Recently, Hobbs, O'Brien, and Westmarland (2007) explored how female door staff in the night-time economy mediate gender and violence as part of their work role. Monaghan (2002) points to the tensions implicated in door work at dance clubs, especially since the disciplinary power it imposes strongly contrasts with a liminal, body-oriented economy that promotes a carnivalesque hedonism devoid of social constraints.

11. In addition to different institutional styles, the role of door supervisors is also shaped by particular outlooks and norms of behaviour. Professionalization of this role in Britain came relatively recent through the Private Security Act 2001 (see Chapter 2), which introduced obligatory training and registration schemes.

It altered the role and image of door supervisors, partly reframing the control of admission as a measure of security. Yet, the authority of these private policing bodies is still strongly grounded in subcultural codes of (male) honour, physical strength and, if necessary, the threat of violence (Hobbs et al. 2003). Nevertheless, with the professionalization of this role, emotional labour of self-restraining stress and anger and seeking non-violent resolutions to conflicts has gained more importance (as has the employment of female door staff). Additional surveillance measures at the door (CCTV) put the door-supervisors themselves under scrutiny (Monaghan 2002: 407, 414; Hobbs et al. 2007: 24–25).

12. Apparently, door work is indeed seen by some members of staff as an opportunity to meet women (Monaghan 2002: 411, 414).

13. As Rodaway (1994: 91) points out, it is easier to distance oneself from a visual world than an auditory one. Sound constructs an auditory sphere without fixed boundaries. By contrast, visual objects subsist in space and time, have location and duration. Thereby, vision provides a geographical and temporal continuity (ibid.: 114, 125).

14. The grid-group model was originally developed by Mary Douglas and other anthropologists and initially evolved from a Durkheimian concern with classification as the central element of cultural processes. The grid-group model casts four types of social organization along the two dimensions of grid and group, that is, the strength of regulation and integration (although the exact definitions of these dimensions are subject to much debate). The typology generated includes the positional or hierarchist type (high grid/high group), the enclave (low grid/high group), the isolate (high grid/low group) and the individualist type (low grid/low group) of social organization (see Douglas 2007, Mamadouh 1999). Of course clubs may vary in terms of the degree of grid and group; higher grid and group structures may develop in smaller clubs which have a regular audience base drawn from a particular local area or which feature stricter style codes (music or fashion-wise).

15. In his writings on fashion, Georg Simmel (1997b: 188–189, 194) already pointed to the dialectic of imitation and individual differentiation built into the institution of fashion.

16. By contrast, as Melechi argued, dancing in rave and acid-house settings was about the disappearance from the gazes of spectators into dark and anonymous zones (Melechi 1993: 37).

17. This distinction of the classical and the grotesque body stems from Bakhtin (1968; see also Featherstone 1991: 79, Stallybrass and White 1986).

18. Turner distinguished the 'subjunctive mood of culture', the 'maybe', 'might be', 'as-if', from the indicative mood of ordinary life embracing cause and effect, rationality and common-sense (1986: 42).

19. As Welsch (1997) demonstrates, the concept of the aesthetic has no single ultimate meaning, but comprises a range of semantic elements and groups. In a general sense it refers to the sensuous basis of perception; more narrowly, it circumscribes theories of the beautiful and of artistic form.

20. The concept of mimesis also captures the key moments of aesthetic reflexivity: mimesis involves understanding and expression through the senses and the body rather than through theoretical thinking. It evolves from practical experience and simulates or represents something in a concrete way with qualities that are similar to qualities in other phenomena (Gebauer and Wulf 2003). Interaction orders are movement orders (Klein 2004b: 141) that are based on the 'shared vocabularies of body idiom' (Goffman 1963: 35).

21. Lury's (1998) argument is that a prosthetic culture is beginning to emerge in Euro-American societies; however, it is neither seen to have replaced 'synthetic' culture (and possessive individualism), nor is prosthesis as such

considered to be specific for contemporary Euro-American societies alone. The focus of interest are the new forms that prosthetic culture takes on, expanding from mere mechanical replacement or perceptual prosthesis to soft technologies interiorized into the body. Not all members of Euro-American societies participate equally or on the same terms in prosthetic culture.

22. Husserl distinguishes between primary remembrance (retention) and secondary remembrance (recollection). While retention is a 'still-being-conscious of the just having-been', the identity of an object is constituted in recollection (see Schütz 1967: 48–49).

23. For instance, a common idealization is that a car cannot go forwards and backwards simultaneously (Pollner 1987: 26).

24. Pollner tagged the dismissal of some experiences as deficient representations of reality as 'ironicizing', for example, through notions of 'illusion', 'repression' or 'hallucinations' (Pollner 1987: 70–71).

25. Schütz referred in this regard to Husserl's distinction between predications of existence (or non-existence) and predications of reality (or fiction) (1971: 237). Authenticity has many shades of meaning shaped in the discourses of Romanticism in the late eighteenth century and the romantic critiques of modernity and alienation. Berman (1971) pointed out a key difference between inauthenticity as insincerity or as self-alienation, in the sense that modern society makes impossible the expression of, and distorts, authentic modes of being.

26. While perception is a more cognitive and reflexive evaluation favouring long-range senses, sensation is a more sensual evaluation of pleasure or displeasure related to vital interests of the body (see Welsch 1997: 60–64).

27. This distinction also loosely correlates with two of Caillois' categories of games, in particular with mimicry and ilinx (Caillois 1961).

28. Even personhood was described as simulacra (see Deleuze and Guattari 1984: 366).

29. On mimesis, dance and simulation see also the discussion in Klein (2004a).

30. This point is indebted to Brian Massumi's elaboration of the Deleuze-Guattarian notion of 'becoming' as bodily thought and unhinging of habit when a zone of indeterminacy opens up between stimulus and response (Massumi 1992: 99).

31. On the dialectic of innovation and sedimentation underlying the acquisition of habit and the significance of habit for the construction of identity see Ricoeur (1992: 121–122).

32. Symbolic boundaries, moreover, 'are often used to enforce, maintain, normalize, or rationalize', but also to 'contest and reframe' social boundaries, 'the objectified forms of social differences manifested in unequal access to and unequal distribution of resources (material and nonmaterial) and social opportunities' (Lamont and Molnár 2002: 168, 186). The concept of boundary work was originally developed by Thomas Gieryn in his analysis of ideological practices in the science field (Gieryn 1983). He described boundary work as an attempt to attribute qualities and to draw lines of demarcation against rivals in order to stake out claims to authority, resources and status.

33. 'It is indeed by comparing a thing with itself in different times that we form the ideas of identity and diversity' (Ricoeur 1992: 125). Ricoeur distinguishes between two meanings of identity as either sameness (*idem*) or selfhood (*ipse*) (1992: 116). Similarly, from a psychoanalytical, Lacanian perspective identity rests on the exclusion of, and the simultaneous fascination by, an abject other (for example, Butler 1993: 113). From a philosophical or deconstructionist Derridian viewpoint identity is a relation of difference, as each meaning or term contains itself and its other, A and non-A (Sampson 1989: 8).

34. '*Oneself as Another* suggests from the outset that the selfhood of oneself implies otherness to such an intimate degree that one cannot be thought of without the other, that instead one passes into the other, as we might say in Hegelian terms' (Ricoeur 1992: 3).
35. A related point was made by Lamont and Molnár, who stated that the relationality of identity may not only rest on a binary logic of difference and opposition, but also on a multiplex logic of 'juxtaposition to a number of possible "others"' (Lamont and Molnár 2002: 174).

NOTES TO CHAPTER 5

1. As was explained in Chapter 4, this does not refer to predications of existence or non-existence, but of authenticity vs. falseness, delusion, dream, or else.
2. Blacks as well as working classes were positioned in similar ways.
3. He developed his DJing also into music production. His future plan was to become a film director. Chapter 6 expands on cultural production and work involvement in dance culture and elaborates on the term 'identity project'.
4. A similar example of the imagination of a dance club as a space of dis-alienation, freedom, security and home can be found in Measham et al. (2001: 163). See also Pini (2001), who similarly elaborated on new forms of belongingness.
5. See Pollner (1987: 70–71) and the discussion in Chapter 4 (part 2).
6. Life-time rate = having used the drug at least once in life. Past-year and past-month rates are defined accordingly.
7. This study was based on 2,000 brief interviews and 362 in-depth interviews. Similar findings were discussed in the Release survey carried out in London and based on a sample size close to 500 (Release 1997). According to Release, 87 per cent of the club visitors would use at least one illegal drug on the night when being interviewed, the favourite drugs for men and women being cannabis (59 per cent) and ecstasy (53 per cent), followed by amphetamines (39 per cent), LSD (16 per cent) and cocaine (8 per cent; Release 1997: 12–13). Compared with the British Crime Survey of 1994, the club population researched by Release was three times more likely than the general population to have tried cannabis and fourteen times more likely to have tried ecstasy. Despite a higher level of experimentation with LSD, poppers, magic mushrooms and cocaine, the most widely used drug, Release found, was alcohol.
8. GHB or 'liquid ecstasy' is a salty liquid that diminishes inhibitions to open up, creates a sense of delight and has a reputation as an aphrodisiac (Reynolds 1998: 308). In high doses it has narcotic effects. Its chemical structure and its effects bear no similarities to ecstasy.
9. Despite higher life-time rates, which suggest a higher level of experimentation with drugs, the majority of young people do not use illicit drugs on a regular basis. According to the British Crime Survey 2000 around 50 per cent of young people age 16 to 24 had tried drugs in their lives, 29 per cent had consumed an illicit drug within the past year and 18 per cent within the past month (Sharp, Baker, Goulden, Ramsay, and Sondhi 2001). While the life-time rates give the impression of widespread drug-use in the youth population, the past-year and past-month rates point out that current and regular consumption of drugs is limited to a significantly smaller share of young people. Breaking this down to different classes of drugs, only one to five per cent of all 16- to 24-year-olds had used Class A drugs in the preceding year whilst the most widely used drug in all age groups was cannabis, with a life-time rate of 44 per cent followed

by amphetamines with a life-time rate of 22 per cent and a past-month rate of 2 per cent. The Misuse of Drugs Act 1971 classifies drugs on the basis of the supposed harm they may cause. Class A comprises heroin, cocaine, ecstasy and hallucinogens, Class B includes amphetamines and barbiturates. Class C includes steroids, benzodiazepines and growth hormones, ketamine and cannabis. The most recent findings of the British Crime Survey 2007/08 (Kershaw, Nicholas, and Walker 2008) confirm these points and indicate a slight decrease in the use of illicit drugs in both the general as well as the young population. The past-year rates of 16- to 24-year-olds were 5 per cent for cocaine powder, 3.9 per cent for ecstasy, 2.4 per cent for amphetamines and 17.9 per cent for cannabis. Even if measured by frequent use (i.e. the use of any drug more than once a month in the past year), which was at 7.3 per cent, it would not be apt to speak of the normalization of drug use among the young population in general. But higher levels of drug use exist among certain, vulnerable segments of the young, e.g. young offenders, truants, those who were excluded from school, homeless or young people in care (J. Becker and Roe 2005).

10. For example, this involves, amongst other things, the display of the zero-tolerance policy towards illicit drug use and the responsibility of confiscating drugs and reporting to the police. See Chapter 2 for more details.

11. A recent exception to this critical observation is the work by Fiona Hutton (2006), who explored the meanings of drugs in relation to female clubbers' negotiation of risk, pleasure, gender and sexuality. Earlier qualitative studies primarily investigated decision-making processes (Boys et al. 2000; Measham et al. 1998), underscoring people's employment of coping strategies and rational cost–benefit assessments in relation to recreational drug use. On long-term dimensions of drug consumption see for example Parker et al. (1998). The work of Plant and Plant (1992) discussed causes of drug use. The collection of South (1999b) provides useful discussions. The essayistic accounts of Garratt (1998), Collin (1997), Reynolds (1998) and Saunders (1995, 1997) are also helpful.

12. This is in contrast to literary fiction, which constitutes imaginative, mimetic variations around the pre-supposed invariant of the corporeal existence and conditions of acting in the world (Ricoeur 1992: 150).

13. A commentator at the end of the 1980s remarked, 'a lot of people were born again. . . . They gave up their relatively normal lives, 'cos they thought "Why am I doing this shitty job?" You got all these people suddenly deciding to go off and travel' (quoted by Reynolds 1998: 46–47). Melissa Harrison's collection of clubbers' accounts contains more examples (Harrison 1998: 19–23, 26–27).

14. See also Valverde (1998) and Sedgwick (1992).

15. See Roland Barthes' (1977: 94) model of structural analysis of narrative.

16. This recalls Turner's (1969, 1980) notion of ritual structure: separation, margin and re-aggregation.

17. To some extent, this also reflects age, as some of the men referred to in the analysis were older than most of the women, who were in their late adolescence and early twenties.

18. Hutton (2004) drew attention to the ambivalence of sexuality in relation to drug use. On the one hand, women described how ecstasy reduced their inhibitions around body image and forged more intense sensual experiences as well as it opened up scope for experimentation. On the other hand, women felt that their drug taking could increase some men's expectations that they were 'up for it' and could put unwanted pressure on women to have casual sex.

19. Dependency in relation to dance-drugs was usually not described as substance addiction, but more in terms of a 'process-addictive behaviour'. This notion accentuates drugs as an integral part of a series of addictive activities

or interactions. The differentiation between forms of addiction stems from Anne W. Schaef and Diane Fassel (1988, quoted from Ettorre 1992: 130).
20. Before its de-legalization, MDMA was used in some therapeutic settings and in the US. As a response to its popularization in the nightclub scenes, e.g. in Dallas, it was banned in the 1980s. In the UK, MDMA is an illegal Class A drug since the Misuse of Drug Act 1971 (Modification) Order of 1977 (Reynolds 1998: xxiii–xxiv).
21. The view that drug use may exacerbate pre-existing depressive states was also expressed in research (Measham et al. 2001: 130).
22. This may be due to 'cocktail' pills that contained MDA rather than MDMA. MDA may have hallucinatory effects similar to LSD (Reynolds 1998: 192).
23. Drug taking was not a very central topic in the narratives of lesbian-identified interviewees.

NOTES TO CHAPTER 6

1. This is similar to philosophical notions of 'project'; for example, in Heidegger's existential philosophy, project (or *Entwurf*) is a central term. In understanding, the human being interprets the pre-existing meaning or 'project' of the world. This project of the world opens a space for a mode of existence of projecting, e.g. wishing, planning, deciding, willing. Vilém Flusser too embraces the term project in a positive way, as a process through which a 'subjective' attitude is being substituted for a 'projective' imaginativeness (Flusser 1998).
2. Philosophically speaking this can be seen along the lines of a teleological form of justification (as in utilitarian philosophies) in contrast to a deontological ethic. The latter evaluates actions as either good or bad in terms of general moral principles; the former justifies actions with reference to a morally respected goal they are oriented to.
3. In the UK three-quarters of the 18- to 24-year-olds attend nightclubs, compared to two-thirds of the 25 to 35 age group (Mintel 2004: 27).
4. Barbara Bradby pointed to the prolongation of youth in relation to femininity (1993). Pini took the stance that this evidences the 'formation of new modes of *adult* femininity' (2001: 16).
5. This conceptual differentiation somewhat differs from Giddens' notion of social positioning, but nevertheless resonates with his theory of structuration (1984). Social position in Giddens' sense comprises the positioning of social actors in space and time and in relation to other actors. 'Social positions are constituted structurally as specific intersections of signification, domination and legitimation which relates to the typification of agents' (ibid. 83). Social positioning involves the placement of individuals within symbolic categories and the ascription of social identities which carry normative aspects circumscribed by rights and obligations. It occurs at the levels of co-presence, the life-cycle and institutionalized practices.
6. The method of interpretation that these case studies are based on is sequential analysis (Rosenthal 1995, Oevermann 1993) and thematic analysis. The former was applied to the initial narrative prompted by the first interviewer question. The latter was extended to the whole transcript and involved the identification of significant and recurring themes and how they were connected to each other. The underlying assumption of sequential analysis is that a narration consists of a series of selections from a range of possible narrative acts, and therefore, has to be interpreted in the light of the course of its generation. It follows an 'abductive' procedure of interpretation (see the writings of Charles S. Peirce edited by Hartsphorne and Weiss 1980: 7.218).

7. One other case analysis was carried out as a contrastive example. Relevant passages from other interviews too were drawn on for the same purpose.
8. Paul Heelas sketched the models or (partly) contradictory aspects of the self that were propagated by Thatcherist 'character reform' (Heelas 1991: 73–76). It featured an energetic, persuasive and competitive 'enterprising self'; a 'sovereign consumer' centring on the extension of choice; an 'active citizen' committed to taking up responsibilities for the community; and a 'conservative self' oriented to values of hard work, family and education.
9. A similar point was made by Kevin Hetherington (1992: 95) in relation to traveller culture and free festivals. He pointed to the entanglement of the ethos of the gift with real cutthroat business.
10. The way in which Chuck presented this called up the Christian story-type of the 'prodigal son returning home'. However, this cannot be followed up here.
11. In particular, in the light of the association of lesbian identity with working-class butchness (see Skeggs 1997: 118), femininity can protect from being recognized through such class categories.
12. Yong, by contrast, in describing his role as a DJ, articulated mind, knowledge of the music genre and the mastery of technology (see Chapter 5). He framed his DJing as artistic activity and not as work.
13. This can be compared to Valerie Walkerdine's (1984: 173) analysis of feminine agency in narratives of romance as an 'actively passive' state of waiting for being found and selected.
14. Žižek elaborated this point quite neatly: 'Therein lies the paradox of the notion of the 'performative' or speech act: in the very gesture of accomplishing an act by uttering words, I am deprived of authorship; the 'big Other' (the symbolic institution) speaks through me. It is no wonder then, that there is something puppet-like about people whose professional function is essentially performative (judges, kings . . .): they are reduced to a living embodiment of the symbolic institution' (Žižek 1997a: 110).
15. This also has an interesting resonance with different techniques of acting. One approach is to base the performance of feelings on observation and mimicry, with the actor maintaining an inner distance to the role. Another one was Stanislavsky's technique, which proposed that a performer should come to live the character and should use one's memory of certain feelings as a source for authentic performance. This opposition is also sometimes referred to as 'acting from the outside in versus acting from the inside out' (see Dyer 1979: 132).
16. For a discussion of the middle classes in the countryside see also Urry (1995), Cloke, Phillips, and Thrift (1995), Fielding (1995) and Howkins (2001).

NOTES TO CHAPTER 7

1. Unfortunately, the photographs discussed cannot be included here for copyright reasons. Several attempts at tracking down the copyright holders have remained unsuccessful.
2. The US equivalent is *Billboard* magazine, and the German equivalent would be *SPEX* magazine.
3. The notion of visual scenario was adopted from William Simon's concept of cultural scenario as set out here.
4. Elizabeth Wilson pointed to the changing perceptions of 'homosexual relations . . . as a lifestyle choice rather than a transgressive destiny' (1999: 22).
5. Phelan calls this the 'ideology of the visible', which presumes a correspondence between the representation of physical markers and desire/identity (Phelan 1993: 7).

6. *Mixmag*, July 2000: 4. This style of portraying clubbers is now featured as 'Rogues' Gallery' (see *Mixmag*, September 2008: 6–7).
7. Images of stardom often allude to sexual ambiguity; see Dyer (1979: 58).
8. For an extended discussion of how the cultural configuration of butch style occupied the place of real lesbian identity, see J. Harding (1998: 131–133) and Munt (1998: 54).
9. On this point see Lisa Walker's essay, in which she criticized that 'what has been historically defined as a "feminine" sexual style is tacitly constructed as evidence of her desire to pass for straight and not of her desire of other women' (Walker 1993: 879).
10. *Ministry*, May 2000: 22.
11. Williamson argued that in contemporary media, ads, fashion and popular culture sexism has been re-constructed as 'retro-sexism'; that is, either as a period style of the 1960s or 70s, or through fetishistic imagery of S&M sex. In the frame of these styles, sexism can continue to be articulated in a self-aware, 'tongue-in-cheek' fashion. In her view, this expresses both sexism and the gender conflict over social power.
12. This is similar to the construction of female agency as 'actively passive' (see Walkerdine 1984: 173).
13. While in this situation drugs seemed to have compromised her agency and will, when first 'seducing' her later fiancé, a drug helped increase her agency and confidence. See in more detail the discussion in Chapter 5.

NOTES TO CHAPTER 8

1. In a later publication, Muggleton acknowledged that despite the transformation of traditional boundaries between youth subcultures, boundaries continue to exist (Muggleton and Weinzierl 2003a: 19).
2. This point is indebted to Goffman's notion of institutional reflexivity as a circular process of the naturalization of gender difference (1977). Goffman points out how gender is institutionalized in such a way that those qualities are emphasized and affirmed which supposedly motivated the institutionalization of gender difference in the first place (e.g. socialization, labour market, sports, etc.).
3. The agenda of community building in the wake of the gay liberation movement was based on an ethnic model of sexual identity. However, this never succeeded in creating unified gay and lesbian communities. Processes of fragmentation and exclusion prompted much debate as to whether or not gay culture ever constituted a community at all (see also Buckland 2002: 86-89).
4. The analysis mainly relates to the period when the bulk of ethnographic fieldwork and narrative interviewing was carried out (1999–2002) and does not necessarily reflect the most recent developments. See the introductory chapter for a detailed description of the research design.
5. Spatial marginalization is not necessarily peculiar to these spaces, but is part of the wider segmentation of club cultures. However, the specificity of residual spaces of sexual, and also, not to forget, of ethnic minorities is that such spatial location often translates into risk of harassment and violence because of the ongoing inequalities in the occupation of public space.
6. However, such safety is not guaranteed, especially not outside of clubs. Moreover, the visible exposure as meeting places for a predominantly gay audience sometimes turns them even more into targets for homophobic violence (as demonstrated by the Soho bombings in 1999 and other attacks against visitors leaving from gay venues; for example, David Morley, a survivor of the

Soho bombings, was beaten to death near a Central London nightclub in November 2004).

7. Sexually mixed night-life environments have mostly been promoted by proponents of the gay scenes.

8. Base = 838. The survey was conducted by the market research company Mintel at the London Mardi Gras festival in 2000.

9. Some exceptions in the early and mid-1990s were, for example, the night 'Venus Rising' at the Fridge in Brixton (see Pini 1997) and the techno night 'Kitty Lips' (see Dixit 1997).

10. For brief overviews of Soho's recent history and transformation see Mort (2003), Collins (2004) and Binnie (1995). Soho has a historical legacy and image as an area that hosts avant-garde culture, artistic and bohemian lifestyles and small-scale, family-run trades with a diverse ethnic basis. Prostitution, homosexual culture and entertainment are also part of its historical legacy. Especially in the 1950s and 1960s it had a seedy image, but the exposure to music-based youth cultural influence reinvigorated its image as a place of youth, fashion and creativity. New populations migrated to Soho. Service-sector and media-related industries (especially film, design and advertising) benefited from the place-image and from low rents and property prices. With the crackdown on the sex and porn industry, more commercial venues became available since the mid-1980s into the 1990s. These were turned into new cafés, bars, pubs and clubs and helped promote a new vision of gay identity built around a hedonistic lifestyle, fashion and glamour modelled on images of continental European, especially Parisian and Italian urban consumption. Soho has evolved into a central destination for gay tourism and also spurred the growth of non-gay businesses and cafés. Unlike other gay villages in the UK it is not the result of a planned development, but happened piecemeal and ad hoc. It never received explicit municipal support as other gay villages did, for example, in Manchester.

11. After the privatization of British Rail, the venue was leased from the company Railtrack.

12. http://www.heaven-london.com (accessed: 30 January 2002).

13. http://www.heaven-london.com (accessed: 28 August 2008). This was the case until August 2008. However, the most recent changes since then—Jeremy Josephs's G.A.Y. club now running at Heaven—could not be followed up anymore.

14. http://www.candy-bar.co.uk (accessed: 30 January 2002). The latter clearly alludes to the mobility of the brand, see Moore (2003a: 42).

15. http://www.thecandybar.co.uk (accessed: 28 August 2008).

16. See on this point the discussion of stylization and identification in Chapter 4.

17. See Chapter 4 for a detailed discussion of door policies and the strategic vagueness and tactical improvisation of security work (Monaghan 2002: 421).

Bibliography

Akin, F. (2005). *Crossing the Bridge. The Sound of Istanbul*. Documentary, Germany.

Andermahr, S. (1994). 'A queer love affair? Madonna and lesbian and gay culture'. In D. Hamer and B. Budge (Eds.), *The Good, the Bad and the Gorgeous: Popular Culture's Romance with Lesbianism*. London: Pandora.

Anthias, F. (2005). 'Social stratification and social inequality: Models of intersectionality and identity'. In F. Devine, M. Savage, J. Scott, and R. Crompton (Eds.), *Rethinking Class: Culture, Identities and Lifestyles*. Basingstoke, England: Palgrave Macmillan.

Attwood, F. (2006). 'Sexed up: theorizing the sexualization of culture'. *Sexualities*, 9 (1): 77–94.

———. (2007). 'Sluts and riot grrrls: Female identity and sexual agency'. *Journal of Gender Studies*, 16 (3): 233–247.

Augé, M. (1995). *Non-Places*. London: Verso.

Bailey, P. (1990). 'Parasexuality and glamour: The Victorian barmaid as cultural prototype'. *Gender and History*, 2 (2): 148–172.

Bakhtin, M. (1968). *Rabelais and His World*. Cambridge, MA: MIT Press.

Barthes, R. (1977). *Image, Music, Text*. London: Harper Collins.

Bartu, A. (1999). 'Who owns the old quarters? Rewriting histories in a global era'. In C. Keyder (Ed.), *Istanbul: Between the Global and the Local*. New York and Oxford, England: Rowman & Littlefield.

Bassett, K., Smith, I., Banks, M., and O'Connor, J. (2005). 'Urban dilemmas of competition and cohesion in cultural policy'. In N. Buck, I. Gordon, A. Harding, and I. Turok (Eds.) *Changing Cities: Rethinking Urban Competitiveness, Cohesion and Governance*. Basingstoke, England: Palgrave Macmillan.

Bateson, G. (1972). *Steps to an Ecology of Mind*. London: Intertext.

Baudrillard, J. (1983). *Simulations*. New York: Semiotext(e).

Baudrillard, J., Krauss, R., and Michelson, A. (1982). 'The Beaubourg-effect: Implosion and deterrence'. *October*, 20 (Spring 1982): 3–13.

Bauman, Z. (1993). *Postmodern Ethics*. Oxford, England: Blackwell Publishing.

Beck, U. (1992). *Risk Society: Towards a New Modernity*. London: Sage.

Becker, H.S. (1967). 'History, culture and subjective experience: An exploration of the social bases of drug-induced experiences'. *Journal of Health and Social Behaviour*, 8 (3): 163–176.

Becker, J. and Roe, S. (2005). 'Drug Use Among Vulnerable Groups of Young People: Findings From the 2003 Crime and Justice Survey'. London: Home Office.

Bell, D. and Binnie, J. (2004). 'Authenticating queer space: Citizenship, urbanism and governance'. *Urban Studies*, 41 (9): 1807–1820.

Bell, D. and Valentine, G. (Eds.). (1995). *Mapping Desire: Geographies of Sexualities*. London: Routledge.

Benjamin, W. (1955). 'Über einige Motive bei Baudelaire'. In S. Unseld (Ed.), *Illuminationen*, Frankfurt am Main, Germany: Suhrkamp Verlag.

———. (1982). *Das Passagen-Werk*. Frankfurt am Main, Germany: Suhrkamp Verlag.

Bennett, A. (1999). 'Subcultures or neo-tribes? Rethinking the relationship between youth, style and musical taste'. *Sociology, 33* (3): 599–617.

———. (2000). *Popular Music and Youth Culture: Music, Identity and Place*. London: Macmillan.

———. (2001). *Cultures of Popular Music*. Buckingham, England and Philadelphia: Open University Press.

Bennett, A. and Harris, K. (Eds.). (2004). *After Subculture: Critical Studies in Contemporary Youth Culture*. Basingstoke, England: Palgrave Macmillan.

Bennett, T. (1998). *Culture: A Reformer's Science*. London: Sage.

Berman, M. (1971). *The Politics of Authenticity*. London: Allen & Unwin.

Bianchini, F. (1995). 'Night cultures, night economies'. *Planning, Practice and Research, 10* (2): 121–126.

Binnie, J. (1995). 'Trading places: Consumption, sexuality and the production of queer space'. In D. Bell and G. Valentine (Eds.), *Mapping Desire: Geographies of Sexualities*. London: Routledge.

Boltanski, L. and Chiapello, È. (2005). *The New Spirit of Capitalism*. London: Verso.

Bora, T. (1999). 'Istanbul of the conqueror: The "alternative global city" dreams of political Islam'. In C. Keyder (Ed.), *Istanbul: Between the Global and the Local*. Oxford, England: Rowman & Littlefield.

Boratav, H.B. (2005). 'Negotiating youth: Growing up in inner-city Istanbul'. *Journal of Youth Studies, 8* (2): 203–220.

Bordo, S. (1995). *Unbearable Weight: Feminism, Western Culture and the Body*. Berkeley, Los Angeles, London: University of California Press.

Bourdieu, P. (1984). *Distinction: A Social Critique of the Judgement of Taste*. London: Routledge and Kegan.

Boys, A., Fountain, J., Marsden, J., Griffiths, P., Stillwell, G., and Strang, J. (2000). 'Drugs Decisions: A Qualitative Study of Young People'. London: Health Education Authority.

Bradby, B. (1993). 'Sampling sexuality: Gender, technology and the body in dance music'. *Popular Music, 12* (2): 155–176.

Brenner, N. (2001). 'State theory in the political conjuncture: Henri Lefebvre's "Comments on a new state form"'. *Antipode, 33* (5): 783–809.

Brenner, N. and Theodore, N. (2002). 'Cities and the geographies of "actually existing neoliberalism"'. *Antipode, 34* (3): 349–379.

Buckland, F. (2002). *Impossible Dance: Club Culture and Queer World-Making*. Middletown, CT: Wesleyan University Press.

Butler, J. (1990). *Gender Trouble: Feminism and the Subversion of Identity*. London: Routledge.

———. (1993). *Bodies that Matter: On the Discursive Limits of 'Sex'*. London: Routledge.

Butler, T. (2005). 'Gentrification'. In N. Buck, I. Gordon, A. Harding, and I. Turok (Eds.), *Changing Cities: Rethinking Urban Competitiveness, Cohesion and Governance*. Basingstoke, England: Palgrave Macmillan.

Caillois, R. (1961). *Man, Play and Games*. New York: Free Press.

Callon, M., Méadel, C., and Rabeharisoa, V. (2004). 'The economy of qualities'. In A. Amin and N. Thrift (Eds.), *The Blackwell Cultural Economy Reader*. Oxford, England: Blackwell Publishing.

Carrington, B. and Wilson, B. (2004). 'Dance nations: Rethinking youth subcultural theory'. In A. Bennett and K. Kahn-Harris (Eds.), *After Subculture: Critical Studies in Contemporary Youth Culture*. Basingstoke, England: Palgrave Macmillan.

Casey, M. (2004). 'De-dyking queer space(s): Heterosexual female visibility in gay and lesbian spaces'. *Sexualities*, 7 (4): 446–461.

Castells, M. (1983). *The City and the Grassroots*. London: Edward Arnold.

Chamberlayne, P., Bornat, J., and Wengraf, T. (Eds.). (2000). *The Turn to Biographical Methods in Social Science: Comparative Issues and Examples*. New York: Routledge.

Chatterton, P. (2002). 'Governing nightlife: Profit, fun and (dis)order in the contemporary city'. *Entertainment Law*, 1 (2): 23–49.

Chatterton, P. and Hollands, R. (2003). *Urban Nightscapes: Youth Cultures, Pleasure Spaces and Corporate Power*. London: Routledge.

Chee, R. (27 December 2005). 'The order of the day is: party'. *The Straits Times*.

Cieslik, M. (2003). 'Introduction: Contemporary youth research: Issues, controversies and dilemmas'. In A. Bennett and M. Cieslik (Eds.), *Researching Youth*. Basingstoke, England: Palgrave Macmillan.

Cloke, P., Phillips, M., and Thrift, N. (1995). 'The new middle classes and the social constructs of rural living'. In T. Butler and M. Savage (Eds.), *Social Change and the Middle Classes*. London: UCL Press.

Cohen, E. (1979). 'A phenomenology of tourist experiences'. *Sociology*, 13 (2): 179–201.

Cohen, P. (2003). 'Mods and shockers: Youth cultural studies in Britain'. In A. Bennett and M. Cieslik (Eds.), *Researching Youth*. Basingstoke, England: Palgrave Macmillan.

Collin, M. (1997). *Altered State: The Story of Ecstasy Culture and Acid House*. London: Serpent's Tail.

Collins, A. (2004). 'Sexual dissidence, enterprise and assimilation: Bedfellows in urban regeneration'. *Urban Studies*, 41 (9): 1789–1806.

Crewe, L. and Beaverstock, J. (1998). 'Fashioning the city: Cultures of consumption in contemporary urban spaces'. *Geoforum*, 29 (3): 287–308.

DCMS (2007). 'Alcohol, Entertainment and Late Night Refreshment Licensing. England and Wales, April 2006–March 2007' [statistical bulletin]. London: Department for Culture, Media and Sport.

Deleuze, G. (2000). *Cinema 2: The Time-Image*. London: Athlone Press.

Deleuze, G. and Guattari, F. (1984). *Anti-Oedipus: Capitalism and Schizophrenia*. London: Athlone Press.

———. (1996). *A Thousand Plateaus*. London: Athlone Press.

Devine, F., Savage, M., Scott, J., and Crompton, R. (Eds.). (2005). *Rethinking Class: Culture, Identities & Lifestyle*. Basingstoke, England: Palgrave Macmillan.

Dixit, T. (1997). *Techno Babes*. Documentary, Waves Production, UK.

Dokmeci, V., Altunbas, U., and Yazgi, B. (2007). 'Revitalisation of the main street of a distinguished old neighbourhood in Istanbul'. *European Planning Studies*, 15 (1): 153–166.

Douglas, M. (2007). 'A history of grid and group cultural theory'. Online. Available HTTP: <http://www.chass.utoronto.ca/epc/srb/cyber/douglas1.pdf> (accessed: 14 July 2008).

Douglas, M. and Isherwood, B. (1979) *The World of Goods: Towards an Anthropology of Consumption*. Harmondsworth, England: Penguin.

du Gay, P. (1996). *Consumption and Identity at Work*. London: Sage.

Duggan, L. (2002). 'The new homonormativity: The sexual politics of neoliberalism'. In R. Castronovo and D.D. Nelson (Eds.), *Materializing Democracy: Toward a Revitalized Cultural Politics*. Durham, NC: Duke University Press.

Durkheim, E. (1995). [1912] *The Elementary Forms of Religious Life*. New York: Free Press.

Dyer, R. (1979). *Stars*. London: British Film Institute.

Eder, K. (1993). *The New Politics of Class: Social Movements and Cultural Dynamics in Advanced Societies*. London: Sage.

Edwards, R. (30 September 2005). 'Threat to party time as police try to close Hippodrome club'. *The Evening Standard*, 5.

Edwards, T. (2003). 'Sex, booze and fags: Masculinity, style and men's magazines'. In B. Benwell (Eds.), *Masculinity and Men's Lifestyle Magazines*. Oxford, England: Blackwell Publishing/Sociological Review.

Eimer, D. (2 July 2006). 'The great leap backward'. *Mail on Sunday*, 25.

Elias, N. and Dunning, E. (1986). *Quest for Excitement: Sport and Leisure in the Civilising Process*. Oxford, England: Blackwell Publishing.

Entwistle, J. (2002) 'The aesthetic economy: the production of value in the field of fashion modelling', *Journal of Consumer Culture* 2 (3): 317–339.

Ergun, N. (2004). 'Gentrification in Istanbul'. *Cities*, 21 (5): 391–405.

Ergun, N. and Dundar, B. (2004). 'Functional change as an indicator of transformation near the old city centre of Istanbul'. *European Planning Studies*, 12 (5): 723–738.

Erkip, F. (2000). 'Global transformations versus local dynamics in Istanbul'. *Cities*, 17 (5): 371–377.

Ettorre, E. (1992). *Women and Substance Use*. Basingstoke, England: Macmillan.

Eves, A. (2004). 'Queer theory, butch/femme identities and lesbian space'. *Sexualities*, 7 (4): 480–496.

Ewenstein, B. (2004). 'Post-subculture and reflexivity: Cultural learning in London and Berlin'. Unpublished PhD thesis, University of London.

Falk, P. (1994). *The Consuming Body*. London: Sage.

Featherstone, M. (1991). *Consumer Culture and Postmodernism*. London: Sage.

Fielding, T. (1995). 'Migration and middle-class formation in England and Wales, 1981–91'. In T. Butler and M. Savage (Eds.), *Social Change and the Middle Classes*. London: UCL Press.

Florida, R. (2002). *The Rise of the Creative Class: And How it is Transforming Work, Leisure, Community and Everyday Life*. New York: Basic Books.

Flusser, V. (1998). *Vom Subjekt zum Projekt*. Frankfurt, Germany: Fischer.

Forsyth, A. (1998). 'A quantitative study of dance drug use'. Unpublished PhD thesis, University of Glasgow.

Foucault, M. (1977). *Discipline and Punish: The Birth of the Prison*. London: Allen Lane.

———. (1979). *The History of Sexuality, Vol.1: The Will to Knowledge*. London: Allen Lane.

———. (1986). 'Of other space'. *Diacritics*, 16 (Spring 1986): 22–27.

Frank, S. (2003). *Stadtplanung im Geschlechterkampf*. Opladen, Germany: Leske + Budrich.

Frith, S. (1978). *The Sociology of Rock*. London: Constable.

———. (2004). 'Afterword'. In A. Bennett and K. Kahn-Harris (Eds.), *After Subculture. Critical Studies in Contemporary Youth Culture*. Basingstoke, England: Palgrave Macmillan.

Gadsden, G.Y. (2002). 'Crooked men and straightened women: Images of homosexuality across race in two women's magazines, 1986–1995'. *Journal of Homosexuality*, 43 (2): 59–76.

Gampell, J. (1 March 2006). 'Social order takes the life out of night life letter from Bangkok'. *The New York Times*. Online. Available HTTP: <http://query. nytimes.com/gst/fullpage.html?sec=travel&res=9505E0DC1231F932A3575

0C0A9609C8B63&scp=1&sq=gampell%20social%20order%20&st=cse>
(accessed 20 February 2008).

Garett, S. (18 February 2000). 'Talking about a revolution'. *The Pink Paper*, 13.

Garratt, S. (1998). *Adventures in Wonderland: A Decade of Club Culture*. London: Headline.

Gebauer, G. and Wulf, C. (1998). *Spiel—Ritual—Geste. Mimetisches Handeln in der sozialen Welt*. Reinbek bei Hamburg, Germany: Rowohlt.

———. (2003) *Mimetische Weltzugänge. Soziales Handeln—Rituale und Spiele— ästhetische Produktionen*. Stuttgart, Germany: Kohlhammer.

Gershuny, J. (2000). 'Social position from narrative data'. In R. Crompton, F. Devine, M. Savage, and J. Scott (Eds.), *Renewing Class Analysis*. Oxford, England: Blackwell Publishing.

Gerson, J.M. and Peiss, K. (1985). 'Boundaries, negotiation, consciousness: Reconceptualizing gender relations'. *Social Problems*, 32 (4): 317–331.

Gibson, C. and Pagan, R. (1998). 'Rave culture in Sydney, Australia: Mapping youth spaces in media discourse'. Online. Available HTTP: <www.cia.com.au/peril/youth/> (accessed: 20 November 1999).

Giddens, A. (1984). *The Constitution of Society: Outline of the Theory of Structuration*. Cambridge, England: Polity Press.

———. (1991) *Modernity and Self-Identity*. Stanford: Stanford University Press.

Gieryn, T. (1983). 'Boundary-work and the demarcation of science from non-science: Strains and interests in professional ideologies of scientists'. *American Sociological Review*, 48 (6): 781–795.

GLA (2002). 'Late-Night London: Planning and Managing the Late-Night Economy'. London: A Report Commissioned by the Greater London Authority, London Development Agency, Transport for London.

———. (2004). 'The London Plan. Spatial Development Strategy for Greater London'. London: Greater London Authority. Online. Available HTTP: <http://www.london.gov.uk/mayor/strategies/sds/london_plan/lon_plan_all.pdf> (accessed: 12 February 2008).

———. (2006). 'Draft Further Alterations to the London Plan' London: Greater London Authority. Online. Available HTTP: <http://www.london.gov.uk/mayor/strategies/sds/further-alts/docs/alts-all.pdf> (accessed: 12 February 2008).

———. (2007) 'Managing the night time economy: Best practice guidance'. Online. Available HTTP: <http://www.london.gov.uk/mayor/strategies/sds/bpg-night-time-economy.jsp> (accessed: 14 February 2008).

Glaser, B. and Strauss, A. (1964). 'Awareness contexts and social interaction'. *American Sociological Review*, 29 (5): 669–679.

———. (1967) *The Discovery of Grounded Theory*. Chicago: Aldine.

Goffman, E. (1963). *Behaviour in Public Places: Notes on the Social Organisation of Gatherings*. New York: Free Press.

———. (1972). *Relations in Public: Microstudies of the Public Order*. New York: Harper & Row.

———. (1977). 'The arrangement between the sexes'. *Theory and Society*, 4 (3): 301–331.

Goodman, M. (23 December 2007). 'Ministry of Sound plays down its profits'. *The Sunday Times*, Business & Money, 3.

Griffiths, P., Vingow, L., Jansen, K., Sherval, J. Lewis, R., and Hartnoll, R. (1997). 'New Trends in Synthetic Drugs in the European Union'. Lisbon, Portugal: EMCDDA.

Grossberg, L. (1990). 'Is there rock after punk?' In S. Frith and A. Goodwin (Eds.), *On Record: Rock, Pop and the Written Word*. London: Routledge.

———. (1992). *We Gotta Get out of this Place: Popular Conservatism and Postmodern Culture*. London: Routledge.

Hackney, C. (2005). 'Statement of Licensing Policy 2005'. London: Hackney Council.

Hall, P. (2000). 'Creative cities and economic development'. *Urban Studies*, 37 (4): 639–649.

Hannigan, J. (1998). *Fantasy City: Pleasure and Profit in the Postmodern Metropolis*. London: Routledge.

Hänninen, V. and Koski-Jännes, A. (1999). 'Narratives of recovery from addictive behaviours'. *Addiction*, 94 (12): 1837–1848.

Haraway, D. (1991). 'Situated knowledges'. In D. Haraway (Eds.), *Simians, Cyborgs and Nature*. London: Free Association Books.

Harding, A. (2005). 'Governance and socio-economic change in cities'. In N. Buck, I. Gordon, A. Harding, and I. Turok (Eds.), *Changing Cities: Rethinking Urban Competitiveness, Cohesion and Governance*. Basingstoke, England: Palgrave Macmillan.

———. (2006). 'Devolution in England: Cause without a rebel?' In W. Salet and J. Jorgensen (Eds.), *Synergy in Urban Networks*. Amsterdam: Sdu Uitgevers.

Harding, J. (1998). *Sex Acts: Practices of Femininity and Masculinity*. London: Sage.

Harrison, M. (Ed.). (1998). *High Society: The Real Voices of Club Culture*. London: Piatkus.

Hartsphorne, C. and Weiss, P. (1980). [1933] *Collected Papers of Charles Sanders Peirce*. Cambridge: Belknap.

Heath, T. (1997). 'The twenty-four hour city concept—a review of initiatives'. *Journal of Urban Design*, 2 (2): 193–205.

Hebdige, D. (1979). *Subculture: The Meaning of Style*. London: Methuen.

Heelas, P. (1991). 'Reforming the self: Enterprise and the characters of Thatcherism'. In R. Keat and N. Abercrombie (Eds.), *Enterprise Culture*. London: Routledge.

Hemmings, C. (1997). 'Bisexual Theoretical Perspectives: Emergent and Contingent Relationships'. In Bi Academic Intervention (Eds.), *The Bisexual Imaginary: Representation, Identity and Desire*. London and Washington: Cassell.

Henderson, S. (1999). 'Drugs and culture: The question of gender'. In N. South (Ed.), *Drugs: Cultures, Controls and Everyday Life*. London: Sage.

Hennessy, R. (1995). 'Queer visibility in commodity culture'. In L. Nicholson and S. Seidman (Eds.), *Social Postmodernism: Beyond Identity Politics*. Cambridge, MA: Cambridge University Press.

———. (2000). *Profit and Pleasure: Sexual Identities in Late Capitalism*. London: Routledge.

Hesmondhalgh, D. (2002). *The Cultural Industries*. London: Sage.

Hetherington, K. (1992). 'Stonehenge and its festival: Spaces of consumption'. In R. Shields (Ed.), *Lifestyle Shopping*. London: Routledge.

———. (1998). *Expressions of Identity: Space, Performance, Politics*. London: Sage.

Hitzler, R., Bucher, T., and Niederbacher, A. (2005). [2001] *Leben in Szenen: Formen jugendlicher Vergemeinschaftung heute* (2nd ed.). Wiesbaden, Germany: Verlag für Sozialwissenschaft.

Hobbs, D., Lister, S., Hadfield, P., Winlow, S., and Hall, S. (2000). 'Receiving shadows: Governance and liminality in the night-time economy'. *British Journal of Sociology*, 51 (4): 701–717.

Hobbs, D., Hadfield, P., Lister, S., Winlow, S., and Waddington, P.A.J. (2003) *Bouncers: Violence and Governance in the Night-Time Economy*. Oxford: Oxford University Press.

Hobbs, D., O'Brien, K., and Westmarland, L. (2007) 'Connecting the gendered door: Women, violence and doorwork'. *British Journal of Sociology*, 58 (1): 21–38.

Hollands, R. and Chatterton, P. (2003). 'Producing nightlife in the new urban entertainment economy: Corporatization, branding and market segmentation'. *International Journal of Urban and Regional Research*, 27 (2): 361–385.

Horkheimer, M. and Adorno, T.W. (1969). [1944] 'Kulturindustrie, Aufklärung als Massenbetrug'. In M. Horkheimer and T.W. Adorno (Eds.), *Dialektik der Aufklärung*, Frankfurt, Germany: Fischer.

Howkins, A. (2001). 'Rurality and English identity'. In D. Morley and K. Robins (Eds.) *British Cultural Studies: Geography, Nationality, and Identity*. Oxford, England: Oxford University Press.

Howorth, A. (21 June 2003). 'Twelve-month revamp planned for UK's Ministry of Sound'. *Billboard*, 51.

Hutton, F. (2004). '"Up for it, mad for it?" Women, drug use and participation in club scenes'. *Health, Risk and Society*, 6 (3): 223–237.

———. (2006). *Risky Pleasures: Club Cultures and Feminine Identities*. Aldershot, England: Ashgate Publishing.

Huyssen, A. (1986). *After the Great Divide: Modernism, Mass Culture, Postmodernism*. Bloomington: Indiana University Press.

Islington (2005). 'Statement of Licensing Policy 2005-2008'. London: Islington Council.

Jackson, P. (2004). *Inside Clubbing: Sensual Experiments in the Art of Being Human*. Oxford, England: Berg Publishers.

Jackson, S. (2006). 'Interchanges: Gender, sexuality and heterosexuality: The complexity (and limits) of heternormativity'. *Feminist Theory*, 7 (1): 105–121.

Jacobs, J.M. (1961). *The Death and Life of Great American Cities*. New York: Vintage.

———. (1998) 'Staging difference: Aestheticization and the politics of difference in contemporary cities'. In R. Fincher and J.M. Jacobs (Eds.), *Cities of Difference*. New York, London: Guilford Press.

James, W. (1952). [1890] *The Principles of Psychology*. Chicago: Benton.

Jameson, F. (1991). *Postmodernism, or, the Cultural Logic of Late Capitalism*. London: Verso.

Jayne, M., Holloway, S.L., and Valentine, G. (2006). 'Drunk and disorderly: Alcohol, urban life and public space'. *Progress in Human Geography*, 30 (4): 451–468.

Jordan, T. (1995). 'Collective bodies: raving and the politics of Gilles Deleuze and Feliz Guattari'. *Body & Society*, 1 (1): 125–144.

Kershaw, C., Nicholas, S., and Walker, A. (2008). 'Crime in England and Wales 2007/08: Findings from the British Crime Survey and Police Recorded Crime' [statistical bulletin]. London: Home Office.

Keyder, C. (1999). 'The setting'. In C. Keyder (Ed.), *Istanbul: Between the Global and the Local*. New York and Oxford, England: Rowman & Littlefield.

Key Note Ltd. (2005). 'Leisure and Recreation Market: Market Review October 2005'. Key Note database.

Klaic, D. (2005–2006). 'Istanbul's cultural constellation and its European prospects'. Online. Available HTTP: <http://www.esiweb.org/pdf/turkeynetherlands/istanbulreport.pdf> (accessed: 17 September 2007).

Klein, G. (2004a). *Electronic Vibration: Pop Kultur Theorie*. Wiesbaden, Germany: Verlag für Sozialwissenschaften.

———. (2004b). 'Bewegung denken: Ein soziologischer Entwurf'. In G. Klein (Ed.), *Bewegung. Sozial- und kulturwissenschaftliche Konzepte*. Bielefeld, Germany: transcript Verlag.

Kocabas, A. (2005). 'The emergence of Istanbul's fifth urban planning period: A transition to planning for sustainable regeneration?' *Journal of Urban Technology*, 12 (2): 27–48.

Laing, R.D. (1967). *The Politics of Experience*. London: Penguin.

Lamont, M. and Molnár, V. (2002). 'The study of boundaries in the social sciences'. *Annual Review of Sociology*, 28 (1): 167–195.

Landry, C. (2000). *The Creative City: A Toolkit for Urban Innovators*. London: Earthscan.

Landry, C. and Bianchini, F. (1995). *The Creative City*. London: Demos.

Lash, S. (1990). *Sociology of Postmodernism*. London: Routledge.

———. (1993). 'Reflexive modernization: The aesthetic dimension'. *Theory, Culture & Society*, 10 (1): 1–23.

———. (1994). 'Reflexivity and its doubles: Structure, aesthetics, community'. In U. Beck, A. Giddens, and S. Lash (Eds.), *Reflexive Modernization: Politics, Tradition and Aesthetics in the Modern Social Order*. Cambridge, England: Polity Press.

———. (1999) *Another Modernity*. Oxford, England: Blackwell Publishing.

Lash, S. and Lury, C. (2007). *Global Culture Industry: The Mediation of Things*. Cambridge: Polity Press.

Lash, S. and Urry, J. (1987). *The End of Organized Capitalism*. Oxford: Blackwell Publishing.

———. (1994). *Economies of Signs and Space*. London: Sage.

Le Galés, P. (1998). 'Regulations and governance in European cities'. *International Journal of Urban and Regional Research*, 22 (3): 482–506.

Leder, D. (1990). *The Absent Body*. Chicago: University of Chicago Press.

Lewis, L. and Ross, M. (1995). *A Select Body: The Gay Dance Party Subculture and the HIV/AIDS Pandemic*. London: Cassell.

Longhurst, B. and Savage, M. (1996). 'Social class, consumption and the influence of Bourdieu'. In S. Edgell, K. Hetherington, and A. Warde (Eds.), *Consumption Matters*. Oxford, England: Blackwell Publishing.

Lovatt, A. (1996). 'The ecstasy of urban regeneration: Regulation of the night-time economy in the transition to a post-Fordist city'. In J. O'Connor and D. Wynne (Eds.), *From the Margins to the Centre*. Aldershot, England: Ashgate Publishing.

Lovatt, A. and O'Connor, J. (1995). 'Cities and the night-time economy'. *Planning, Practice and Research*, 10 (2): 127–133.

Lury, C. (1998). *Prosthetic Culture: Photography, Memory and Identity*. London: Routledge.

MacPherson, C.B. (1962). *The Political Theory of Possessive Individualism*. Oxford, England: Clarendon Press.

Maffesoli, M. (1995). *The Time of the Tribes: The Decline of Individualism in Mass Society*. London: Sage.

Malbon, B. (1998). 'Ecstatic geographies: Clubbing, crowds and playful vitality'. PhD thesis, University of London.

———. (1999). *Clubbing. Dancing, Ecstasy and Vitality*. London: Routledge.

Mamadouh, V. (1999). 'Grid-group cultural theory: An introduction'. *GeoJournal*, 47 (3): 395–409.

Manson, S. (15 December 2006). 'Back when we started, raving in a cold car park in Shoreditch; club talk' *The Evening Standard*, 22.

Massumi, B. (1992). *A User's Guide to Capitalism and Schizophrenia: Deviations from Deleuze and Guattari*. Cambridge, MA: MIT Press.

Matza, D. and Sykes, G.M. (1961). 'Juvenile delinqency and subterranean values'. *American Sociological Review*, 26 (5): 712–719.

McNay, L. (1992). *Foucault and Feminism*. Cambridge, Oxford: Polity Press and Blackwell Publishing.

McRobbie, A. (1984). 'Dance and social fantasy'. In A. McRobbie and M. Nava (Eds.), *Gender and Generation*. London: Macmillan.

———. (1994) 'Shut up and dance: Youth culture and changing modes of femininity'. In A. McRobbie (Ed.), *Postmodernism and Popular Culture*. London: Routledge.

———. (1997a). 'Dance narratives and fantasies of achievement'. In J.C. Desmond (Ed.), *Meaning in Motion: New Cultural Studies of Dance*. Durham, England and London: Duke University Press.

———. (1997b). 'More! New sexualities in girls' and women's magazines'. In A. McRobbie (Ed.), *Back to Reality? Social Experience and Cultural Studies*. Manchester, England: Manchester University Press.

———. (1999a). *In the Culture Society: Art, Fashion and Popular Music*. London: Routledge.

———. (1999b). 'Thinking with music'. In K. Kelly and E. McDonnell (Eds.), *Stars Don't Stand Still in the Sky: Music and Myth*. London: Routledge.

Measham, F. (2004). 'Play space: Historical and socio-cultural reflections on drugs, licensed leisure locations, commercialisation and control'. *International Journal of Drug Policy*, 15 (5-6): 337–345.

Measham, F., Parker, H., and Aldridge, J. (1998). 'Starting, Switching, Slowing, Stopping' [drugs prevention initiative]. London: Home Office.

———. (2001). *Dancing on Drugs*. London: Free Association Books.

Melechi, A. (1993). 'The ecstasy of disappearance'. In S. Redhead (Ed.), *Rave Off: Politics and Deviance in Contemporary Youth Culture*. Aldershot, England: Avebury.

Miège, B. (1987). 'The logics at work in the new cultural industries'. *Media, Culture & Society*, 9 (3): 273–289.

Mimique, P. (2007). 'Biopolitical regulation of the Shoreditch late-night economy'. Online. Available HTTP: <http://www.projectmimique.org.uk/1-13.HTM> (accessed: 12 February 2008).

Mintel (1996). *Nightclubs and Discotheques*. London: Mintel International Group Limited.

———. (2000a). *Nightclubs and Discotheques*. London: Mintel International Group Limited.

———. (2000b) *The Gay Entertainment Market*. London: Mintel International Group Limited.

———. (2003) *Clubbing Holidays*. London: Mintel International Group Limited.

———. (2004) *Nightclubs*. London: Mintel International Group Limited.

———. (2006) *Nightclubs*. London: Mintel International Group Limited.

Monaghan, L.F. (2002). 'Regulating "unruly" bodies: Work tasks, conflict and violence in Britain's night-time economy'. *British Journal of Sociology*, 53 (3): 403–429.

Montgomery, J. (2003). 'Cultural quarters as mechanisms for urban regeneration. Part 1: conceptualising cultural quarters'. *Planning, Practice and Research*, 18 (4): 293–306.

Moore, E. (2003a). 'Branded spaces: The scope of "new marketing"'. *Journal of Consumer Culture*, 3 (1): 39–60.

Moore, K. (2003b). 'E-heads versus beer monsters: Researching young people's music and drug consumption in dance club settings'. In A. Bennett, M. Cieslik, and S. Miles (Eds.), *Researching Youth*. Basingstoke, England: Palgrave Macmillan.

Moran, L., Skeggs, B., Tyrer, P., and Corteen, K. (2003). *Sexuality and the Politics of Violence and Safety*. London: Routledge.

Mort, F. (2003). 'The sexual geography of the city'. In G. Bridge and S. Watson (Eds.), *A Companion to the City*. Oxford, England: Blackwell Publishing.

Muggleton, D. (1997). 'The Post-subculturalist'. In S. Redhead, D. Wynne, and J. O'Connor (Eds.), *The Clubcultures Reader*. Oxford, England: Blackwell Publishing.

————. (2000). *Inside Subculture: The Postmodern Meaning of Style*. New York: New York University Press.

Muggleton, D. and Weinzierl, R. (2003a). 'What is "post-subcultural studies" anyway?' In D. Muggleton and R. Weinzierl (Eds.) *The Post-Subcultures Reader*, Oxford, England: Berg Publishers.

————. (Eds.) (2003b). *The Post-Subcultures Reader*. Oxford, England: Berg Publishers.

Munt, S.R. (1998). *Heroic Desire: Lesbian Identity and Cultural Space*. London: Cassell.

Navaro-Yasin, Y. (1999). 'The historical construction of local culture: Gender and identity in the politics of secularism versus Islam'. In C. Keyder (Ed.), *Istanbul: Between the Global and the Local*. Oxford, England: Rowman & Littlefield.

Nead, L. (1988). *Myths of Sexuality: Representations of Women in Victorian Britain*. Oxford, England: Blackwell Publishing.

Newburn, T. (2001). 'The commodification of policing: Security networks in the late modern city'. *Urban Studies, 38* (5–6): 829–848.

O'Connor, J. (1998). 'The Cultural Production Sector in Manchester: Research and Strategy'. Manchester Institute for Popular Culture.

————. (1999). 'Popular culture, reflexivity and urban change'. In J. Verwijnen and P. Lehtovuori (Eds.), *Creative Cities: Cultural Industries, Urban Development and the Information Society*. Helsinki, Finland: UIAH Publications.

O'Connor, J. and Wynne, D. (Eds.). (1996). *From the Margins to the Centre: Cultural Production and Consumption in the Post-Industrial City*. Aldershot, England: Arena Publishing, Ashgate Publishing.

Oevermann, U. (1993). 'Die objektive Hermeneutik als unverzichtbare methodologische Grundlage für die Analyse von Subjektivität'. In T. Jung and S. Müller-Doohm (Eds.) *'Wirklichkeit' im Deutungsprozeß. Verstehen und Methoden in den Kultur- und Sozialwissenschaften*. Frankfurt am Main, Germany: Suhrkamp Verlag.

O'Hagan, C. (1999). 'British dance culture: Sub-genres and associated drug use'. Paper presented at 'Club Health 2000', Amsterdam, November 1999.

ONS (2007). 'Annual Business Inquiry'. Office for National Statistics, UK.

Parker, H., Aldridge, J., and Measham, F. (1998). *Illegal Leisure: The Normalization of Adolescent Recreational Drug Use*. London: Routledge.

Parker, H., Measham, F., and Aldridge, J. (1995). 'Drug Futures: Changing Patterns of Drug Use Amongst English Youth'. London: ISDD.

Pearson, G. (2001). 'Normal drug use: Ethnographic fieldwork among an adult network of recreational drug users in inner London'. *Substance Use & Misuse, 36* (1–2): 167–200.

Phelan, P. (1993). *Unmarked: The Politics of Performance*. London: Routledge.

Pini, M. (1997). 'Other traces: A cultural study of clubbing and new modes of femininity'. Unpublished PhD thesis, University of London.

————. (2001) *Club Cultures and Female Subjectivity: The Move from Home to House*. Basingstoke, England: Palgrave Macmillan.

Plant, M. and Plant, M. (1992). *The Risk-Takers: Alcohol, Drugs, Sex and Youth*. London: Routledge.

Plant, S. (1999). *Writing on Drugs*. London: Faber and Faber.

Plummer, K. (1995). *Telling Sexual Stories: Power, Change and Social Worlds*. London: Routledge.

Polhemus, T. (1996). *Style Surfing*. London: Thames and Hudson.

Pollner, M. (1987). *Mundane Reason: Reality in Everyday and Sociological Discourse*. Cambridge, MA: Cambridge University Press.

Power, D. and Scott, A.J. (2004). 'A prelude to cultural industries and the production of culture'. In A.J. Scott and D. Power (Eds.), *Cultural Industries and the Production of Culture*. London: Routledge.

Pratt, A.C. (2004). 'Mapping the cultural industries: Regionalization; the example of South East England'. In D. Power and A.J. Scott (Eds.), *Cultural Industries and the Production of Culture*. London: Routledge.

Probyn, E. (1995). 'Lesbians in space: Gender, sex and the structure of missing'. *Gender, Place and Culture*, 2 (1): 77–84.

Rabinow, P. (Ed.). (1997). *Michel Foucault: Ethics, Subjectivity and Truth*. London: Allen Lane.

Radley, A. (1995). 'The elusory body and social constructionist theory'. *Body & Society*, 1 (2): 3–23.

Randeria, S. (17 August 2002). 'The little league'. *The Guardian*, 'Orange' Supplement.

Reichert, T. (2003). 'Sex and the marketing of media'. *Sexuality and Culture*, 7 (3): 3–6.

Release (1997). 'Release Drugs and Dance Survey: An Insight into the Culture'. London: Release.

Reynolds, S. (1998). *Energy Flash: A Journey Through Rave Music and Dance Culture*. London: Picador.

Richards, G. (2000). 'The European cultural capital event: Strategic weapon in the cultural arms race'. *Cultural Policy*, 6 (2): 159–181.

Ricoeur, P. (1991). 'Narrative identity'. In D. Wood (Ed.), *On Paul Ricoeur: Narrative and Interpretation*. London and New York: Routledge.

———. (1992). *Oneself as Another*. Chicago: The University of Chicago Press.

Rittner, V. (1983). 'Zur Soziologie körperbetonter sozialer Systeme'. *Kölner Zeitschrift für Soziologie und Sozialpsychologie, Sonderheft 25: Gruppensoziologie* 233–255.

Roberts, K. (2003). 'Problems and priorities for the sociology of youth'. In A. Bennett and M. Cieslik (Eds.), *Researching Youth*. Basingstoke, England: Palgrave Macmillan.

Roberts, M. (2006). 'From "creative city" to "no-go areas": The expansion of the night-time economy in British town and city centres'. *Cities*, 23 (5): 331–338.

Roberts, M. and Turner, C. (2005). 'Conflicts of liveability in the 24-hour city: Learning from 48 hours in the life of London's Soho'. *Journal of Urban Design*, 10 (2): 171–193.

Roberts, M., Turner, C., Greenfield, S., and Osborn, G. (2006). 'A continental ambience? Lessons in managing alcohol-related evening and night-time entertainment from four European capitals'. *Urban Studies*, 43 (7): 1105–1125.

Robins, K. and Aksoy, A. (1996). 'Istanbul between civilisation and discontent'. *City*, 1 (5-6): 6–33.

Rodaway, P. (1994). *Sensuous Geographies: Body, Sense and Place*. London: Routledge.

Rose, N. (1999a). *Governing the Soul*. London: Free Association Books.

———. (1999b). *Powers of Freedom. Reframing Political Thought*. Cambridge: Cambridge University Press.

Rosenthal, G. (1995). *Erlebte und erzählte Lebensgeschichte: Gestalt und Struktur biographischer Selbstbeschreibungen*. Frankfurt, Germany and New York: Campus.

Ross, M.W. (2005). 'Typing, doing, and being: Sexuality and the Internet'. *The Journal of Sex Research*, 42 (4): 342–352.

Ryan, B. (1992). *Making Capital from Culture*. Berlin and New York: Walter de Gruyter.

Saego, A. (2004). 'The "Kraftwerk-Effekt": Transatlantic circulation, global networks and contemporary pop music'. *Atlantic Studies,* 1 (1): 85–106.

Sampson, E.E. (1989). 'The deconstruction of the self'. In J. Shotter and K. Gergen (Eds.), *Texts of Identity.* London: Sage.

Sassatelli, R. (1999). 'Interaction order and beyond: A field analysis of body culture within fitness gyms'. *Body & Society,* 5 (2–3): 227–248.

———. (2001). 'Tamed hedonism: Choice, desires and deviant pleasures'. In J. Gronow and A. Warde (Eds.), *Ordinary Consumption.* London: Routledge.

Saunders, N. (Ed.). (1995). *Ecstasy and the Dance Culture.* London: Neal's Yard Press.

———. (Ed.). (1997). *Ecstasy Reconsidered.* London: Neal's Yard Press.

Schaef, A.W. and Fassel, D. (1988). *The Addictive Organization.* San Francisco: Harper and Row.

Schneider, W. (2005). 'Der Prothesen-Körper als gesellschaftliches Grenzproblem'. In M. Schroer (Ed.), *Soziologie des Körpers.* Frankfurt am Main, Germany: Suhrkamp Verlag.

Schroeder, S.K. (2006). 'Global electronic dance music meets Anatolian local music: Ethnographies of "glocal" music cultures'. Paper presented at 'Reconfiguring, Relocating, Rediscovering Conference' organized by the International Association for the Study of Popular Music, Nashville, February 2006.

Schütz, A. (1967). [1932] *Phenomenology of the Social World [Der sinnhafte Aufbau der sozialen Welt].* Evanston, IL: Northwestern University Press.

———. (1971). *Collected Papers 1: The Problem of Social Reality.* The Hague: Nijhoff.

Schütz, A. and Luckmann, T. (2003). *Strukturen der Lebenswelt.* Konstanz, Germany: UVK Verlagsgesellschaft mbH.

Schütze, F. (1978). 'Die Technik des narrativen Interviews in Interaktionsfeldstudien: dargestellt an einem Projekt zur Erforschung von kommunalen Machtstrukturen'. *Universität Bielefeld, Fakultät für Soziologie (=Arbeitsberichte und Forschungsmaterialien 1)*

Scott, A.J. (2000). *The Cultural Economy of Cities.* London: Sage.

Sedgwick, E. (1992). 'Epidemics of the will'. In J. Crary and S. Kwinter (Eds.), *Incorporations.* New York: Zone.

Sharp, C., Baker, P. Goulden, C., Ramsay, M., and Sondhi, A. (2001). 'Drug Misuse Declared in 2000: Key Results From the British Crime Survey' [research development and statistics directorate, research findings 149]. London: Home Office.

Shaw, S., Bagwell, S., and Karmowska, J. (2004). 'Ethnoscapes as spectacle: Reimaging multicultural districts as new destinations for leisure and tourism consumption'. *Urban Studies,* 41 (10): 1983–2000.

Sherwin, A. (2 October 2006). 'Nightclub firm poses music sale challenge'. *The Times,* Business, 38.

Sherwood, S. (10 December 2006). 'Amid the minarets of Istanbul. Club music pulses'. *The New York Times.* Online. Available HTTP: <http://www.nytimes.com/2006/12/10/travel/10Istanbul.html> (accessed 28 February 2008).

Shields, R. (1992). 'Spaces for the subject of consumption'. In R. Shields (Ed.), *Lifestyle Shopping.* London: Routledge.

Shilling, C. (2005). *The Body in Culture, Technology and Society.* London: Sage.

Shiner, M. and Newburn, T. (1997). 'Definitely, maybe not? The normalisation of recreational drug use amongst young people'. *Sociology,* 31 (3): 511–529.

———. (1999). 'Taking tea with Noel: The place and meaning of drug use in everyday life'. In N. South (Ed.), *Drugs: Cultures, Controls and Everyday Life.* London: Sage.

Sieder, R. (1982). 'Bemerkungen zur Verwendung des "Narrativinterviews" für eine Geschichte des Alltags'. *Zeitgeschichte,* (5): 164–178.

Simmel, G. (1950). 'Sociability (an example of pure, of formal sociology)'. In K.H. Wolff (Ed.), *The Sociology of Georg Simmel*. New York: The Free Press.

———. (1971). [1918] 'The transcendent character of life'. In D.N. Levine (Ed.), *Georg Simmel: On Individuality and Social Forms*. Chicago and London: The University of Chicago Press.

———. (1995). [1903] 'Die Großstädte und das Geistesleben [The metropolis and mental life]'. In R. Kramme (Ed.), *Simmel: Aufsätze und Abhandlungen 1901– 1908*. Frankfurt am Main, Germany: Suhrkamp Verlag.

———. (1997a). *Simmel on Culture: Selected Writings*. London: Sage.

———. (1997b). [1905] 'The philosophy of fashion'. In D. Frisby and M. Featherstone (Eds.), *Simmel on Culture: Selected Writings*. London: Sage.

Simon, W. (1996). *Postmodern Sexualities*. London: Routledge.

Skeggs, B. (1997). *Formations of Class and Gender*. London: Sage.

———. (1999). 'Matter out of place: Visibility and sexualities in leisure spaces'. *Leisure Studies*, 18 (3): 213–232.

———. (2000). 'The appearance of class: Challenges in gay space'. In S.R. Munt (Ed.), *Cultural Studies and the Working Class*. London: Cassell.

———. (2004). *Class, Self, Culture*. London: Routledge.

———. (2005). 'The re-branding of class: Propertising culture'. In M. Savage, F. Devine, J. Scott, and R. Crompton (Eds.), *Rethinking Class: Culture, Identities and Lifestyle*. Basingstoke, England: Palgrave Macmillan.

Skeggs, B. and Binnie, J. (2004a). 'Cosmopolitan knowledge and the production and consumption of sexualized space: Manchester's gay village'. *Sociological Review*, 52 (1): 39–62.

Skeggs, B., Moran, L., Tyrer, P., and Binnie, J. (2004b). 'Queer as Folk: Producing the real of urban space'. *Urban Studies*, 21 (9): 1839–1856.

Slater, D. (1998). 'Trading sexpics on IRC: Embodiment and authenticity on the Internet'. *Body & Society*, 4 (4): 91–117.

———. (2002a). 'From calculation to alienation: Disentangling economic abstractions'. *Economy and Society*, 31 (2): 234–249.

———. (2002b). 'Capturing markets from the economists'. In P. du Gay and M. Pryke (Eds.), *Cultural Economy: Cultural Analysis and Commercial Life*. London: Sage.

Smith, C. (1998). *Creative Britain*. London: Faber & Faber.

Smith, D.E. (1987). *The Everyday World as Problematic: A Feminist Sociology*. Boston: Northeastern University Press.

Sommerville, S. (21 April 2008). 'Killing kittens'. *Time Out*. Online. Available HTTP: <http://www.timeout.com/london/alternativenightlife/features/4622/Killing_Kittens.html> (accessed 3 December 2008).

South, N. (1999a). 'Debating drugs and everyday life: Normalisation, prohibition and "otherness"', in N. South (Ed.), *Drugs: Cultures, Controls and Everyday Life*. London: Sage.

———. (Ed.). (1999b). *Drugs: Cultures, Controls and Everyday Life*. London: Sage.

St John, G. (1999). 'Alternative cultural heterotopia: ConFest as Australia's marginal centre'. PhD thesis, La Trobe University, Australia.

Stallybrass, P. and White, A. (1986). *The Politics and Poetics of Transgression*. London: Methuen.

Stauber, B. (2004). *Junge Frauen und Männer in Jugendkulturen: Selbstinszenierungen und Handlungspotentiale*. Opladen, Germany: Leske + Budrich.

Stoker, G. (2004). *Transforming Local Governance: From Thatcherism to New Labour*. Basingstoke, England: Palgrave Macmillan.

Stokes, M. (1999). 'Sounding out: The culture industries and the globalization of Istanbul'. In C. Keyder (Ed.), *Istanbul: Between the Global and the Local*. New York and Oxford: Rowman & Littlefield.

Strathern, M. (1992). *After Nature: English Kinship in the Late Twentieth Century*. Cambridge, England: Cambridge University Press.

Sujin, T. (7 April 2006). 'Ministry's uncivil servants'. *The Straits Times*.

———. (17 November 2007). 'Ministry of Sound parent sues Singapore franchise'. *The Straits Times*.

Sweetman, P. (2003). 'Twenty-first century dis-ease? Habitual reflexivity or the reflexive habitus'. *The Sociological Review*, 51 (4): 528–549.

———. (2004). 'Tourists and travellers? "Subcultures", reflexive identities and neo-tribal sociality'. In A. Bennett (Ed.), *After Subculture: Critical Studies in Contemporary Youth Cultures*. Basingstoke, England: Palgrave Macmillan.

Swindells, D. (9 November 2005). 'Nightlife - a switch in time'. *Time Out*, 120.

Talbot, D. (2004). 'Regulation and racial differentiation in the construction of night-time economies: A London case study'. *Urban Studies*, 41 (4): 887–901.

———. (2006). 'The Licensing Act 2003 and the problematization of the night-time economy: Planning, licensing and subcultural closure in the UK'. *International Journal of Urban and Regional Research*, 30 (1): 159–171.

———. (2007). *Regulating the Night: Race, Culture and Exclusion in the Making of the Night-Time Economy*. Aldershot, England: Ashgate Publishing.

Talbot, D. and Böse, M. (2007). 'Racism, criminalization and the development of night-time economies: Two case studies in London and Manchester'. *Ethnic and Racial Studies*, 30 (1): 95–118.

Taylor, C. (1989). *Sources of the Self: The Making of Modern Identity*. Cambridge, England: Cambridge University Press.

Thornton, S. (1995). *Club Cultures: Music, Media and Subcultural Capital*. Cambridge, England: Polity Press.

Thrift, N. (1997). 'The still point: Resistance, expressive embodiment and dance'. In M. Keith and S. Pile (Eds.), *Geographies of Resistance*. London: Routledge.

Tierney, J. (2006). '"We want to be more European": The 2003 Licensing Act and Britain's night-time economy'. *Social Policy and Society*, 5 (4): 453–460.

Tiesdell, S. and Slater, A.-M. (2006). 'Calling time: Managing activities in space and time in the evening/night-time economy'. *Planning Theory & Practice*, 7 (2): 137–157.

Tilly, C. (2006). *Identities, Boundaries and Social Ties*. Boulder: Paradigm Publishers.

Tseëlon, E. (1992). 'Is the presented self sincere? Goffman, impression management and the postmodern self'. *Theory, Culture & Society*, 9 (2): 115–128.

Turkle, S. (1996). *Life on the Screen: Identity in the Age of the Internet*. London: Weidenfeld & Nicolson.

Turner, V. (1969). *The Ritual Process: Structure and Anti-Structure*. Chicago: Aldine.

———. (1974). *Dramas, Fields and Metaphors*. London: Cornell University Press.

———. (1980). 'Social dramas and stories about them'. *Critical Inquiry*, 7 (1): 141–168.

———. (1982). *From Ritual to Theatre: The Human Seriousness of Play*. New York: Performing Arts Journal Publication.

———. (1986). 'Dewey, Dilthey, and drama: An essay in the anthropology of experience'. In V. Turner and E.M. Bruner (Eds.), *The Anthropology of Experience*. Urbana, IL and Chicago: University of Illinois Press.

Ünsal, D. (2006). 'How to talk about the cultural sector in Turkey'. Online. Available HTTP: <http://www.labforculture.org/de/directory/region_in_focus/previous_regions_in_focus/turkey/how_to_talk_about_the_cultural_sector_in_turkey_by_deniz_uensal> (accessed: 17 September 2007).

Urban, P. (2007). 'Shoreditch Night-Time Economy Study. Evidence Base Review'. Report by Urban Practitioners. London: Hackney Council.

Urry, J. (1990). *The Tourist Gaze: Leisure and Travel in Contemporary Societies.* London: Sage.

——— (1995). 'A middle-class countryside?' In T. Butler and M. Savage (Eds.), *Social Change and the Middle Classes.* London: UCL Press.

Valentine, G. (1993). 'Negotiating and managing multiple sexual identities: Lesbian time-space strategies'. *Transactions of the Institute of British Geographers,* 18 (2): 237–248.

Valverde, M. (1998). *Diseases of the Will: Alcohol and the Dilemmas of Freedom.* Cambridge, England: Cambridge University Press.

———. (2003). 'Police science, British style: Pub licensing and knowledges of urban disorder'. *Economy and Society,* 32 (2): 234–252.

Walker, L.M. (1993). 'How to recognize a lesbian: The cultural politics of looking like what you are'. *Signs: Journal of Women in Culture and Society,* 18 (4): 866–891.

Walkerdine, V. (1984. 'Some day my prince will come: Young girls and the preparation for adolescent sexuality'. In A. McRobbie and M. Nava (Eds.), *Gender and Generation.* London: Routledge.

Walkowitz, J. (1992). *City of Dreadful Delight: Narratives of Sexual Danger in Late-Victorian London.* Chicago: University of Chicago Press.

Welsch, W. (1997). *Undoing Aesthetics.* London: Sage.

Westminster (2005). 'Statement of Licensing Policy'. London: Westminster City Council.

———. (2008) 'Licensing Policy. Statement of Licensing Policy 2008'. London: Westminster City Council.

Whittle, S. (Ed.). (1994). *The Margins of the City: Gay Men's Urban Lives.* Aldershot, England: Arena Publishing.

Widdicombe, S. (1993). 'Autobiography and change: Rhetoric and authenticity of "gothic" style.' In E. Burman and I. Parker (Eds.), *Discourse Analytical Research: Repertoires and Readings of Texts in Action.* London: Routledge.

Widdicombe, S. and Wooffitt, R. (1990). '"Being" versus "doing" punk: On achieving authenticity as a member'. *Journal of Language and Social Psychology,* 9 (4): 257–277.

———. (1995). *The Language of Youth Subcultures: Social Identity in Action.* Hemel Hempstead, England: Harvester Wheatsheaf.

Williamson, J. (31 May 2003). 'Sexism with an alibi'. *The Guardian.* Online. Available HTTP: <http://www.gaurdian.co.uk/media/2003/may/31/advertising.comment> (accessed 20 August 2008).

Willis, P. (1976). 'The cultural meaning of drug use'. In S. Hall and T. Jefferson (Eds.), *Resistance through Rituals: Youth Subcultures in Post-War Britain.* London: Hutchinson.

Wilson, E. (1999). 'The bohemianization of mass culture'. *International Journal of Cultural Studies,* 2 (1): 11–32.

Wolfe, M. (1992). 'Invisible women in invisible places: Lesbians, lesbian bars, and the social production of people/environment relationships'. [Special Issue: Women, Space and Cultural Changes] *Architecture and Behaviour,* 8 (2): 137–157.

Wolfe, T. (1968). *The Pump House Gang.* New York: Farrar, Straus & Giroux.

Wynne, D. (1998). *Leisure, Lifestyle and the New Middle Class.* London: Routledge.

Young, J. (1971). *The Drugtakers: The Social Meaning of Drug Use.* London: Paladin.

Zerubavel, E. (1999). *Social Mindscapes: An Invitation to Cognitive Sociology.* Harvard: Harvard University Press.

Žižek, S. (1997a). *The Plague of Fantasies*. London: Verso.

———. (1997b). 'Multiculturalism, or the cultural logic of multinational capitalism'. *New Left Review*, 38 (225): 28–51.

Zukin, S. (1996). *The Cultures of Cities*. Oxford, England: Blackwell Publishing.

Index